Peter Freeman

CAPE HORN BIRTHDAY

Record-Breaking
Solo Non-Stop Circumnavigation

Seaworthy Publications, Inc.
Melbourne, Florida

Cape Horn Birthday
Record-Breaking Solo Non-Stop Circumnavigation

Peter Freeman
200 Ensilwood Road
Salt Spring Island, BC V8K 1N1
Canada
http://petersfreeman.ca

Published in the USA and distributed worldwide by:
Seaworthy Publications, Inc.
6300 N. Wickham Rd
Unit 130-416
Melbourne, FL 32940
Phone 310-610-3634
email orders@seaworthy.com
www.seaworthy.com

Library of Congress Cataloging-in-Publication Data

Names: Freeman, Peter, 1952- author.
Title: Cape Horn birthday : record-breaking solo non-stop circumnavigation /

Peter Freeman.
Description: Melbourne, FL : Seaworthy Publications, Inc., 2018. | Includes index.
Identifiers: LCCN 2018009741 (print) | LCCN 2018011360 (ebook) | ISBN 9781948494069 (E-book) | ISBN 194849406X (E-book) | ISBN 9781948494052 (hardcover : alk. paper) | ISBN 1948494051 (hardcover : alk. paper) |
ISBN
9781948494045 (pbk. : alk. paper) | ISBN 1948494043 (pbk. : alk. paper)
Subjects: LCSH: Freeman, Peter, 1952—Travel. | Voyages around the world | Single-handed sailing. | Sailors–Australia–Biography.
Classification: LCC GV810.92.F74 (ebook) | LCC GV810.92.F74 A3 2018 (print)| DDC 910.4/1–dc23
LC record available at https://lccn.loc.gov/2018009741

Dedication

To my father, who gave me my sense of adventure
To my mother, who gave me my sense of destiny

Contents

Foreword

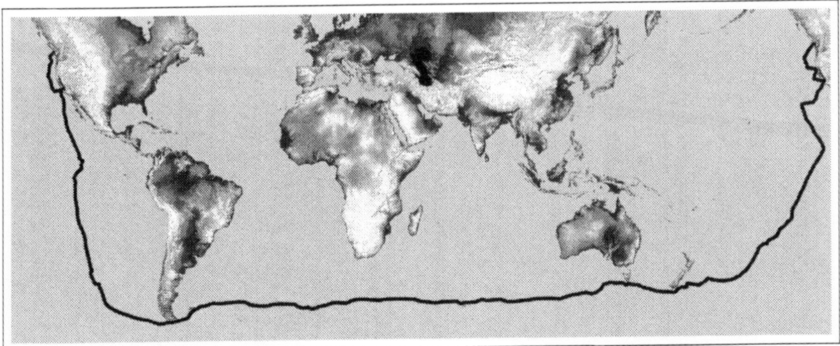

Figure 1: Route of the Hartley thirty-two-foot sloop Laiviņa

What is the meaning of life? We all have so many different interpretations for our short existence on this planet, which we share with so many other creatures. We like the feeling of seeing birds aloft and large mammals below the surface. We love the excitement of experiencing the raw power of nature when right in the midst of its turmoil.

We lead safe lives. While this provides us with the security and flexibility to tailor our existence, it can often leave us with the feeling that some intangible thing is missing. Humans are designed to develop skills in adversity and gain knowledge from challenges.

You may not have a plucky little yacht with which to roam the wide oceans. You may not know of the many strange terms used on board a sailing vessel. As you read my story, you will gradually learn the ways of the sea. Every day, and many times through the day, you will scan the sky, notice the changes in the clouds and tap the barometer to watch the needle settle into a more relaxed position. You will know the ways of the sea.

Come with me on a journey. Come experience what it is to be a seafarer, a rover of oceans and a lover of the ocean's incredible beauty. Voyage with me through these pages and experience rich emotions as you discover what it is really like to be alone, self-reliant, and resourceful.

While you are constantly rolling, pitching, and yawing on a tiny boat, you will learn the most important things you will need to survive. You will discover how to engineer solutions out of the most primitive of supplies. You will understand the physics of materials, their breaking point, and their strengths. You will make many choices, some on which your life will depend. You will realize that disaster does not occur from one choice, but from a string of seemingly innocuous poor choices. Your little sailboat will be your only home for many months, and you will come to know every square foot of surface of your small vessel.

You will not be using tools powered by electricity. Instead, you will wield a hacksaw and a hammer, cutting pieces of stainless steel tube and peening them over washers to make new grommets for sails. They will be just as strong, reliable, and effective as the originals. You will learn to splice laid and braided lines using a marlinespike and a fid. And you will sew... and sew... and sew, because your life depends on movement, and movement depends on your sails.

Your hands will toughen, your muscles will harden, your body will strengthen, and you will have the balance of a gymnast. You will take care of your health and your well-being, physically and mentally, because you are your own physician and your own psychiatrist, and your boat is your own hospital. You will learn to judge risks quickly yet carefully. You will put in place methods that you will exercise with rigorous discipline because any casual moment can turn into a life-threatening event.

You will not have access to all of the modern technological tools that instantly and continually give you your position. Instead, you will be using some of the same equipment that guided the early explorers across the vast oceans of the world: a sextant, chronometer, compass, and analog barometer. You will wait patiently in the cold wind for hours for that momentary glimpse of a feeble sun poking through a cloud-filled sky. You will be quick with your hands and eyes as you bring the sun down to kiss the horizon before it disappears for the rest of the day.

You will experience what it is like for the few who sail alone around the world, following in the wake of all who have sailed before them. It is a challenging life, but a rewarding one. And the world will not seem so large and overwhelming as it once was.

Peter Freeman

Introduction

Figure 2: Laiviņa is about to be launched for the first time

The sleet had finished falling, leaving puddles of water in the hollows of the concrete wharf. A faint sun filtered through grey clouds. Off the edge of the wharf lapped the harbour water, darkened by the fresh wind. I tightened the top of the red jacket around my neck as a gust of wind struck and sent sheets of old newspapers tumbling across the deserted yard at the edge of the wharf. I felt a tug at my sleeve and I turned around.

"They're lifting her up now," Arvita said quietly.

I walked over to the heavy crane and watched carefully as the slings were placed around *Laiviņa*'s belly. The load came on the thick wire rope. Into the air sailed a vessel designed and destined for water but not yet settled into its embrace. With infinite care, the crane driver eased *Laiviņa* over the edge of the wharf and lowered her down until the keel was ten centimetres from the waiting wavelets. Another gust of wind whistled through the heavy arm of the crane, drowning out all but a few snatches of conversation.

"... and may God protect all those who sail upon her."

The diesel engine roared and the winch drum turned as I watched the waves lap at the keel for the first time. Into the water *Laiviņa* went until she floated free of the slings and bobbed against the pilings. A ragged cheer broke out from the small group of friends who had braved the inclement weather to witness a birth. From the shed where Arvita and I had spent countless hours building our dream, *Laiviņa* had come into the world.

Since that wet and windy day in Dunedin, New Zealand, the miles started to flow under her keel. Before a year was out, *Laiviņa* had travelled 3,000 nautical miles from weekend sailing and races with the Otago Yacht Club. At the end of the racing season, she had collected a number of trophies and had taken the series for the season. During the southern winter of 1981, I set out with Arvita, my father, and my brother, Carl, from Nelson, New Zealand, bound for Australia. It was to be *Laiviņa*'s first ocean crossing.

Two weeks later, after being battered by the Tasman Sea, we docked in Brisbane, Queensland, before heading up the coast to Noosa Heads, my childhood home. In June 1982, Arvita and I set off for a crossing of the Pacific Ocean to Canada. It was a gentle voyage, arriving at Victoria, British Columbia, after sixty-five days of sailing. A short time later, our marriage of six years foundered, and out of the ensuing depression a dream was born.

CHAPTER 1

Preparations

On the floor, scattered at random, lay a number of books tossed down among some clothes and shoes. Outside, the rain lashed against the small, high window, the only source of feeble light from the winter sky. I got up, walked across the cold floor to the refrigerator, fetched another piece of ham and climbed back into my cozy bed. I had just finished another of the many books I had been reading in order to avoid thinking of the marriage that had failed a month before. For a while I lay staring up at the ceiling with my head filled with murder mysteries and science fiction. A feeling of loneliness washed over me, and slowly the germ of an idea appeared in my mind.

My voyage to Victoria from Australia had ended in turmoil. I felt homesick and wanted to sail back to Australia yet couldn't bring myself to accept defeat. I had made up my mind the year before that I was going to make something of myself in this foreign land. I didn't want to let go of that sense of purpose, but my despondency was encouraging me to give up.

To sail back across the Pacific would not achieve anything new. I had already done that. In my mind I saw the chart of the Pacific Ocean with its many islands, Japan, the Philippines, and Australia in the west, and the United States, Mexico, and South America in the east. South America...South America and Cape Horn. Now that would be a challenge!

My brain instantly came alive. I could feel the adrenaline racing around under my scalp, causing it to start tingling. Yes! That's it. Go back to Australia the long way, via Cape Horn. Where would I stop? No, why stop at all? Do it in one go! Who would I take? What if no one wanted to go? I would have to go by myself. By myself. Alone. Of course! Great!

After my sense of euphoria had died down, I began to take stock of the realities of such a venture. Could it really be done? I would have to do some research and see if such a trip was feasible. I knew it would be a while before I would have sufficient funds for such a voyage, as I was earning a subsistence wage, struggling just to save a few dollars. I would have to hunt for a better-paying job.

The wet weekend passed and gave way to better weather. I briskly walked the two kilometres to work in the cold winter air, past early blooming crocuses. My day went by quickly, and when evening came, I stayed behind typing on the word processor. It was the start of a voyage plan that was to fill with ideas over the succeeding months. I had a purpose again.

My visits to the Victoria Public Library became more frequent, and I scanned the newspaper for jobs. I wrote letter after letter to apply for a more lucrative job, to no avail. The voyage plan was becoming thicker and thicker, and more detailed.

Sailing from Victoria in British Columbia to Tasmania, Australia, was two-thirds of the way around the world. Solo. Without stopping. If I kept going back across the Pacific to Victoria, I would have completed a solo non-stop circumnavigation. It was something that only a handful of sailors had done since 1968, when Robin Knox-Johnston was the first to successfully complete such a feat. What a challenge! What a voyage it would be. It would also allow me to make a life in Canada. I would not give up. I adjusted my voyage plan and continued to do research at the library.

In September of 1983, my lucky break came. A friend of mine had accepted a job offer in Vancouver, leaving his previous job available. If I took over his old job, I would be making three times the salary I was currently earning. I went for it in spite of his warnings that the company was on shaky ground, likely to go under in a few months. What did I have to lose? Anything would be better than the pittance I was now earning.

To my immense pleasure, I got the job and my bank balance started to rise sharply. Four months later, his predictions proved to be correct and I was on the street again. There wasn't much full-time work around, but a number of businesses that I had supported in my previous job still needed someone to handle their information and technology needs. As well, there were quite a few smaller companies with computer projects that they wanted done. I incorporated my first limited company and set to work.

After a good deal of planning, I chose the month of departure. It would have to be October. It was the only time of the year in which I could leave to have the best weather conditions for the whole voyage, avoiding hurricanes and the worst of Cape Horn storms. It was only six months away now. Would I be ready, or would I have to postpone the voyage for another year? I felt that if I were to postpone it for another year, I would never go, as life has a way of changing our direction and focus whether we like it or not. I had to sail this voyage. So much of my day was now part of this quest. I felt it had become my destiny, and I would not give it up without a struggle.

I set the date of departure, October 14. By now the planning had been completed and the preparations were under way. Only a few of my friends had any inkling of my plans as this voyage was a very personal one, and I wanted to keep it that way. I told them that I was going to sail down into the South Pacific and would be back in nine months, which was as close to the truth as I would dare reveal.

Four months before I was due to leave, I ran into an unexpected hitch. While swimming at the Oak Bay Recreation Centre, I met Penny. Penny was the nurse on duty when I had been hospitalized with a fever a couple of months before. I had only been in the hospital for a day and didn't remember any of the nurses who took care of me as I was eager to get out of the hospital and back on my feet. But she recognized me, and we ended the evening with a dinner invitation.

Well, one thing led to another, and I found myself becoming more and more attracted to her. This was the last thing I wanted. I was going to be gone for nine months, so I told her not to get too involved, as I was going for "a bit of a sail." It didn't work. She figured out where I was going. In spite of the fact that I would be at sea for nine months, she continued to see me and started to help me prepare *Laiviņa* for the long voyage ahead.

Time was now getting short, and my activity around *Laiviņa* became more intense. Friends were helping me prepare *Laiviņa* for the heavy conditions I was to put her through, but my money was running short. Cheques for work I had done over the past month only arrived in the mail a couple of days before I was due to depart. I spent those last days furiously rushing around to purchase the final important items on my list.

The day before my departure, I drove along the Victoria waterfront loaded up with boxes of food as the West Coast's first winter storm raged. Large waves pounded the Ross Bay sea wall leaving a deep pool of water across the road. The car was drenched with spray as I drove slowly through the saltwater rushing along the asphalt. The radio announced the death of a number of fishermen who drowned after their vessel foundered near the Swiftsure Banks. I was becoming apprehensive and hoped that the storm would abate before I departed. Fortunately the barometer was rising and the storm had blown its worst.

My fears caused me to recall the conversation I had a week before. While I was waiting to slip *Laiviņa* to put on a fresh coating of antifouling paint, I mentioned to a fisherman that I was planning to head off soon.

"Where are you going?" he asked.

"Down the coast and into the South Pacific," I replied.

"Now?" he stared at me in amazement. "You're leaving in October?"

"Hey, Tom!" he shouted to his friend. "This fool wants to commit suicide!"

He turned to me, looked me in the eye and said, "You're nuts!"

The wind shrieked through the trees fringing the Ross Bay cemetery, and the waters of the nearby Juan de Fuca Strait were whipped into a white fury. I began to worry that I had bitten off more than I could chew. The words of that fisherman played over and over in my brain. I shrugged my shoulders and decided I would see how the weather was the next day. That night, in spite of my fears, I savoured the last sleep I was to have in a real bed for some time.

CHAPTER 2

Departure

Sun, Oct 14, 1984: 48°25′N 123°23′W, Previous Day's Run: 0

The wind had died down noticeably, and in spite of the rain squalls, the sun was starting to pierce the grey sky. Cars pulled up alongside the ramp leading down to the floating docks where *Laiviņa* was moored, her fenders squeaking against the hull.

Down below, I was putting away the final items and attending to numerous last-minute jobs when Ed Buscall stuck his head in the hatch and spoke quietly.

"Peter, someone has blabbed. A television crew has just pulled up with their van and there's a reporter here from CHEK TV who wants to have a word with you."

"Oh, no," I whispered. Publicity. This was the last thing I wanted. I was under enough stress as it was without having to deal with the media. When I revealed my plans, I had asked my friends not to contact the press. I did not believe in receiving credit before it was due, and I would feel foolish if bad weather forced me to turn back a day or so later. I did not want my judgment clouded by public expectation. I came on deck.

"Yes?" I asked.

"I heard that a solo sailor just arrived from New Zealand on his way around the world. Is it you?" the reporter said.

Mentally, I breathed a sigh of relief. I could easily avoid this unwanted publicity.

"Well, I came from New Zealand, but that was two years ago now and I've been living here in Victoria since. I think you have incorrect information."

Looking at *Laiviņa*'s red flag with its Union Jack and four white-bordered red stars, he replied, "But you're from New Zealand."

"Yes, but I have been living here for two years," I answered.

He was visibly disappointed.

"Do you know who it might be?"

"No."

After he left, we smiled at how I had sidestepped that problem.

"Well, you did answer him truthfully," said Penny.

It was now an hour before noon. With a group of my friends on board, we cast off the mooring lines, set the mainsail, and sailed out of the wharf enclosure towards the customs dock a half mile away. The wind had died down and we were only heeling a little. I felt weak from a cold I had caught a few days before and tense after having to deal with the television crew. They might not have been so easily fooled.

After docking and securing *Laiviņa*, I grabbed the ship's papers and headed for the customs building.

"I'll come up with you," Barry said.

As we walked briskly along Wharf Street, avoiding the puddles left over from the rain, Barry and I talked about the watches he had given me as a backup to my chronometer.

"You'll find that those batteries should last until you get back, so long as you don't use the alarm, or display the time too much on the LED ones. I put a fresh battery in the stopwatch, and you have those spares just in case."

"Yeah. . . I shouldn't have any problems then even if my shortwave radio packs it in," I answered. "I'll be getting the time signal from the shortwave radio broadcast stations. I can check their accuracy and correct their gain or loss."

We reached the correct floor in the customs building and started with the paperwork.

"Do you have your ship's papers?" the customs officer asked.

I handed them over.

"What port are you bound for?" he asked.

"Victoria."

"No, what port are you *bound* for?" he asked once more.

"Victoria."

"No, you are leaving Victoria. Where is your next port of call?"

"Victoria. I am circumnavigating the globe," I explained.

"Yes, but where will you be calling in next?"

"Victoria," I said. "I won't be calling in anywhere as I intend to circumnavigate without stopping."

Without raising an eyebrow, he filled out the clearance form and handed it to me.

Figure 2.1: A heavily laden Laiviņa at the customs dock

The next problem was my re-entry application. I had yet to become a Canadian citizen and was still classified as a landed immigrant. Because I was going to be out of the country for more than six months, I needed s to ensure that I would be welcomed back into Canada.

"You need two passport-style photographs to go with this application, and it has to be signed by an immigration officer."

"Where can I find an immigration officer?" I asked.

"She's out at the airport now and won't be back in town until three."

I groaned. Weeks before, I had been assured that I could get everything done on the day I left. I had not taken into account that they might have only one immigration officer on duty and at the airport twenty-six kilometres away. There was nothing we could do other than get a couple of passport photos and wait.

When the photos were developed, I saw how tired and worn out I was. They weren't very flattering. In the hope that perhaps the immigration officer was back in town, I went back to the customs office. I was in luck. Her duties at the airport had finished earlier than expected, and she had returned for a cup of coffee before going to the Coho Ferry Terminal. The papers were soon signed, and I was off at a fast pace back to the dock.

At last I could leave. I had planned to leave at noon, and as it was now almost half past two in the afternoon, the little crowd of friends was getting thinner.

"Hey, Pete! Which line do you want off first?" Fred called out.

"Take them all off as there is not much wind blowing now," I answered.

"Now let's turn *Laiviņa* around to face the other way," I added.

Taking care not to damage the self-steering system mounted on the transom, they warped *Laiviņa* around until the bow pointed towards the harbour entrance.

"Dug, would you like to keep the bow out as I give her a push off?"

With a good long shove, *Laiviņa* slid away from the dock; I leaped over the pushpit rails and grabbed the tiller. I was away! Unfortunately there was no wind, and after coasting about sixty metres, *Laiviņa* slowly came to a stop, leaving me standing at the tiller with a silly grin on my face. Here I was, becalmed at the start of this epic voyage.

A few fitful puffs of wind drifted my way, and we slowly worked out of the Inner Harbour and into the Outer Harbour. I was gently gliding past Fisherman's Wharf when I heard Barry calling me. He was standing at the end of the floating finger near where he moored his boat. He waved and I waved back, still feeling that I was going out of the harbour for a bit of a sail.

Figure 2.2: Laiviņa departs with the Princess Marguerite II beyond

In the light airs, *Laiviņa* tacked slowly past the Ogden Point breakwater light where Dug and others were standing to cheer me on. A quarter of a mile further on, I went below to fix up something to eat for dinner, and there on the quarter berth was a disk grinder belonging to my friend Bill! I was horrified. I couldn't take that around the world with me. I turned back towards the breakwater, rounded it, and sailed in to the cruise ship wharves.

"That was a quick trip around the world, Pete!" said Dug, as I passed the grinder to him.

Feeling sheepish, I set off again. By this time there was a little more wind, and I moved away from the breakwater at two knots.

Laiviņa sailed quietly in the light airs towards Race Rocks, some ten miles away. I glanced back and could still see Dug on the wharf watching me leave. As he was standing there alone for some time, I wondered what he was thinking. I went below and discovered that he had left me two big steaks along with a prepared meal of curry for the first night. His support touched my heart.

The light wind finally disappeared and left *Laiviņa* and I slowly drifting in the ebb current past the brightly lit penitentiary on William Head. It had been dark for some hours when at 9 p.m. I glanced up at the sound of a jet aircraft high up, and flying almost overhead. In the aircraft, invisible save for its winking lights, sat Penny on her way to Australia.

Before I had met her, she had booked a vacation in Australia and, serendipitously, had to leave on the same day I was departing. I rushed below, grabbed the big spotlight, and aimed it at the aircraft. I flashed it on and off hoping that she would see the strong light. It was a fantastic feeling knowing exactly where she was, right up there in the night sky. Later, I reflected that it wasn't such a smart thing to do as it could have been construed as a distress signal.

The swift current carried me past black rocks that pierced the night sky. By the starlight, I could see the swirling eddies spinning *Laiviņa* slowly around in the whispering breezes as we shot out into the Juan de Fuca Strait. I felt divorced from the reality of the situation in which I found myself. I reflected on those hours in the afternoon when I had been chatting to my friends before setting out on what might have been just another afternoon sail out beyond the Ogden Point breakwater.

The silence of the night had dissolved the real world I had once lived in, reducing it to a thirty-two foot deck. This was the beginning of a dream over a year old. At last I was living in the world of solitary sailing I had envisioned almost every evening since my dream had been conceived.

Up ahead, the Sheringham Point lighthouse bathed the self-steering vane in an eerie green light. The vane turned slowly in the cold October air as *Laiviņa* eased her way towards the open sea. The exhaustion of the final week of preparation caused me to easily feel the cold air penetrating my thick clothes. I shivered and tightened the neck of the cruiser suit I was wearing. It would be a long night, and I had to keep a watch for ships and fishing boats. Later, a light breeze filled in and I worked on my first chore of the voyage. The self-steering was still a bit sluggish as the new parts I had fitted were stiff. The grease had not yet worked into the new bearings. I pumped some more grease into the nipples and hoped it would improve the sensitivity of the system.

Mon, Oct 15, 1984: 48°30′N 124°15′W, Previous Day's Run: 39

The fitful wind died again, and all through the night we made slow progress. In spite of the hustle and bustle of the days before, I had no trouble staying awake. By dawn I had only reached Sheringham Point, just past Sooke. On the two-burner kerosene pressure stove, I cooked the steaks Dug had given me, as they would not stay fresh for long. My appetite must have been greater than I had originally thought. Into the frying pan went two eggs while I toasted a couple of pieces of bread. What a hearty breakfast! With a warm feeling inside, I went on deck to relax and watched *Laiviņa* move slowly past the Douglas firs that appeared to march down the hillsides.

During the day, I kept on the Canadian side of the Juan de Fuca Strait despite knowing that I would get better currents on the American side. I did not want to cross the strait and be becalmed in the shipping channel, particularly if fog rolled in. As we sailed along the Canadian shore, past the firs and cedars, I checked the gear on deck, tightening shackles and seizing the pins. I would soon be entering the open sea, so I rigged running lifelines down both sides of the deck from the bow right to the stern. Now I could be attached with a harness and walk the complete deck in safety without fear of falling overboard and watching *Laiviņa* sail away from me. The work completed, I settled back with a sandwich in hand and watched our slow progress towards the entrance of the strait.

I was almost opposite Neah Bay when I started to cross over to the American side of the strait and head for what would be my last shelter in the event of sudden bad weather. Luckily, the barometer was still steady and I felt sure that I would be able to make enough sea room before the next depression arrived. On the way across the strait, I retrieved a length of two-by-four dressed cedar floating on the water. On a voyage such as I was attempting, I never knew what calamities might befall me, and lengths of lumber were always handy on board to effect repairs. Dug had already given me a long length of four-by-four lumber, so I lashed the new piece together with the old along the side deck.

Once past Neah Bay, the wind started to blow from the southeast, putting it dead astern. Up went the spinnaker on one side and a poled-out genoa on the other. Away we went for the first time at a speed of between five and six knots.

Little did I know that I was being observed. Thirty miles behind me at Point No Point, Dug sat behind a powerful telescope belonging to an amateur astronomer. I approached Cape Flattery with *Laiviņa* slowly rolling from side to side in the even Pacific swells coming into the strait while Dug watched me trimming sails and moving about on deck. For him it had been an emotional experience. Colourfully spread across the whole of his vision, he watched a small vessel boldly entering the open ocean.

It was getting dark just as I was abeam Cape Flattery. The fatigue I now felt was causing me to shamble about the deck, my limbs shaking from poor muscular coordination. Large swells were starting to roll under *Laiviņa*, and as I hadn't gained my sea legs, I had to be extremely careful. My mind wandered away from the task at hand, forcing me to continually snap it back and will myself to concentrate.

The hours of work and lack of sleep the previous night were taking a toll on my body. I craved sleep. I yearned to put my head down and drift away, but I dared not. Astern, the Cape Flattery lighthouse on Tatoose Island winked at me menacingly, warning me to get away. All around the horizon, a fleet of fishing vessels moved, their masthead strobe lights briefly igniting the dark sky. Ships thudded past, and tugs towing their dangerous cargo of logs added to the confusion of lights. Throughout the night, I sat on the aft hatch cover, my spine against the backstay. Minute by minute, hour by hour, I jerked my nodding head back into wakefulness and scanned the horizon. Slowly, the number of lights decreased until in the early hours of the morning I was quite alone.

CHAPTER 3

Setbacks

TUE, OCT 16, 1984: 47°00′N 126°10′W, PREVIOUS DAY'S RUN: 128

I was well clear of shipping by the time dawn caressed the horizon, so, I lay down on my bunk and tried to sleep. Not a chance. My body and mind had not yet attuned themselves to the motion and conditions of life at sea. At least *Laiviņa* was moving fast, so by the time I took my noon sight, we had completed a noon-to-noon run of 128 miles. Throughout the day I rested, but I wasn't able to sleep. After I ate my evening meal, I put blankets on the bunk, set the alarm for midnight to check on the wind, and fell into a deep, deep sleep.

WED, OCT 17, 1984: 44°50′N 125°10′W, PREVIOUS DAY'S RUN: 137

In spite of the alarm jarring me awake at midnight and at dawn, I felt better than the previous day but still didn't feel well rested. Unfortunately, there was still a lot of work to be done around the boat as various items needed to be restowed in better positions. I set to the task, but the fast rocking and rolling motion made lugging things around difficult. It was a full-time job just preparing my meals to get enough energy to keep *Laiviņa* moving fast, and I was constantly adjusting the self-steering as the wind shifted in direction.

After processing my noon sight, I was impressed with an even better noon-to-noon run than the previous day. Adding another 137 miles, I had quickly caught up to my planned schedule. I had been about seven hours behind schedule at Cape Flattery; now I was starting to get ahead.

THU, OCT 18, 1984: 43°38′N 126°10′W, PREVIOUS DAY'S RUN: 84

Life at sea was becoming enjoyable. I was starting to catch up on my sleep, and, with the cabin properly organized, a routine was beginning to emerge. Around 4 a.m. I noticed that the wind had picked up and *Laiviņa* was becoming hard pressed running under the full sail she was carrying. I tapped the barometer and it was high and still rising. Although this was a bit unusual, I had experienced it before. Sometimes near the top of a rise a stronger wind may blow, a sort of last fling.

With this thought in mind, I decided to take only enough sail area off *Laiviņa* to stop her being over pressed. I dressed warmly, put my cruiser suit on over the top of my clothes and went on deck. Down came the number one genoa and up went the number two. After snugging everything down, I went below, peeled off my clothes and climbed into my bunk. I was just getting comfortable when I noticed that *Laiviņa* was being hard pressed again. Damn! What a nuisance.

Rubbing my eyes, I climbed out of my bunk, dressed again and went on deck, where I changed the genoa for the next headsail, the number one jib. As I was getting a little wary, I also deep-reefed the mainsail to the number three reef position, the maximum I could reduce that sail. *Laiviņa* was now sailing close-hauled with the wind coming from the southeast, so I started to suspect that a gale was on its way.

I went below, tapped the barometer and noticed that it had dropped a lot.

"Aha!" I thought. "Now I know what's happening."

The sail changes were wearing me out, particularly since I hadn't fully recovered from the previous days. The demanding physical activity necessary to solo sail a boat fast was taking its toll. Although I considered myself fit and strong, it had been some time since I had worked my body so hard.

I peeled off the cruiser suit and discovered that my clothes were saturated. I had believed the suit to be waterproof; it wasn't, and my clothes were soaking up water like a sponge. It was now around 9 a.m., and I had been changing sails since four in the morning. Although I had only made two sail changes, it had taken five hours. On shore, tied up to a dock, a sail change would take fifteen minutes maximum, yet at sea it took a couple of hours. Just pulling off my wet clothes inside a pitching and rolling cabin took half an hour.

I dried myself off with a towel, climbed into my bunk, and tried to rest. Impossible. I had to reduce sail again. On deck this time, the wind was starting to howl through the rigging. Carefully working my way forward, I reached the mast, uncoiled the headsail halyard and back-coiled it beside the dinghy. With my back against the cap shroud and my harness lifeline holding me tight, I waited for a break between seas and then whipped off the turns on the cleat and winch. The jib cracked like a whip as I let go the halyard and ran forward, crouching to keep my weight low. At the bow, I hauled the sail down the forestay. As soon as it was down, I bundled the sail against the rail, braced myself against the pulpit and whipped off the hanks in quick succession.

I had to quickly get the sail safely below without it being washed overboard. I opened the tack snap shackle and rolled the sail up towards the clew. With the wet and heavy bundle in my arms, I opened the main hatch and threw it below with the sheet still attached so it could not be lost overboard. As soon as it was safe below, I opened the clew snap shackle, cleared the hatchway and closed the hatch. Now for the number two jib.

I was still determined to sail *Laiviņa* as hard as I could. In the increasing wind I gave ground only when forced to. I waited for a break between seas, quickly slid open the companionway hatch and leaped over the storm board onto the companionway. Now that I was safe, I unclipped my harness from the running lifeline and closed the hatch.

I hauled the number two jib on deck and attached the tack snap shackle. After hanking the sail onto the forestay in the heaving seas, I clipped the sheets onto the clew and hoisted it. The moment the sail was halfway up, *Laiviņa* surged forward again, leaping over the waves like a dolphin with the spray flying over her. I watched her driving to windward, tossing off the seas as they ran at her, one by one.

I was getting cold, so went below to warm up. At the foot of the companionway lay the wet number one jib. I dragged it forward and added it to the already sopping-wet pile of sails in the head. The pile was now up to the cabin top, and I couldn't get through to the forward berth area, not that I wanted to, as it was much too rough up there. I undressed, towelled my tired body as best I could, and crawled into the bunk. A short while later, I opened my eyes and sighed. I had to reduce sail again.

On with my wet clothes and back on deck to replace the number two jib with the storm jib. I also changed the mainsail for the trysail, which took a while as it was getting quite rough. We were sailing as close-hauled as we could into the wind and waves, and *Laiviņa* was flying along. I could have slowed down, but if I wanted to get around the world in good time I couldn't afford to dawdle. The wind was coming from the south, exactly where I wanted to go. The best course I could hold was a westerly one, so out to sea we went, leaping and racing over the waves.

Fortunately the veering wind meant that on the port tack, the heavier seas were not meeting us head on. I went below, stripped off my wet clothes, dried off and climbed into my bunk, expecting to reduce sail even further. In my mind I worked out my next move. I would lower the trysail and go on a reach with just the storm jib.

However, the wind didn't increase. It eased. Completely. The barometer stopped falling, and we were crashing around in the short, heavy swell. It was now 4 p.m. I had spent the last twelve hours changing sails, changing clothes and fooling myself that there was time to rest.

Back on deck, I hoisted the full mainsail and the number two genoa. There was only a little wind, so I considered using the number one genoa, but the barometer had started rising. If the wind freshened again, I would be getting dangerously low on energy and it would be challenging changing sails in good time. I did not want to make any stupid mistakes.

I changed onto the starboard tack, trimmed the sails as best I could in the sloppy leftover seas and adjusted the self-steering system. *Laiviņa* was now heading in a southeasterly direction towards the land. The Oregon coastline was over eighty miles away, and I expected the wind to veer more around to the west. We could then make some pure southing again.

The night fell over the tormented sea as I dropped my head onto the pillow and slept.

Fri, Oct 19, 1984: 41°55′N 126°20′W, Previous Day's Run: 103

During the day following the first gale of my voyage, I ate, slept and did not touch the sails. It was perfect weather for recovering my energy. At times the wind freshened, but never enough to require reefing. I just ate, rested and slept. The only necessary chores were snatching sun sights through faint holes in the cloud-filled sky.

At night, I stood on the bridge deck and sighted back along the fore and aft line to see Polaris, the North Star, directly behind the backstay as we sailed due south.

Sat, Oct 20, 1984: 39°28′N 126°55′W, Previous Day's Run: 149

What a joy it was to feel energy coursing through my body. Life at sea was filling me with happiness. I was starting to develop a deeper friendship with *Laiviņa* than I had ever experienced before. In keeping her part of the bargain, *Laiviņa* roared along with a bone in her teeth clocking up the best previous day's run for the voyage, an excellent 149 miles, averaging a bit over six knots.

Below decks, my saturated clothes refused to dry. The wet sails and wet cabin kept the air down there at maximum humidity. Above decks, a weak sun occasionally shone through the fog and mist, and the sails and rigging rained moisture on the decks each time *Laiviņa* rolled. These minor discomforts did not disturb me. Most important, we were moving. And fast.

Sun, Oct 21, 1984: 37°28′N 125°45′W, Previous Day's Run: 132

Another day of mist and rain and still we surged southward, ever southward towards warmer waters and the sunshine of the tropics. The spinnaker and the genoa were wing and wing, pulling *Laiviņa* hard, surfing with the swells and slicing through a world of grey.

During the afternoon, I was reading in the cabin when I heard a heart-stopping sound. As I froze with all my senses attuned, the spinnaker tore itself right across the middle, from luff to luff. As quickly as I could, I threw on my wet-weather gear and clambered up on deck to retrieve the pieces. From the masthead, high up in the air, flew the top half like the flag of a besieged nation while alongside in the water, the bottom half dragged like a wet dishrag.

It was a struggle to get the piece from the water up onto the deck. Luckily, there was only a genoa left to catch the wind and pull *Laiviņa* along. Her speed had been reduced somewhat. I tossed the clammy nylon down the forward hatch and puzzled over the reason for the tear. The wind wasn't that strong, but the sail was sopping wet from the fine rain. From time to time it collapsed, and in one of these collapses, it must have hooked around the spreader or a mast step. When it filled with wind again, the point loading had been too much for such an old sail and gave way.

I still had to get the other half down from the top of the mast somehow. I hoisted the mainsail and adjusted the self-steering so that the piece of sailcloth fell into the wind shadow behind the mainsail. It was then an easy job lowering it onto the deck.

A big fix-up job! I could see that I was going to have some work ahead of me, and I wondered if I might be pushing *Laiviņa* too hard. I lowered the mainsail again and set the old number one genoa on the port side where the spinnaker had been. Away we went again with the two big genoas wing and wing pulling us along almost as fast as with the spinnaker.

Mon, Oct 22, 1984: 35°15′N 125°10′W, Previous Day's Run: 136

Victoria, with its coming winter, was now eight days behind us. I noticed the distinct change in both the seawater and air temperature. The warmer conditions relaxed me as the possibility of encountering a severe early winter storm decreased day by day, mile by mile. I was excited by the rapid changes of temperature. It was like experiencing a fast and early spring.

One of the real joys of sailing from north to south and vice versa was the illusion of seasons, each lasting only a couple of weeks. I now anticipated sailing for "spring" in the temperate areas, suntanning in the "summer" of the tropics, dressing for "autumn" in the variables, and bundling up for "winter" in the high latitudes. Although the weather was still cool and I was wearing a sweater all day, I was going on deck barefooted.

Before I left Victoria, Barry and Dug put up the money for me to buy a programmable calculator. After spending some time shopping around, I purchased a Hewlett Packard HP-11C. I planned to program it to process a sun sight. Just a few days before leaving, another friend gave me an excellent book that included a number of formulas commonly used by astronomers. I was able to modify and combine the formulas to reduce the time I was taking to calculate our position by the Sight Reduction Tables method.

Settling in to the basic routine of changing sails, navigating, eating, and sleeping, I was starting to crave mental stimulation. After dragging out a pile of mathematics textbooks, I spent the day throwing around formulas and tossing ideas from one side of my head to the other.

Tue, Oct 23, 1984: 33°31′N 123°50′W, Previous Day's Run: 123

The two big genoas whispered as the stiff north wind pressed them hard, straining the sheets and hurtling *Laiviņa* down the face of wave after wave. Tucked neatly up against the transom, the self-steering system clicked away as the rudders swung quickly from side to side, correcting her course. *Laiviņa* was eating up the miles and putting us three to four days ahead of schedule and into the trades well before expected.

On the kerosene pressure stove in the cozy cabin, two eggs crackled away as I prepared my eighth breakfast of the voyage. I moved the pan off the heat, sat the toaster on the flame, and put on two slices of bread, their sides wet from the misting I had given them to reconstitute the bread from its previously dry state.

Laiviņa heeled sharply, and I grabbed the post beside the galley as we slew around in a broach, backing one of the big genoas with a heavy thump. The wave passed under the keel as I waited for the self-steering to take command again and bring her back on course. I waited and waited. Nothing happened, so I went on deck, unlashed the tiller, and helped *Laiviņa* back on course. After she had settled down, I lashed the tiller back into position and then noticed that something was funny with the self-steering. This was not uncommon as sometimes a pin would pop out and I would simply pop it back. I looked at the rudder and saw that the little trim tab that turns the auxiliary rudder had disappeared.

This was a serious setback. Luckily I had a length of Malaysian hardwood; I figured that it would take me a day or so to make a new trim tab and fit it. I looked closer. From the waterline down, the auxiliary rudder was missing as well! It had sheared off and taken the intact trim tab with it.

As soon as I could, I tackled the job of lowering the two big genoas. *Laiviņa* wallowed in the seas as I carried the number one jib up to the bow and hanked it to the forestay. After turning into the wind, I hoisted the reefed mainsail and set a close-hauled course. I needed to return to the place where I had lost the auxiliary rudder and try to find some of the debris. From atop the mast I scanned the sea looking for the telltale colour of red antifouling paint.

After two hours of tacking back and forth searching for the missing rudders, I decided to accept the loss of this most vital part of *Laiviņa*. Without self-steering, I could not hope to complete the voyage as I had planned. I went below and sat down. I was shocked. I had not expected this as I believed that the little wooden shear pins would break before the auxiliary rudder reached a critical stress limit. Apparently not. I realized very quickly that I couldn't go on without the auxiliary rudder. I had to call in somewhere and rebuild the rudders. At first I thought of San Diego but decided upon Santa Barbara as it was closer. My heart sank as I turned *Laiviņa*'s bow towards Santa Barbara, 400 miles away, and prepared myself for the long hours of steering by hand.

CHAPTER 4

Making for Land

As I steered through the day, I racked my brain for a solution to the self-steering problems now facing me. Steering a close reach with *Laiviņa*'s fin keel and balanced rudder was easy, even in these strong winds. To windward in steady winds, all sailboats would hold a course with the tiller lashed to provide the right amount of weather helm. *Laiviņa* was no exception. I had often been able to lash the tiller and leave the helm for hours at a stretch. In variable winds, the amount of weather helm must be adjusted to suit the changes in wind strength.

On a broad reach and on a dead run, *Laiviņa* was too lively to hold her own course for even a minute. In the past I had tried other methods of self-steering and had only little success. In spite of my extensive experimentation, sheet-to-tiller steering worked only a little better than a lashed tiller.

I had to devise some method to steer *Laiviņa* so we could make progress day and night. After rummaging around in the locker in which I kept materials, I came up with a couple of bicycle inner tubes, some blocks, and a length of line. At first I tried rigging a line from the genoa sheet, directing it across the cockpit and then back with a turning block to the port side of the tiller. To oppose this force, I doubled a bicycle inner tube and attached it to the starboard side of the tiller. I sat back to watch how the steering would respond to this jury-rigged system.

It failed, so I adjusted the elasticity of the rubber tubing and sat back to watch it again. Again it failed. I felt the force on the sheet and tried to adjust the elastic tension of the bicycle inner tube by doubling it a number of times. It still failed.

Next, I changed the attachment point of the sheet to the tiller by fixing it closer to the rudder shaft. I sat back and watched it attempt to control *Laiviņa*'s course. It did not work. I tried a number of different sheet attachment positions but to no avail. It just didn't work.

This system would steer *Laiviņa* for perhaps a minute or so before it went wildly off course and either gybed or tacked. Next, I rigged the mainsail to steer *Laiviņa.* This had the same result of working for a while before it went wildly off course. Then I tried both systems together. Still no luck.

I could see what was happening. If *Laiviņa* went into the wind, the tension on the sheet would decrease as the sail feathered. If she turned downwind, the tension on the sheet would also decrease due to the dropping apparent wind speed. It was like trying to balance a stick on its end. All day I played with the system until I decided I was losing mileage and it would be better to steer by hand. At sunset, I hove to, ate my evening meal, and bunked down for the night.

Wed, Oct 24, 1984: 33°42′N 123°04′W, Previous Day's Run: 40

By noon I had sailed only 40 miles. It was poor mileage, but as I had to sleep, I was forced to heave to. I was not impressed with our previous day's run, and my morale suffered from the loss of the rudders and the poor mileage. I felt the lack of spirit, the lack of determination in my body and mind. I was becoming discouraged. Inconveniences annoyed and upset me. Throughout the day, I grumbled to myself as I steered towards land.

After the sun went down, I sheeted in the sails, set a close-hauled course on the starboard tack, and lashed the tiller to give it a bit of weather helm. It meant I was steering about thirty degrees off course to the north, but at least *Laiviņa* would continue sailing through the night as I slept and refreshed my tired body for the next day of steering. When I awoke, I would be closer to Santa Barbara.

Thu, Oct 25, 1984: 33°52′N 121°28′W, Previous Day's Run: 80

Through the night, the wind veered slowly so that by dawn our close-hauled course was now heading in the direction of Santa Barbara. I was able to relax and regain my energy through the day with the tiller lashed and *Laiviņa* in charge. My noon-to-noon run of eighty miles was more encouraging. I conserved my energy as I sailed towards the coast to cover the last hundred miles. It would be that stretch that would tax my endurance. I needed to stay awake to get through the shipping and into Santa Barbara.

Unfortunately, the breeze that had helped me so much died down soon after noon and left me becalmed. However, it was an opportunity to repair the spinnaker. I spread the two torn pieces of spinnaker out over the cabin top in the bright sunshine, and while I waited for the torn pieces to dry, I started reading the first of the 150 books given me by my friends. When the spinnaker was dry, I brought it inside the cabin and started repairing it.

I felt my morale improving and the feelings of helplessness and despair giving way to resolve. I was confident that I could repair the self-steering and continue on my voyage. For the rest of the day, *Laiviņa* rolled in the leftover swell, as the seas went down and the ocean surface smoothed to an oily sheen. I ate my evening meal, set the alarm for 3 a.m., and fell into an easy sleep.

Fri, Oct 26, 1984: 34°14′N 120°28′W, Previous Day's Run: 55

At 3 a.m. the alarm jarred me awake. We were no longer becalmed as a light breeze had sprung up, ruffling the water with gentle cat's paws. I dressed quickly, came on deck, and started steering. Resolve flowed through me as I set my mind to the task of a long and gruelling sail ahead. The night dissipated, the sky lightened, and when the sun rose, it shone weakly through the heavy air pollution that persists along this coastline.

I had been steering for some hours when hunger began creeping up on me. With the genoa backed and the tiller lashed down to leeward, I hove to for breakfast. On the kerosene pressure stove, I cooked up a hearty meal of cereal, eggs, and toast, polishing off every last crumb before I came back on deck. I was fortified for the long day ahead.

Around 10 a.m. I spotted land. Five miles away, in the gloom of smog, lay Santa Rosa Island. With an accurate position fix on my chart, I shaped a course for the Santa Barbara Channel. I noticed a fishing vessel ahead of me and took the opportunity to head for it to ask some questions about the facilities at Santa Barbara. As I approached, I could see that the fishermen were tending crab or lobster pots. When I was getting within hailing range, they took off to another pot a half mile away. I lost that opportunity.

Approaching the Santa Barbara Channel, I noticed the wind increasing. I figured that it was due to the funnelling effect of the channel. We were sailing along fast on a beam reach under full sail, and it was becoming more difficult to prevent *Laiviņa* from heading up into the wind. The extra effort was tiring me quickly, and the hearty breakfast I had eaten was losing its potency. I had to have lunch. Now that *Laiviņa* was clear of the rocks off the northwestern end of Santa Rosa Island, I hove to and went below for another feast. After lunch, I resumed steering and, although we were being hard pressed with the number one genoa, I was reluctant to reduce sail as I would soon be turning downwind.

In spite of the smog, the visibility was reasonable as I approached the edge of the inbound shipping lane. In the offing, a large oil tanker was making its final approach, and I calculated that we would be on a collision course. I headed into the wind a little more, and the strain on the tiller increased. If we could hold this course without the sails tearing, I should safely pass astern of the tanker.

Closer and closer we came to each other, but I could now see that the tanker would pass safely ahead of me. The danger was over. With a heavy thrumming of engines and a boiling wake, the tanker slid ahead, right in front of me. Its bow wave lifted *Laiviņa* high into the air with a lurch, and a minute later we were sailing in its turbulent wake.

With such a stiff breeze, *Laiviņa* quickly cut across from the inbound and into the outbound channel. As the day progressed, we worked our way into the waters off the mainland shore. The sun crept towards the western horizon, and the wind decreased slowly. By sundown, the Santa Ynez Range was blocking the prevailing breezes and giving us light and fitful airs. At least I was out of the shipping lanes. The exertion of helming almost non-stop for the past fourteen hours was beginning to take its toll. Now, helming demanded even more concentration as I trimmed and retrimmed the sails to catch the little blasts of wind descending from the adjacent tall mountain peaks.

I surveyed the new landscape around me. The tall offshore oil platforms, standing on stilts in the water, caused me to feel alienated. I was sailing like a ghost ship, wandering along the coast, viewing other men and their boats moving to and fro. It was as though I didn't exist in this world. I felt as if I were in another dimension and people couldn't see me.

Night was coming on, so I fixed my position by the shore landmarks I could still see. I needed my position to be as accurate as possible to sail through the oncoming darkness. It would be a long night of vigilance to ensure that we didn't run aground or tangle with the service vessels running from oil platform to oil platform.

The darkness became more complete, and the bright yellow lights on the oil platforms dominated the horizon. Sounds of motors, trucks blasting along the coastal highway, and the clanking of heavy machinery came easily across the still water. Foot by foot, cable by cable, I coaxed *Laiviņa* eastward in the confusing winds. Fatigue plagued me, and I fought the weariness trying to overcome me. I had to stay awake.

Sat, Oct 27, 1984: 34°25′N 119°40′W, Previous Day's Run: 40

Through the night, I snacked on sandwiches and fruit to keep my stamina up. We crept closer to the bright lights of Santa Barbara as I worked in nearer to the beaches to try to find the harbour entrance. As this was an unscheduled stop, I had only a medium-scale chart, and there was insufficient detail on the chart of the coastline along which I was now carefully groping my way.

With an eye cocked on the depth sounder and another on the shore, we crept along, right beside the coast. I saw a person with a flashlight walking along the beach and was able to use the relative scale of his shape to better judge the distance from the shoreline. We were too close! I turned away from the coast, and we crept slowly away until I was satisfied we were in much deeper waters.

The hands of the alarm clock crept around the dial as I stared at the eastern horizon for the telltale glow of first light. With the continuing lack of sleep, my muscles jerked in spasms. I moved in an ungainly way around the deck, setting the genoa on first the port side, then the starboard side and then back again. Dawn came in a blaze of yellow glory, sparkling the water and painting the patches of fog in pink. I relaxed as my metabolism came alive with the new day and took over the task of keeping me awake. I fixed my position from the lighthouse on a clifftop and waited for the thermal breezes to pick up. Eventually, the wind ruffled the water and at last filled the sails. I was able to steer *Laiviņa* in towards the coast again, now that I could see the forest of sailboat masts in the harbour.

It was 9 a.m. when I reached the entrance to the harbour. At the end of Stearns Wharf, a crowd of people had gathered. Some were fishing and others just sitting on the tops of the pilings. I lowered the genoa as I passed the wharf and asked a young woman for directions to the harbour master's office.

I turned my attention back to the task of tacking under mainsail between the rows of boats tied to the floating pontoons. I came up to the bright red harbour dredge at the narrow entrance to the harbour and noticed a sailboat motoring up astern wanting to pass me. I brought *Laiviņa*'s head into the wind and kept the mainsail luffing until it motored past me. With the helm hard over, *Laiviņa* fell onto the starboard tack, and I continued carefully working my way deeper into the maze of boats. Ahead, a large coast guard vessel lay docked alongside a fixed wharf, and nearby the ship, I spied the public float. That was where I would head.

Even though I had been at the helm for the past thirty hours, I felt charged up with energy and pleased with my skill at having safely sailed this far. I judged the final approach and quietly touched alongside the float. As soon as we were alongside, I leaped over the lifelines, landed on the dock, and started securing my little ship with the stout mooring lines I had at the ready.

"Haven't you got a motor on that thing?" an idle bystander shouted across from the other wharf.

I just smiled and waved back.

CHAPTER 5

Repairs

I walked up the flight of stairs on the outside of the harbour master's office and past the glass doors to be confronted by armed personnel. It always seems strange that people in such jobs need to be armed with revolvers and rubber truncheons. Having grown up in an environment where even police officers were unarmed, I was disturbed by the blatant display of firearms.

In spite of their outward appearance, they were friendly and co-operative.

"My self-steering rudders broke about 400 miles offshore, so I've called into Santa Barbara to rebuild them," I said. "Can you tell me where I can clear customs?"

"There is no customs office here, but here's the phone number of U.S. Customs," he replied.

He scribbled a number on the back of a requisition form and handed it to me.

"Telephones are down there on the dock," he added.

It was not as easy as it seemed. Some time and money departed through the metal bandit in the weatherproof cubicle. I had to make numerous long-distance phone calls to Los Angeles to get some preliminary information. I became frustrated with the difficulties I was encountering and decided to try a new tack. The coast guard vessel tied alongside seemed like a likely source of information. I went on board and spoke with the commander.

"I'm having a lot of trouble locating U.S. Customs. Isn't there an office in Santa Barbara?"

"No. What number are you trying?" he asked.

I showed him the back of the requisition form, now covered with a long list of numbers.

"Hmmm...just a moment."

He picked up the ship-to-shore telephone and dialed. As I waited, I leaned against a bulkhead and looked around me at the navigation and communication equipment arrayed around the bridge. Quite a bit more sophisticated than what I was using.

The day warmed quickly. I felt the sun pouring onto my back, relaxing me. In my tired state, I half closed my eyes and listened to a mixture of familiar and unfamiliar sounds in the background. Occasional cries of seagulls and the persistent sound of flags fluttering in the strong thermal winds. Disembodied voices floating out of the dark hatchways of the coast guard cutter, combined with the shrill voices of female tourists.

"...have him here. Do you want to speak to him?...Okay. Just a moment."

The commander looked up and caught my eye.

"I have the customs officer on the line; you can talk to him now," he said, handing me the smooth black telephone, and settling back to listen to a one-sided conversation.

"Hello?"

"Yes, I was forced to make an unscheduled stop for repairs."

"The rudders, the self-steering rudders."

"Oh...three or four days, no longer than a week to rebuild them."

"*Laiviņa.* Lima–Alpha–India–Victor–India–November–Alpha. My registration is 380142. Port of registry, Dunedin, New Zealand. That's Delta–Uniform–November–Echo–Delta–India–November."

"Okay, thank you very much."

"Bye."

I turned and handed the receiver back to the commander and explained.

"He said he doesn't need to come out and see me, so long as I contact him before I leave. Thank you for your help."

The commander pushed himself into up a standing position and he waved a farewell.

"Take care now," he said, as I descended the steep set of stairs leading from the bridge to the main deck.

I needed to find a lumberyard so headed for the telephones. After I phoned a few yards, I found that it was too difficult to choose over the phone the best lumber for the task. I needed to visit the yard to get anywhere in my quest for good-quality hardwood. Grateful for the opportunity to exercise my legs, I bounded up the stairs to the harbour master's office. I decided to take a berth for the night and shelled out ten dollars of my emergency funds.

Down the stairs and back to the transient's dock, I walked to where *Laiviņa* rested. The motor fired up after the weeks of inactivity with just a little coaxing, and I untied the mooring lines. With a steady "Bang! Bang! Bang! Bang!" *Laiviņa* cut through the oily water to a spare berth in among the crowded array of vessels of all shapes and sizes. With mooring lines cleated and the ends cheesed down, I moved back along the float. The New Zealand flag flying from *Laiviņa*'s stern was attracting some attention. Just as I was climbing over the lifelines, a burly fellow approached me.

"Have you just arrived from New Zealand?" he asked me.

"No, I've just come down from Canada. I was on my way into the South Pacific when I broke my self-steering rudder," I replied. "Here, I'll show you."

I climbed back over the lifelines and onto the dock.

"That's too bad," he said after he surveyed the splintered end of the auxiliary rudder. "How many sailing with you?"

"Just myself, just *Laiviņa* and me. By the way, I'm Peter."

We shook hands, and he introduced himself as Al. I asked him if he knew where I could buy some good marine lumber. His face wrinkled as he rubbed his head.

"Well, there is one place that's open, but they only sell cheap stuff, you know, fir and other rubbish. Most of the lumberyards around town don't open on the weekend, and with tomorrow being Sunday, well, you'll probably have to wait until Monday," Al responded.

"I guess I'll go for a wander around town and have a look anyway. How far is that place you said would be open?" I asked.

"About a mile or so," he said. "Here. Come with me. We'll go in my car and I'll show you."

"You sure it's no trouble?" I inquired.

"No trouble at all!"

As Al drove me around Santa Barbara, he spoke in his easy and expressive manner of a number of items of interest around town.

"And this is the rough part of town. Doesn't look it now, but wait until after the shops close and the bars open. Real seaman's place, that one," he said, pointing to a low, roughly built tavern.

"Most of the banks are in this street, and the lumberyards start a few blocks over," he continued.

Al drove me back to the docks, and I was very glad to have had this small but important tour. When it came to the legwork I was going to have to do on Monday, this would quicken my search.

"Anything else you need?" he asked in parting.

"No, I don't think so. I have glue, clamps, and woodworking tools," I answered.

"How many clamps do you have?" he asked.

"A couple, I'll use wood screws to laminate the rudder."

"Hell! You'll need more than a couple of clamps to do the job properly. I don't have the kind of clamps you need, but I'll talk to Peter. He lives on his boat a couple of floats down from mine. He's always working on his boat. I bet he has exactly what you'll need. Yeah, I'll talk to Peter tomorrow," Al said as he departed.

The sun had gone down by the time I stepped wearily into *Laiviņa*'s cabin for the last time that day. After a simple meal, I sat at the saloon table writing the events of the last couple of days into my diary by candlelight. Afterwards, I climbed into my bunk, closed my eyes, and thought about the things that had happened. I still had a good chance of completing what I set out to do, a solo non-stop circumnavigation. I would start again, from Santa Barbara. However, on the way back I would have to call in again to Santa Barbara before heading on to Victoria. The soft bunk comforted my tired body, and with my head resting on the cool pillow, my awareness dissolved into dreams.

Sun, Oct 28, 1984: 34°25′N 119°40′W, Previous Day's Run: 0

The rigours of the last few days did not stop me from waking at dawn. I fixed breakfast and started giving *Laiviņa* a good cleaning. A bit before noon, I was ready to remove the broken remains of the self-steering rudder. After pulling the long stainless steel pintle shaft out of the gudgeons, I used the main halyard to winch the rudder up and over the pushpit rails. Next, I sawed through the rudder to remove the bronze gudgeons and, with a bit of chiselling, salvaged the fittings. By the early afternoon, the job was done, leaving me with a pile of parts. The task of repairing the rudder had started.

After drying and folding *Laiviņa*'s sails, I headed for the shower rooms with my pass-key in one hand and a bag of salty clothes in the other. Three-quarters of an hour later, I emerged from a long shower with a heavy sail-bag dripping a steady stream of water from the wet

Figure 5.1: Broken auxiliary rudder

clothes inside. I hung the clothes on hangers from the mast steps and prepared to leave the harbour for the anchorage outside. My time was up as I had only booked the berth for one night. *Laiviņa* was showing a strange sailing rig as I motored out of the harbour with towels draped over the boom and the mast decorated like a Christmas tree with my drying clothes.

Just to the east of the harbour and Stearns Wharf was an area reserved for anchoring. I found a large clear spot among the many boats at anchor or on permanent moorings. It puzzled me that there should be such an open space amid the crowd of boats. Perhaps it was a restricted area? There weren't any buoys or signs marking the area as such, although there was a restricted area near the wharf. Thinking how lucky I was, I dropped anchor in the centre of this empty space and settled down for the night. Later I was to find out why this area was devoid of anchored vessels.

Mon, Oct 29, 1984: 34°25′N 119°40′W, Previous Day's Run: 0

After breakfast the next morning, I rowed the dinghy over to Stearns Wharf. I tied it to an iron ladder beside one of the piers and, after timing the swell, sprang onto a rung and climbed the six metres or so to the deck of the wharf and clambered over the rail. I looked to seaward and saw the end of this wharf jutting out into the bay for about five hundred metres. It was huge! I had not seen such a wharf before. It supported a number of restaurants, boutiques, and souvenir shops. In the early morning, as I walked along the smooth, old boards, I met no one, though I figured that it would become busy later in the day. At least it wasn't the weekend when I would have to work my way through a press of tourists. I passed the attractive buildings, their facades made of light material contrasting the rugged and sturdy pilings.

I quickly reached the shore then walked into town to look for lumber. After trying a couple of places, I was referred to Sobobo Hardwoods, where there was an excellent but expensive selection of hardwoods.

"I'd like to have a look at your Honduras mahogany. Where do you keep it?" I asked.

A strong-looking old lady answered my question.

"Over there," she pointed. "It starts near that wall and ends a few feet past that beam."

I walked to where the mahogany was stacked and pulled out piece after piece. Sobobo had some nice straight and wide lengths of mahogany of varying thickness, so I selected a two-inch-thick piece that was eleven inches wide as the central lamination. I decided to purchase six feet, which would be long enough for the long blade-shaped auxiliary rudder. To pad out the rudder to the correct thickness, I chose two additional pieces that were an inch and a quarter thick, ten inches wide, and about five feet long. I would glue these lengths on either face of the central piece. It was just enough lumber to do the job with little waste.

I guessed that Sobobo Hardwoods was a family business, as I noticed a young man, probably the woman's son, making ornate doors.

"How much will it cost for these two pieces and a six-foot length cut from this piece?" I asked him.

The young man looked up from the door frame he was working on, put down his plane, and moved over to the lumber. He took a pencil from behind his ear and a tape from the leather apron he was wearing.

"Two by nine, six feet long, and two by twelve, let's see." He scribbled some figures down on the newspaper lying on the bench and looked up. "That's all you're getting?"

I nodded.

"Okay then, it comes to $96.50." He put the pencil back atop his ear.

While he played with the tape, sliding it in and out of its holder, I scratched my head and thought. I knew that I had only ninety dollars in U.S. funds, twenty dollars Canadian, and a little loose change.

"Ahhh... would you mind keeping this lumber aside? I have to go to the bank to get some Canadian money changed."

"Sure," he answered. "Make sure you're back before we close at five."

"No problem, I'll be back."

As I walked up the long streets towards the centre of town, I worried about the amount of money that would be left after buying the lumber. It would only be a few dollars. I reached the bank and presented my Canadian notes.

"There's a twenty-five percent charge for exchanging these notes," the teller reminded me.

"How much will I get for this then?" I asked, feeling very much like her poor cousin begging for a handout. I laid every cent of Canadian money I had on the vinyl pad in front of me. She looked down her nose at the paltry sum.

"We don't take change," she asserted.

I scooped my miniature fortune back into my dusty wallet. Staring at me through the slot in the glass, she sighed, looked from side to side and probably hoped I would leave so she could serve a more affluent customer. I didn't move. She sighed again and started to calculate the exchange rate on the twenty-dollar note. With a bored look, she slid a ten-dollar note and some silver halfway towards my eagerly waiting hands. I was shocked at the value of my Canadian twenty-dollar bill. I put the money in my wallet and moved away to a quiet corner of the bank to count out my net worth. One hundred dollars and seventy-nine cents. After paying for the lumber, I would have only a small amount of change left with which to get around the world.

I ambled back along the street, racking my brain for any way I could raise some money. At first I thought I might be able to sell something, but I couldn't think of anything I had on board that anyone would want. Perhaps I could sell some of the cans of tuna. That might work. Then an idea struck me. I could sell my blood. I had heard some years ago that in the United States, people could make a fortune by selling their blood. That is, if they possessed a rare type of blood. Unfortunately, my O-positive blood didn't fall into the rare category. My blood betrayed my common ancestry. Still, maybe I could make a dollar or two.

At the next phone box, I searched through the Yellow Pages for the blood bank. Fortunately, the address showed it to be only a mile or so away, so I set off in the correct direction towards what in my heart felt like Transylvania. Arriving at the low, uninspiring building, I approached in trepidation. What would I say? I ran through my mind some possible openers.

"Hi! Wanna buy some blood?" Too breezy.

"Say, mister, can you spare a couple of bucks? I'll give you a pint or two of the liquid of life."

I didn't want to fawn. Perhaps honesty was the best policy.

"I was just passing by four hundred miles out to sea when I ran into this problem, and..." They wouldn't believe me. It would have to be an oblique approach.

"I'm interested in giving blood. Can you explain how the system works?" I asked, afraid that the nurse in the starched uniform would see through me and realize that I only wanted the money. She handed me a group of pamphlets and informed me that I would find all the information I needed inside the pages.

I sat down on an empty seat and glanced at the others around me. Perhaps I could ask some of the patients. There weren't many. Just an old man asleep with his hat over the corner of his left eye and a swarthy woman firing rapid Spanish at her truculent children. Not much hope there, I thought. I approached the desk again.

"What happens after I give blood? I mean, this is a blood bank, right? Can I get it back later if I need it?" I asked.

She looked at me strangely. "We give you a deposit book with a record of the deposits you make. In the event of an accident, for free you can get half of the blood you have deposited."

I didn't think too much of that banking scheme. An interest rate of minus fifty percent didn't seem too encouraging.

"What if I want to make a withdrawal? I mean, say I want just the cash value of my deposits."

"We don't pay cash for blood, sir," she answered.

"Well...ahhh...I've got to get back to work, so I'll be in again later," I said as I backed out the swinging glass doors.

Outside I berated myself for being such a fool. I had raised my hopes too much. The day was getting on, and I had to walk back to Sobobo Hardwoods before the place shut. While I strode down the low hill, I reflected that at the very least I was getting some much-needed leg exercise. I would be missing such a luxury in the succeeding months.

I reached the lumberyard with a quarter of an hour to spare, collected my lumber, and caught the eye of the man with whom I had talked previously.

"I'll pay for this lumber now, please. I only want six feet of this piece, though," I said.

He took the long length of mahogany from me and placed it in front of the cut-off saw. After marking off the correct length, he neatly sliced off the unwanted piece and placed it back in the rack.

"Let's see. That'll be a $101.50," he told me.

"But you said it would be $96.50!" I said.

"There's a five-buck cutting charge."

I was shocked. I hadn't allowed for this.

"I'll see if I have enough with me," I mumbled as I groped in the dark recesses of my thin wallet.

"What do you want this lumber for anyway?" he asked.

He listened intently as I told him of my solo sail down the coast from Canada and how I discovered the broken rudder. I didn't tell him of my plans to sail around the world, as I still wanted to keep it under close wraps. He watched as I eased the wrinkled bills out of my wallet for the last time and counted the money out on the table.

"Listen, don't worry about the cutting charge. It'll be on the house. Good luck with making the rudder and have a good voyage!"

With a grin, he waved goodbye. I heaved the three pieces of lumber onto my shoulder and marched out of the yard.

At first, the lumber was easy to carry, and I was confident I could get back to Stearns Wharf without too much bother. However, the weight started to take its toll. I found I was counting my steps and making goals to reach the next block before changing shoulders. At last my footsteps echoed hollowly on the heavy timbers of the wharf. I reached the spot above the dinghy, stacked the lumber by the rail, and looked around while I rested. There were a number of tourists now, some strolling slowly, while others looked over the rails and gazed at the swell below.

I picked up the heaviest piece and swung myself over the railing and onto the invisible ladder below the bulwark. With one arm around the plank and the other holding on to the top rail, I descended carefully by letting go each rung and grabbing the next rung an instant later. Some tourists came over to watch me descend the six-metre ladder to the dinghy swirling around in the swell below. They seemed to be secretly hoping I would end up taking an unscheduled swim. Fortunately I transported the three pieces safely to the dinghy.

Once in the dinghy, I carefully stacked the lumber on the thwarts. My next task was to borrow some clamps that had been offered. However, I first needed to take the lumber out to *Laiviņa*. Climbing back into the dinghy, I rigged it for sail, slid the centreboard and rudder in place, and headed for where *Laiviņa* was anchored.

When I arrived at the boat, I discovered why no one had anchored in the empty spot. To windward was a low platform floating on the water and moored to a buoy. This platform had become a haven for numerous seabirds, and the daytime sea breezes carried an almost overpowering stench of guano right through the boat. The other live-aboards must have chuckled when they saw me anchored there.

After unloading the lumber, I climbed back into the dinghy and set a course for the harbour. From *Laiviņa* to the harbour docks, the rhumb line went right under Stearns Wharf, past a dredge and into the harbour. With barely enough clearance below the cross-braces for the dinghy mast, I sailed under the wharf, among the piers, and out the other side. At the docks, I made my way to Al's boat and knocked on the hull.

"Ahoy there!" I called.

A head popped out of the lit hatch opening.

"Oh, it's you, Peter. Listen, we're just finishing dinner, but you can come aboard anyway," Al said.

"That's okay, I just came to borrow those clamps you said you had," I replied.

He disappeared down the companionway; a short time later, he reappeared with the clamps in his hand.

"It's about all I have, but you're welcome to 'em. Hey, I talked to Peter and he gave me his friend's telephone number. Just a minute, I wrote it down somewhere. This guy's name is Chris. He's a woodworking instructor. Give him a call," Al said.

I set off at a sprint for the pay phones on the dock, found a quarter, and phoned Chris. I introduced myself when he answered and briefly told him of my dilemma. He was only too glad to help. He told me to wait and he would come to the docks with the clamps. A half-hour later, a Volkswagen turned onto the wharf, and a slightly built man approached me.

"Chris?" I ventured.

"Peter?"

I nodded as he stretched out his arm. We shook hands, he walked back to his car and dragged out a cardboard box containing two dozen heavy-duty clamps.

"Will these be enough?" Chris asked

"More than enough!" I replied. "This is great! Thank you very much for the loan of the clamps. I should be finished with them in a day or so. I'll try not to get any glue on them."

"Oh, I'm always getting glue on them. Don't worry about that," he answered.

We chatted on the dock for some time about a variety of nautical subjects. I learned that he had built a boat and tried to sail to Hawaii, but in spite of his drive and love of the sea, he suffered so badly from seasickness that he had to return after a few days.

The conversation ran out, and we shook hands once more. After he left, I untied the dinghy and rowed unhurriedly back to *Laiviņa* in the still air.

Tue, Oct 30, 1984: 34°25′N 119°40′W, Previous Day's Run: 0

After a breakfast of eggs on toast garnished with the strong odour of guano, I hauled up onto the deck the pieces of mahogany I had bought. I laid a sheet of black plastic on the deck as a drop cloth, greased the clamps, and mixed up a batch of epoxy glue. I had to work fast, spreading glue on the faces of the mahogany and putting the pieces into position in their final lamination arrangement. I clamped them together before the fast-setting glue went hard.

Once the job was done, I cleaned up my tools, rigged the sails on the dinghy and headed back into the harbour to pick up my battery. I had left it with Al's friend Peter, who offered to charge it up on his battery charger for me. The day was still warm, and the late afternoon sun had set behind the Santa Ynez mountains as I tacked back and forth towards Peter's boat. He wasn't there, but he had left instructions to invite myself aboard. I switched off the charger, disconnected it from the battery terminals, hoisted the heavy battery over the side and into the dinghy, sheeted in the dinghy sail, and pointed the bow back towards Stearns Wharf. By the time I reached *Laiviņa*, it was quite dark. I had a quick snack, flopped onto my bunk, and soon fell asleep.

Wed, Oct 31, 1984 34°25′N 119°40′W, Previous Day's Run: 0

Soon after dawn, I awoke and went on deck to look at the result of my gluing job of the day before. The glue was hard, and the greased clamps came away easily. I carried the heavy mass of wood below and, using Chris's clamps, attached the rudder to the saloon table. A while later I had planed off the glue runs, taken a shaving off all surfaces, and marked in pencil the outline of the rudder.

I sat back, rested for a while and worked out a plan of action. My first job was to saw eighteen inches along the grain of what was now a piece of mahogany five inches thick. I cleaned the grease off my handsaw, wobbled it back and forth in the air, and eyed the thick pencil line. Staring at the line wasn't going to get the job done, so I climbed up onto the saloon table and set to work.

Luckily my saw was brand new and sharp. It still took some time, and my hands, as tough as they were from sailing, were getting a little red in places. I was relieved when the piece of scrap lumber fell with a thump on the sawdust-covered cabin sole. Next, I had to rough out the curved shape to remove most of the excess lumber. I remembered how

Figure 5.2: Glued laminations ready to shape

long it had taken me the first time I built the auxiliary rudder, and that rudder was made of Oregon pine, a lot easier to plane than mahogany. I knew that I was in for some blood, sweat, and tears.

The hot sun climbed into the sky as the level of the curly red shavings rose on the floor. By the afternoon, I was ankle deep in a sea of shavings. I had stripped down to my shorts, and my chest glistened with rivulets of sweat. The red mahogany dust stained my hands as I pushed the plane along the resisting surface. Slowly, the irregular slab of wood took on the shape of a long, sleek blade. Eventually I dared not take off any more wood as I had yet to make templates of the hydrodynamic curves at different points along the blade, so I decided to shape the trim tab instead. Now I really had to work.

The original trim tab had been made out of a piece of Malaysian lumber called balau. It was one of the denser hardwoods, something like Australian jarrah. In the aft locker, I still had the original plank of balau from which I cut the first trim tab. I dragged it out, marked out the shape, and started to saw a five-foot-long cut, the length of the plank.

Tough wasn't the word. The saw protested as I hacked back and forth. At long last, the pitch of the shrieking saw rose higher and higher until the piece dropped amid the shavings. Now I had to plane it. First I sharpened the plane blade and honed it. I needed a razor-sharp blade to hack into the solid wood; otherwise, the plane would just skip over the surface.

The sun was sinking as I took the last shaving off the trim tab. I turned the long five-centimetre-wide wooden blade, letting the light reflect off the surface. It looked good. With a spoke-shave I smoothed off the high spots and sanded the plane lines away. One part completed. I was getting excited as my new rudder would be very strong and I would soon be on my way again.

After dinner, I lit the Tilley storm lantern and started making the templates for the shape. Using my programmable calculator, I worked out the curves and marked them on a piece of stiff cardboard. The cardboard, once a "Bon Voyage" sign given to me on my departure, was now in fifteen pieces covered in pencil marks. With a pair of scissors, I cut the hydrodynamic curves out of the templates. I was ready for the final shaping.

It was Halloween and I went to bed thinking of the little ghosts and goblins running from house to house trick-or-treating. Penny had given me a gift to unwrap at Halloween, but I decided not to open it until

I reached the start of the northeast trades. I would have been at that latitude if the rudder had not broken. Just another carrot to hold in front of my nose!

Thu, Nov 1, 1984: 34°25′N 119°40′W, Previous Day's Run: 0

I awoke to another clear morning, breakfasted quickly, and started work on the rudder. Using a spoke-shave and the templates from the evening before, I whittled out the correct shape at various points along the rudder and, using the grooves as a guide, planed the rudder until I had removed all of the excess wood down to the whittled grooves. A rubdown with sandpaper and the rudder was a beautiful, smooth, hydrodynamic shape.

The next job was to make a new bearing and mount for the bottom of the trim tab. I drilled a hole in the trim tab and rudder and bent a piece of five-sixteenth-inch stainless steel rod in the vice. After cutting some straps out of a stainless steel sheet, the job was done. All that remained was to fit the gudgeons, paint the wood, and remount the rudder onto the transom.

The sun had disappeared behind the mountains, and it would soon be dark. I wanted to continue working. I was all fired up, now that I knew I was nearly finished. The last thing I wanted was to spend days doing a proper paint job, but the wood had to be sealed and coated with antifouling. I decided to do it after dinner.

With my belly full, I felt stronger. I mixed up some epoxy resin and painted it over the whole of the rudder except where the gudgeons were to be fitted. The wood under the gudgeons would be sealed the next day, after I bonded the gudgeons into place. After the epoxy had gone tacky but not yet dry, I painted on the antifouling so that the epoxy would bond to the antifouling.

At midnight, I sat back on the settee and finally rested. There was nothing more I could do. My hands were sticky, and the kerosene smoke from the Tilley storm lantern stung my eyes. I was tired. I washed my hands, laid back on the bunk, and threw the blankets over me. The weariness did not prevent me from savouring the mood that was encompassing me. I scorned myself for the low morale I suffered when the rudder had broken. Now, I had a strong new rudder. I smiled silently in dark of the cabin and fell softly asleep.

Fri, Nov 2, 1984: 34°25′N 119°40′W, Previous Day's Run: 0

When I awoke, the wind had sprung up a little, chopping up the surface of the water. It was too rough to fit the rudder; I needed still water to do the job properly. At anchor in the bay, *Laiviņa* was in constant motion pitching up and down and rolling from side to side. While I sat on deck planning the day, I noticed the harbour master in his power boat heading in my direction.

"Ahoy!" I called to him.

He saw me waving, so he turned and manoeuvred the craft over to me.

"How are you doing?" he asked.

"Good! I've finished the rudder. Here, I'll show you."

I ducked down the hatch, picked up the rudder and carefully carried it up the companionway.

"Looks good," he said.

"The problem is, it's too rough out here to fit it. Would it be okay if I used the visitor's dock to fit it on the transom?" I asked.

"When do you want to do that?" he returned.

"This morning."

He scratched his beard for a moment.

"I guess it'll be okay," he replied. "As long as you leave room for other boats coming and going. It's only Friday, so it shouldn't be too busy. How long are you going to take?"

"Maybe a couple of hours. I have to bed the fittings down with epoxy, but I'll try to get it done as quick as possible," I replied.

"Okay."

With a wave of his hand, he pushed the throttle forward and headed off, disappearing among the anchored boats. I took the rudder back into the cabin and started the motor.

It took a while to break out the anchor, well bedded in from the last few days of steady sea breezes. It came up clean from the sandy bottom, so I pulled it quickly onto the bow fitting, ran back to the tiller and steered for the end of Stearns Wharf.

Once *Laiviņa* reached the visitor's dock, I secured the mooring lines and set about fitting the rudder. I borrowed an electric drill from a fisherman to bore a security hole through the trim tab and the rudder. With a safety line through these holes, I would not lose the rudders if any of the fittings were to come loose. I carefully lowered the rudder over the side and into the water. I was feeling a bit nervous, concerned that I would lose a vital fitting into the water, so it took some careful manipulation of the various parts before the fittings were assembled. Fortunately, I had taken the precaution of tying safety lines onto all the parts that I could in case I dropped anything. I didn't relish diving in the cool water, searching for a fitting or two.

With the pintle shaft slid into place, I drove mahogany wedges between the gudgeons and the rudder to hold the rudder in the correct location. Next, I sealed the bottom of the gudgeons with silicone rubber and poured epoxy into the gap between the bronze gudgeon and the bare wood. It would be near impossible to separate the fitting from the rudder once the epoxy hardened. Not that I wanted to, as I felt the rudder would never need to be disassembled again, and I wanted it to be as strong as possible.

During the afternoon, while I waited for the epoxy to harden, I chatted with a couple who thought I was from England. The Union Jack in the corner of *Laiviņa*'s New Zealand flag had convinced them I was English.

"So, where are you off to?" the man asked.

"Oh, down into the South Pacific for a bit," I replied, as usual.

We talked boats for a while, and I expounded on my various sailing theories and techniques. Soon the epoxy was hard, and the couple left me to finish cleaning up. I posted my mail and walked to the nearest phone box to contact customs. After the important and necessary task of clearing out of the United States was done, I walked back to the dock. I went aboard and started swinging on the crank handle. With the engine chugging quietly away, I untied the mooring lines.

I was standing on the dock coiling one of the lines when I felt a tap on my shoulder. I turned to find the couple back again, the man holding a steaming hot mug of soup in an outstretched hand.

"Here," he said, thrusting the mug into my hands. "You certainly taught me a lot, and I'm grateful for it. Have some clam chowder."

I laughed "You're welcome to the knowledge, it's free," I said, taking the mug from him. "Thank you, I appreciate your generosity."

It didn't take long to finish the soup as I had been too busy to eat a proper meal through the day. Soon I was alone again as *Laiviņa* chugged quietly out to anchor in the bay. Tomorrow I would be away!

CHAPTER 6

Second Departure

SAT, NOV 3, 1984: 34°22′N 119°45′W, PREVIOUS DAY'S RUN: 5

My first thoughts as I awoke were tinged with excitement. I was going to be on my way again. I was impatient to start sailing and determined to make up the time I had lost. Almost exactly one week after arriving in Santa Barbara, I was leaving. If I counted the time from when the rudder had broken, I had lost more than ten days. If I combined that with the time I took to sail to Santa Barbara, I had two weeks to make up and today's wind was not going to co-operate. Dawn had brought only a light breeze and filled the main shipping channel with smog.

I hurried through breakfast and went on deck to prepare for my departure. After sniffing the wind, I pre-set the self-steering for a close-hauled course on the port tack and hoisted the mainsail. As soon as the sail was up, I pulled *Laiviņa* up to the anchor, waited until she fell off onto the correct tack, and broke the anchor out of the bottom.

Slowly we crept forward under the single sail as I hauled quickly on the genoa halyard. We gained a little more speed now as the larger sail filled, and we headed for the other anchored boats at a hair-raising speed of almost one knot! Although we were not travelling that fast, *Laiviņa* was inexorably moving straight towards one of the anchored boats. Running back to the stern, I grabbed the wind vane and turned it to force *Laiviņa* off the wind and around the transom of the vessel dead ahead. By steering with the wind vane, we dodged around two more boats before we were in the clear.

Ahead lay the end of Stearns Wharf. I wondered if I would clear it in one tack. It looked as though I would be forced to put in a tack, but as I drew closer the wind lifted us a little and I knew *Laiviņa* would clear the end piles. As I drew closer, a couple of cautious fishermen began to reel in their lines, no doubt fearing that *Laiviņa* was going to collect their hooks as souvenirs. I managed to weather the end of Stearns Wharf without tacking and worked across the harbour entrance.

After crossing the entrance, we were off the breakwater when the wind dropped to a zephyr. Backwash from the breakwater chopped the surface up into a mess of clapotic waves, slowing *Laiviņa* down until we were making very little headway. I was a bit concerned as sailing past steep cliffs and rock walls in a light breeze can be dangerous. The backwash can stall forward motion, and consequently a vessel can drift onto the rocks. With the anchor ready to let go, I persevered. I knew that I could not tack as it would kill every bit of speed we had, which would create a worse situation.

I eased the sheets and pointed *Laiviņa*'s bow a little more downwind to keep what little speed we had. Slowly we eased along the breakwater, getting closer and closer to the rocks. I did not want to give in and drop the anchor to wait for the wind. Eventually *Laiviņa* passed the end of the breakwater and was off the beach where the backwash ended. I was able to sail closer to the wind and away from the shore.

Approximately five miles from the anchorage, the wind quit altogether. It was noon, and I was left basking in the warm sunshine on the edge of the Santa Barbara Channel. The heavy thrumming of ship's engines came from out of the fogbound channel. Thankfully, I wasn't in the fog bank when the wind dropped. I fixed lunch, brought it on deck, and stripped off for a suntan. I was all alone, enjoying the quiet conditions and resting on top of the underside of the dinghy. An hour passed in the quiet, still air while I dozed off with dreams and visions unfurling in my brain.

Suddenly, I awoke to the sound of a motor close by. Looking up, I saw a group of fishermen coming closer and closer in a fast, open, planing hulled boat. I groped madly for my trousers, and after a couple of attempts to put my foot into the correct trouser leg, I was dressed again. I wasn't sure, but it looked as though they were smirking as they roared past, leaving *Laiviņa* rocking in their wake.

We wallowed through the day without making any real progress. I chafed at the slow speed. By nightfall, I was at the edge of the outbound shipping lane. Though tired, I had to stay awake as *Laiviņa* had now entered the fog bank. Around me, I could hear ships slowly passing us with their heavy foghorns vibrating the thick misty air that surrounded my world. The radar reflector on top of the mast must have been working well as they all seemed to avoid me. Little by little, as the night drew on, I worked through the outward-bound lane and on into the relative safety of the central separation zone.

Sun, Nov 4, 1984: 34°14′N 120°11′W, Previous Day's Run: 23

Slowly the blackness of night softened into grey as the invisible sun climbed from beneath the horizon. It was a misty noon before I was able to finally cross the inbound shipping lane. Although the channel was only about ten miles wide, it had taken me eighteen hours in the non-existent wind to cross it. That afternoon, the breeze picked up a little and the fog thinned to reveal the vague outlines of Santa Rosa Island and San Miguel Island. At last I started to make reasonable progress towards the channel between the two islands, hoping to arrive at the entrance before dusk.

Laiviņa was now occasionally rolling to swells coming in from the North Pacific Ocean, and it was while I was walking along the side deck that it happened. In the light, almost non-existent wind, the tightly sheeted boom suddenly swung over to the weather side. I saw it coming and ducked, but not far enough. With a crack, the mainsail filled on the opposite tack, flicking the boom against the side of my head. I fell to the deck, stunned from the painful blow, with a sharp sound ringing in my ear.

Pain washed over me as I clung to consciousness in desperation, holding my head with clenched fists. A groan slowly escaped from between my lips as the shock subsided. I pushed myself up onto my knees and caught my breath. That was too close. I had thought I was clear of the boom's arc of travel and had I been a few centimetres further away, I would have never been struck. I resolved to be more careful and discipline myself rigorously so I could survive the next nine months. I really could not afford to be hit by the boom and knocked unconscious. In a heavy sea, I might have been hurled overboard and be hanging underwater by my lifeline.

At sunset, the wind dropped away completely, and the fog closed in. I was now in a bit of a predicament. The off-lying rocks exposed to the heavy Pacific swell, the fog, and dark night sky created a significant risk. My navigation had to be very good to pass through the narrow channel under these conditions. I had only the depth sounder to improve my dead reckoning position. However, as the wind was very light, at least I would be able to hear the sound of breaking waves before I got too close to the rocks.

With my eye on the needle of the depth sounder slowly moving upwards, We crept cautiously towards the location of where I judged the channel to be. The soft, continuous roar of breakers on the rocky shore grew louder and louder. Through the thick fog, I suddenly spied the faint outline of individual swells expending their energy among the kelp and barnacles.

Adrenalin surged through my body. We were dangerously close to Santa Rosa Island. I altered course and sailed parallel to the coast, keeping the noise of the waves abeam. I did some quick mental calculations and figured that the largest swells passing under *Laiviņa*'s keel would break in about six metres of water.

As the needle of the depth sounder moved closer and closer to the twenty foot mark, the noise of the waves breaking on the rocks grew louder and louder. A large swell rolled under me and to my horror, broke with a roar barely a hundred metres away. Spray flew skyward and the fizzing of white water came clearly to my ears. This was getting too risky. I turned downwind and worked gradually away from the shore as the sound of the breaking waves diminished.

Once we had travelled a distance away from the island and its dangerous shore, the depth sounder registered a safe amount of water under the keel. I backed the genoa and lashed the tiller to leeward, bringing *Laiviņa* into a hove-to position and on a drift away from danger. I would sit out the night keeping watch.

Mon, Nov 5, 1984: 33°49′N 120°26′W, Previous Day's Run: 28

For the rest of the night, *Laiviņa* lay hove to while I waited for dawn, watching to make sure tidal currents didn't drift us onto the rocks. It was my second night without sleep, and I paced the deck in an effort to prevent my eyelids from closing. When it became apparent that I was still falling asleep, I forced a spurt of adrenaline into my bloodstream by shocking myself with images of fearful situations. This did the trick. Unfortunately, the effects of the adrenaline would wear off after a while, and I would be once again fighting to keep my head up.

After dawn, the fog lifted, and I saw the channel clearly. As we moved closer, I saw many rocks above water and breaking swells identifying those rocks below the surface. Once in the channel, we finally got the wind I had been waiting for since leaving Santa Barbara. *Laiviņa* heeled over and accelerated until we were zipping along.

As I trimmed the sails, I felt the strain of the last three days without sleep weakening me. It was with a weary hand that I waved to a fisherman motoring through the channel from the opposite direction. Soon we were through the channel and into open water. It was reassuring to get away from land quickly as I was burnt out and could not have made it through a third night without sleep.

By the afternoon, I was more than ten miles offshore and could afford the luxury of a couple of hours sleep. Setting the alarm, I climbed into my bunk. In spite of my mental exhaustion, it took a while to get to sleep as my biological clock refused to co-operate. Eventually I lapsed into a deep slumber.

When the alarm finally woke me two hours later, I went on deck and checked the course and the weather. The conditions had remained much the same and we were now more than four hours direct sailing away from the coast. I set the alarm to give me four hours sleep and this time I fell asleep quickly.

When the alarm woke me for the second time, it was dark. In the cool night air, I sniffed the wind, checked the compass, and made a slight adjustment to the self-steering system. Standing on the aft hatch, I watched *Laiviņa* driving along smoothly in the dark cloud-filled night. At this rate, we would soon be safely out to sea. I went below and reset the alarm clock to give me a full eight hours' sleep. We were so far away from the land now that I could safely sleep through the night without the danger of striking land.

I had a strict rule for sleeping close to land. Don't. In spite of the fact that I might be sailing away from the land, an unannounced wind shift could easily send *Laiviņa* sailing directly towards land while I slept. As a policy, I decided to sleep only when I was more than two hours' direct sailing, or approximately ten miles, away from danger. The amount of sleep I allowed myself was less than the time it would take to sail directly towards the nearest danger at *Laiviņa*'s fastest possible speed. If there was any danger of sleeping through the alarm, then I would have to sleep sitting up on deck, so I could be sure that I would not fall into a deep sleep.

Tue, Nov 6, 1984: 33°39′N 120°30′W, Previous Day's Run: 11

What a feeling! I felt very relaxed from the fourteen hours of deep sleep, even if it was broken by the alarm clock's strident clanging. I slept well and woke up to greet the sun and a calm sea. The sound of a powerful aircraft coming closer and closer disturbed my breakfast, so I went on deck to investigate. Above in the sky, a large military plane circled slowly around *Laiviņa*. It swooped down until it was sixty metres above the water and came right at me.

Figure 6.1: Orion

I grabbed my camera and photographed it as it droned overhead. I thought it might have been a surveillance plane looking for drug runners. It circled around and then made another pass over the top of my mast at the same low altitude. It circled once more, and then after finally crossing *Laiviņa*'s bow for the third time, a loud megaphone boomed at me.

"Zero... One... Six..."

"Zero... One... Six..."

Because of the pattern the aircraft had been flying, I interpreted this to mean that the crew was on a search and rescue mission and was requesting me to steer a course of 016 degrees to assist. I swung my body into the cabin, grabbed the crank handle, and slid it into the heavy flywheel. After a few hefty turns, the diesel beat out a steady "Thud... thud... thud," and I bounded back on deck.

I was quite excited at the prospect of saving lives. Where were these drowning sailors I was going to pluck from the cold caress of Davy Jones' locker? Which direction? The megaphone had revealed its secrets in such a perplexing way. Zero-one-six? Was that true, magnetic, or compass? I reasoned that it could not have been a compass course as they weren't able to see *Laiviņa*'s deviation card, pinned to the bulkhead above the chart table. It was either a true or magnetic course. Which was it? I finally decided that it was more likely a magnetic course. The chart showed that this was the direction from which I had just come, between the two islands, Santa Rosa Island and San Miguel Island.

I climbed the mast and scanned the sea towards the northeast. A tanker dead ahead looked as if it was making no way. Bristling with excitement, I imagined myself hauling a dozen oil-covered seamen onto *Laiviņa*'s deck. Quickly reaching the deck, I thrust the long gear lever ahead and headed for the tanker. After a while I noticed that the tanker was moving. So much for that theory. Perhaps it was some fisherman wrecked on San Miguel Island. Yes, that must be it!

All day I motored in the direction I had been given, reaching the islands near sunset. Nothing I had seen resembled anything like sailors in distress. All around me, a constant traffic of ships passed between *Laiviņa* and the islands. I was starting to feel like a fool. Here was a solo sailor with primitive gear, conducting a search and rescue with no idea as to what or where to look, while radio-equipped ship after ship carried on regardless.

Thin wisps of fog diffused the approaching black rocks. What was I doing? Was I going to continue groping around in the fog and dark, tired and looking for what? The time I had taken to get to the islands would have been enough time for the coast guard to have come from Santa Barbara, rescued whomever was in trouble, and returned to Santa Barbara. No aircraft had flown over me with the "search called off" pattern. I was angry and confused. What did zero-one-six mean?

Dejectedly, I turned around after losing another precious day and headed back onto my course. I was beginning to think that I would never get away from smoggy California. It was not until a couple of years later that I realized that zero-one-six was VHF Channel 16. Why did they say *zero*-one-six? Why not just Channel 16? Anyway it was not possible for me to talk to them as *Laiviņa* carried no VHF radio. I only had a shortwave receiver and an emergency transmitter beacon on the aircraft frequency.

The darkening sky brought a steady breeze, gently pushing *Laiviņa* into deeper water and away from land. When the sky finally melted into the sea, I went into the warm cabin, prepared and cooked up a hot meal of rice and cabbage. I longed for the deep ocean swells.

Wed, Nov 7, 1984: 32°01′N 120°24′W, Previous Day's Run: 98

A steady force 3 wind had us reaching along under full mainsail and number one genoa. I lazed about, occasionally wandering on deck, tweaking the sails and fine-tuning the self-steering. *Laiviņa* needed little attention. The wind blew the waves under us with undulating motion. I needed the rest. Selecting a book from the library I had been given, I curled up in a loose ball on the starboard quarter berth and intermittently dozed and read. Life was looking up. I was sailing again. *Laiviņa* was stronger with her new mahogany rudder, and there was still plenty of fresh food, although all the leafy greens were gone. The cabbages were lasting well. Occasionally I needed to peel off a sorry-looking outer layer, but they remained crisp inside.

Thu, Nov 8, 1984: 30°09′N 119°15′W, Previous Day's Run: 127

Hash browns steamed in the frying pan as I sprinkled them with a dash of pepper and a little hot sauce. A blackened and buckled pot held a chunk of cabbage. Onion and potato were going to accompany it on its journey to my inner regions. I was carefully consuming those foods that would go bad first. A monotonous diet of the same foods for all meals over the next week was in store for me. I did not mind it as I would soon be on simpler rations.

Thunder exploded in a painful screaming roar, shaking *Laiviņa* along her deck. My breakfast fell from my lap as fear galvanized my legs into a leap for the open companionway. What monstrous harpy was swooping down to devour us? My eyes followed the crackling roar overhead, revealing the hot glowing hell of a fighter's tail diminishing to an insignificant dot. Anger replaced shock as my caged heart threatened to break free. The sky held no more surprises as the jet fighter became a tiny gnat lost in the blue air. Swinging into the cabin, I caught up the camera and brought it above decks in readiness for the sleek machine's next pass.

Sliced water folded off the reaching bow as the big white genoa murmured gently. With aching neck and squinting eyes, I surveyed the expanse of openness above me. Nothing. I was alone again with my unfinished breakfast.

As the afternoon softened the sky, I spied an aircraft carrier and a destroyer to the east accompanied by swarming fighters buzzing like bees around a hive.

Fri, Nov 9, 1984: 27°45′N 119°04′W, Previous Day's Run: 144

Eagerness to get caught up with my chores gave me the inspiration to repair the spinnaker. I had not yet fixed it, mainly owing to lethargy. It looked like a big job, so I kept avoiding it, and the more I avoided it, the bigger the job looked. Fortified with my usual breakfast of potatoes, onions, and cabbage, I cleared the chart table of its paraphernalia and, with drawing pins, secured the first metre of the spinnaker to the table. Now it would not move.

Taking a piece of copper pipe, I beat it flat and sharpened an edge into a knife. Over the kerosene pressure stove, I heated the knife until it was red hot and then drew it carefully along the line of the ragged tear. The hot knife sliced and sealed the edge and trimmed off the loose fibres. Now there was a straight edge for the patch. I continued pinning, heating, and cutting until both halves of the spinnaker had a zigzag but clean edge. Using contact adhesive, I folded a one-centimetre hem and glued it together. I cut out the long strip patch in the same fashion and glued it to one of the halves. Now it was time to sew.

Figure 6.2: Flying fish to frying fish

I went on deck for a break and was surprised to find my first flying fish lying against the toe rail near a scupper. It was flipping and flapping in a vain attempt to get back into the water. I quickly grabbed it, beheaded it, gutted it, and cleaned it. A fresh meal for lunch! I coated the filet of fish in flour and breadcrumbs and sprinkled some spices on top. Into the frying pan it went. From flying fish to frying fish. It was delicious!

Flying fish were a sure sign of the trade wind zone, and at noon my sun shot confirmed that I had reached the trades. Well, I had reached the latitude where the trade wind was supposed to blow. Except I wasn't experiencing trade winds yet. Instead of the east-northeast wind I expected, the wind was still blowing from the north. Although I was expecting the trade winds, it was wonderful that I was still getting a following wind. It was easier sailing than beating close-hauled into the wind.

Having a following wind was making it easy for me to make as much easting as possible as I would soon be close-hauled, and working towards the east would be more difficult. I wanted to be as close to the North American continent as safety would allow. Once in the southern hemisphere, working eastward would be difficult if not impossible in the southeast trades.

Still, I decided that I would open up my belated Halloween gifts as a form of celebration. Wrapped up in the gift box were a number of chocolate pumpkins, which I decided would be better rationed at one a day until they were finished. This was one of the many ways I learned to tease myself into maintaining focus. In the box was a card from my friend Mhora containing a crossword puzzle and a cryptogram for me to solve. This was very exciting as I love cryptograms!

Penny had enclosed a photo of the Gorge as a reminder of a sailing trip we had done in *Laiviņa*'s dinghy. We had started sailing up the Gorge from Fisherman's Wharf, where *Laiviņa* was moored, passing under the Johnson Street Bridge, the Bay Street Bridge, the Tillicum Road Bridge, and finally the Admirals Road Bridge. When we arrived at the head of the Gorge, the tide was quite low and the depth of water was only ten centimetres. We dragged the dinghy through the mud, sinking up to our knees until we finally reached the shore near the Esquimault and Nanaimo Railway. Our relationship was relatively new at that stage, so it was a kind of "baptism by fire" for Penny.

My intent was to drag the dinghy across the narrow isthmus that separated the head of the Gorge from the Esquimault Basin. From the Esquimault Basin, we would sail out of Esquimault Harbour and head southeast along the coast, enter Victoria Harbour, and sail back to Fisherman's Wharf. All in a little Optimist-class sailing dinghy, loaded down with two adults. The distance across the isthmus was about 400 metres, and three-quarters of that was on the railroad tracks of an active rail line. Our whole day's sailing would total eight and a half nautical miles, or about sixteen kilometres.

We had hauled the dinghy up onto the railway, and it fit easily between the standard gauge rails. The brass-coated runners that acted as handrails on the underside of the hull slid easily on the railway ties, and we made good progress. Just as we were dragging the dinghy off the tracks near the Esquimault Basin, I heard a train whistle blowing and it sounded very close. We had just dragged the dinghy down the embankment into the aptly named Portage Park when the light passenger rail car ran swiftly by. It was a close shave. I had visions of my dinghy being smashed into matchwood had we been a few minutes late in reaching the basin. I put away the photo and turned my attention back to the torn spinnaker.

I fetched the sewing machine from its locker and clamped it to the chart table. This would stop it sliding as I sewed. With a hand on the crank and an eye on the seam, I started to toil. Clattering along the seam, zigzag stitches appeared, rejoining the orange and black ripstop nylon. Work progressed steadily until failing light called a halt to my efforts. I looked at my handiwork. A fifth had been repaired. On deck, I stretched my aching back before adjusting the sails and checking our steady southward course.

Sat, Nov 10, 1984: 25°22′N 119°12′W, Previous Day's Run: 143

Laiviņa was still wing and wing with my two big number one genoas and sailing on a dead downwind run. She was averaging a bit under six knots. We were obviously not yet into the trades, and I knew that we were likely to lose this delightful following wind before I picked up the trade winds. I was up early in the morning at first light and got started on sewing up the rest of the spinnaker. I found that the work now went really fast as I had my techniques down pat. By the end of the day, I had the two halves joined together. All that remained to do was to patch a few small holes I had found when I gave the sail a thorough checking over. It was getting too dark in the cabin to do these small patches, so they would have to wait until tomorrow.

I checked out the two big genoas that were pulling *Laiviņa* along at a fast clip. The boat's motion was chafing the new number one genoa in a couple of places where it was rubbing against the lifelines, so I decided to fix that genoa at the first opportunity.

Sun, Nov 11, 1984: 23°34′N 118°30′W, Previous Day's Run: 115

I finished the small holes in the spinnaker and decided to change the sailing rig. The wind was dying down, and if I wanted to sail my set course, I could no longer run dead downwind, wing and wing. On my set course, the wind would be blowing across the port quarter. It was the right conditions to set the spinnaker and see how it was shaped. After I had hoisted the spinnaker to the top of the mast and it ballooned out in the light wind, I checked it over. It was looking good. There were no wrinkles or misshapen areas. As I was watching it, I got an idea.

Figure 6.3: Jury-rigged bowsprit

I brought up the piece of four-by-four lumber that Dug had given me and planed it smooth, rounded the sharp edges. Next, I chiselled some rope groves at either end. I carried it up to the bow and fixed it as a jury-rigged bowsprit extending some two metres beyond the bow of the boat. Bracing it with ropes, I reset the spinnaker at the end of this jury-rigged bowsprit and then hoisted the genoa to fill in the slot. I now had 1,405 square feet of sail up, and *Laiviņa* was moving well in the light air.

Once done, I checked out the fishing line with the lure I had been trailing every day since I had left Victoria. So far, no fish had decided to bite at the lure, and it remained empty. Today was no exception. As I was checking it out, I spotted two sharks astern and saw one of them go for the fishing lure. After hitting the lure with its side, the shark wasn't interested, and they both swam away.

It was a beautiful, warm, sunny day, so I relaxed on deck sunbathing. By now, I was able to move around without my sea boots and socks, for the seawater that splashed up on deck was warm. I was down to wearing light clothes. After a while, I grew hungry and decided to go down below to get some food. As I swung down the companionway, the little toe of my left foot hooked the edge of the box that covered the engine, and I screamed in pain. I believed I had either broken my toe or torn some tendons. I resolved to take care moving around now that I wasn't wearing footwear to protect my toes.

Mon, Nov 12, 1984: 22°34′N 118°13′W, Previous Day's Run: 62

In the early morning, I awoke to find that the wind had dropped away to almost nothing, and *Laiviņa* had drifted off course and hove herself to. There was still a light breeze, so I was able to get her sailing again. I would have to pay more attention now that we were in light airs. I wondered how long we had been hove to and was frustrated that I had not anticipated this situation.

I was settling into life at sea, and my routine included daily navigation. In the forenoon period, I took a sextant shot of the sun, processed and plotted it. This gave me a position line that formed at least a sixty-degree angle to a line of latitude that I would get later with my noon shot. An angle shallower than sixty degrees would give me a less accurate fix.

In the high latitudes during winter, I would have to "shoot the sun" as early as 9 a.m. in order to get a good angle between the pre-noon and noon position lines. The problem was, I would be sailing for three hours between the two sights and navigating by dead reckoning. This would introduce an accumulated log error and be greater than the error from an acute angle between position lines.

It was getting close to the summer solstice in the southern hemisphere, and the sun would only get as high as fifty degrees above the horizon. I found that 10 a.m. was a good time to get my morning sight. Any earlier and the sextant angle was too acute and less accurate from the bending of the light rays passing obliquely through the atmosphere. I had to balance the error from dead reckoning with the errors of a shallow angle between the two position lines from my morning and noon sights, along with the errors of a low-angle sight.

I had just obtained my usual noon shot, when a big dorado took the lure of my fishing line. I put away my sextant and came back on deck to carefully haul in the fish. A dorado was a fast-moving fish like a tuna, mostly made up of fast-twitch muscle fibres, with tasty dark flesh. Dorado was sometimes called "mahi mahi" or "dolphin fish." Once I had the fish alongside, I hooked it with the gaff and pulled it aboard. Just as I was pulling it inboard, it gave a violent jerk to save itself, came off the gaff, and lost the hook in its mouth. It nearly went back over the side as I dropped the gaff, grabbed its slippery body, and slid it into the cockpit well.

I hadn't eaten lunch yet, so I scaled and cleaned the dorado and cut it up into steaks. After coating four of the steaks in a batter made from flour and water, I cooked them up and filled my belly to capacity. I cut up the rest of the meat into small chunks.

Tue, Nov 13, 1984: 20°41′N 117°55′W, Previous Day's Run: 114

We had truly picked up the trades as the wind was now blowing from the northeast and had increased in strength. To get back on course, I took down the spinnaker and hoisted the old number one genoa and the full mainsail. After setting the self-steering for a reaching course, I settled back to enjoy the morning under the warm trade winds.

This was an exciting milestone. It had only taken two days to pass through the "horse latitudes," a zone of light winds that exists on the polar edge of the trade winds. The trade winds blow towards a spot about seven degrees north of the equator where they rise, cool down, and head back towards the poles to descend at the horse latitudes before heading back towards the equator again. It's a giant conveyor belt of wind.

The horse latitudes were so named because sailing ships carrying horses from Australia would reach these latitudes after many months at sea, when their hulls would have become heavily encrusted with gooseneck barnacles. The barnacles slowed the ships down so much that stores of fresh water needed for both men and horses became very low. Horses were thrown overboard to leave water for men, and later on, other sailing vessels would come across the floating bodies of horses in this area.

Figure 6.4: Dorado, mahi mahi, or dolphin fish

During the day, I cooked up more of the dorado and ate nothing but fish, fish, and more fish. The remainder of the afternoon was spent cooking the rest of the meat in empty peanut butter jars sitting inside my pressure cooker. When the meat was cooked and the pressure was back to normal, I took off the pressure cooker lid and tightened the top of the jars with gloved hands. This meat stayed fresh for many months.

Wed, Nov 14, 1984: 18°37′N 117°09′W, Previous Day's Run: 131

It was so wonderful to be in the trades. The wind was relatively steady, and it came from more or less the same direction day after day. There were few if any sail changes to do, and I could sleep all night knowing that *Laiviņa* would be surging along, holding a steady course and letting the miles flow under her keel.

Now that I was getting deeper into the trade wind zone, I was seeing many flying fish. *Laiviņa*'s silent passage through the ocean would sneak up on a school of flying fish, and they would all leap into the air and fly off together, their fins outstretched like the wings of birds. They would glide for many tens of metres before returning to the water.

Three months before, I was skippering a three-masted schooner from Victoria to San Diego for its owner. It was the vessel's maiden voyage. While we were passing to the south of Catalina Island near the end of the voyage, the wind was very light and the sea calm. The approaching hull of the schooner frightened a thirty-centimetre-long flying fish. It leaped out of the water and fluttered its fins like a slow-motion version of a hummingbird as it flew past us. Prior to witnessing this flight, I had read, heard, and believed that flying fish merely glided and did not flap their fins like a bird flaps its wings. Seeing this display of fluttering, and hearing the sound that the fins made as it flew past, changed my understanding of their means of flight. It sounded like a very loud slow-motion hummingbird.

It was so warm now, there was no reason to wear any clothes at all. The saltwater spray could wet me all over, and I just needed to wipe the dried salt off my skin. I made good speed and rapidly approached the doldrums, that zone of fickle, ever-changing, and sometimes non-existent winds.

Thu, Nov 15, 1984: 16°38′N 115°50′W, Previous Day's Run: 141

This was an even better day's run, the third day of close reaching with the sails full and by. We were driving fast southward and making a little easting at the same time. I noticed a change in the weather. Over the last three days of trade winds, the sky had a lot of cloud cover, about four eight oktas of cumulus clouds. I was now seeing more blue sky and less cloud. I felt that the doldrums were not too far ahead.

Fri, Nov 16, 1984: 14°46′N 114°55′W, Previous Day's Run: 124

During the night, the wind must have increased, because I awoke to the sound of flapping sails. I climbed out of my bunk on the starboard side and went on deck to see the old number one genoa flapping in the breeze. There was a tear from the clew to the tack and another tear from the clew to the head. This was going to be a big repair job. I lowered the torn sail and set the new number one genoa, made by North Sails prior to my departure. It had only been used for a limited number of days while heading down the Oregon and California coasts, so I figured it should stand up to the pressure of the trade winds.

During the day, I enjoyed reading *The Hotel New Hampshire* by John Irving. It was part of a collection of books I had been given by my friends who had helped me prepare for this voyage. Thinking about the books caused me to reminisce.

A week before I left Victoria, I had slipped *Laiviņa* at the small slipway in Victoria Harbour at the foot of Head Street. It was time to put a fresh coat of antifouling paint on her bottom. I recalled my conversation at Trotac Marine, the local ship chandler near Fisherman's Wharf.

"Hi! I need to buy a couple of gallons of antifouling," I told the man behind the counter.

"Yeah, okay. What kind do you want?"

"I've been using a hard copper. The last time I bought antifouling was when I was in Australia, and it was a brand called Epiglass. Do you have that?" I asked.

"Nope. We don't have that. But if it's a copper antifouling you want, we got Triple X."

"Triple X, eh? Is it a hard copper type?"

"I dunno what you mean by hard copper, but it's copper, and the fishermen all swear by it," he assured me.

"That a fact?"

"Yep, it's good."

"Okay. Then I'll take a couple of gallons."

I put the first coat of antifouling on *Laiviņa*, but couldn't find the time to put on the second coat as I was booked to teach computer classes at the Oak Bay Recreation Centre that evening. Dug came to the rescue.

"Don't worry about it, Pete. I'll put it on for you," he offered.

"Would you?"

"Sure. No problem," he said.

"As soon as my class is over, I'll come here and help you finish up," I told him.

After my class, I drove as fast as I could in the heavy rain to the slipway in Esquimault. There was a storm system approached the coast. When I arrived, Dug was standing under the hull, trying to shelter from the pouring rain. It must have been near midnight when we finished rolling on the antifouling. The rain rolled off the wet-weather gear we wore, and it also rolled easily off Dug's stoic personality. Nothing fazed him. A helicopter pilot by profession, doing everything from firefighting to heli-logging, he took the world in his stride.

Sat, Nov 17, 1984: 12°46′N 113°54′W Previous Day's Run 134

It was another wonderful day sailing in the trade winds. I had finished repairing the old Hood number one genoa and could afford the luxury of lazing about. Well, lazing about was a relative term. It was true that I was sleeping well at night. I didn't need to set the alarm clock to wake up multiple times to check our course, the sails, or the barometer, which was slowly dropping as we approached the doldrums.

I did need to do those numerous chores to keep everything "shipshape and Bristol fashion," along with cooking meals, navigating, and conducting my daily fittings check. When I awoke, I would go on deck and see how closely we were keeping to course.

In the trades, I was sailing by the wind rather than by a course. I wanted to keep *Laiviņa* close to the wind and make some easting, while sailing fast southward. If I sheeted in the sails and came hard on the wind, I would lose some speed southward and possibly make too much easting and end up in the middle of the South Pacific high-pressure system. I needed to be west of the high. Like everything in life, it was a balancing act.

After assuring myself that we were sailing well, I would make breakfast. This was usually porridge and raisins with a can of tuna. I had numerous cans of tuna on board. Two hundred and forty, in fact. I remembered how lucky I was in finding a good deal on tuna when I was provisioning before my voyage.

The small Oxford Foods supermarket in Fairfield had advertised a sale on tuna, so I drove to the store and walked in to buy enough for my extended sojourn at sea.

"I see you have tuna on sale here in your flyer," I said, pointing at the picture of a can of tuna adorning the front page of the flyer.

"Yes."

"Can you tell me where it is?" I asked.

He showed me the aisle.

"I need more than what you have there," I said, when I spotted about forty or fifty cans on the shelf.

"How many do you want to buy?" he asked me.

I pulled out my notebook.

"I need 240," I told him.

"240?"

"Yes."

"You're not from another store, are you? Are you going to sell them somewhere else?"

"Oh, no," I assured him. "I'm provisioning my sailboat. I'll be away sailing for a year."

He was not convinced.

"I'm serious. I need this to satisfy my protein needs while at sea. It's important."

"How much did you say you need?"

"Two hundred and forty cans."

"That's... well, there's two dozen to a box..."

"Yep. I need ten boxes," I told him.

He sighed, then turned and went through the doors marked "EMPLOYEES ONLY." About ten minutes later, he returned with a wagon stacked with ten cases of tuna.

"Follow me," he directed.

We went to the cash, and he instructed the clerk to ring it up. I paid for the tuna.

"Can I take the wagon out to my car?" I asked him.

"Yes, but bring it back to me when you're finished. I need to put it back in the storeroom."

"I will."

I drove back to Penny's house and took the paper labels off the cans. Leaving the paper label on would encourage the cans to rust as the paper absorbed and retained moisture from the surrounding air. I sealed the cans in plastic bags with six cans to a bag and then sealed six bags of six cans in a larger bag, then stored the larger bags in large plastic garbage bags inside cardboard boxes that were in turn put inside another garbage bag. There were four layers of plastic between the tin-plated steel can and the corrosive world of ocean sailing.

My reminiscing and breakfast over, I went on deck to check the course and weather.

At noon, I was visited by a tired seabird that landed on *Laiviņa*'s pulpit and perched there trying to keep its balance as we leaped over the low trade wind swells. It was an Arctic tern, a youngster as its feathers had the markings of an immature bird. It sat there all day, and when night came, it fell asleep still doing its balancing act automatically. Even later that night when I checked everything, the bird was still sound asleep, wobbling up and down and from side to side in concert with *Laiviņa*'s motion.

During the day, I solved the cryptogram that Mhora had sent me. It took a lot of effort, but it was worth it. I read the decoded message: "PINS ARE ABOUT THE ONLY THINGS THAT ARE POINTED IN ONE DIRECTION AND HEADED IN THE OTHER."

Tomorrow, I would technically be in the doldrums, but so far there was no sign of them. The trade wind was still blowing steadily, and we were making good progress. We had sailed the trade winds efficiently.

Sun, Nov 18, 1984: 10°49′N 112°45′W, Previous Day's Run: 135

When I awoke in the morning and went on deck to check the sails, I noticed that the Arctic tern had flown away. It must have had enough of *Laiviņa*'s rough motion.

Under the keel, the ocean slid quickly, and the air temperature rose steadily. Flying fish, in large, dense schools, continually shot out of the water ahead of *Laiviņa*'s surging bow, then curved in a sparkling, silvery arc of flashing wings before slipping back into the deep blue waves abeam. The week of idyllic sailing ended abruptly along with sunny skies as we entered the dark and brooding no man's land of the doldrums.

CHAPTER 7

Through the Tropics

Mon, Nov 19, 1984: 8°50′N 111°50′W, Previous Day's Run: 131

We were now in the doldrums. Outside the shelter of *Laiviņa*'s hull, the sky was filled with dark, pendulous clouds releasing squalls of rain upon the deck. When I heard the first pitter-pattering of large drops of rain falling on the mahogany hatches, I raced on deck with a bucket in my hands, eased the mainsail halyard, and took a turn on the old roller furling gear that rotated the boom and produced a gutter between the boom and the Dacron sail. Now the rain lashing the mainsail flowed down the sail and into the gutter. Next, I lifted the clew end of the boom a bit with the topping lift, and the water in the formed gutter ran towards the mast and the gooseneck fitting. Here I held the bucket, catching the precious fresh water that flowed into it.

At first, the water collected was incredibly salty as it washed away weeks of accumulated salt spray that had coated the sail. I dumped that water out of the bucket. As water flowed into the bucket, I constantly tasted it until it was only slightly salty. This I collected and poured into another bucket as it would be suitable for cooking foods such as rice and porridge. When it ran fresh, I topped up my empty fresh water containers. I collected fifteen litres of water, which would last about a week. It was good to have more fresh water.

When I left port, every container was topped up. Every saucepan, the pressure cooker, buckets, cups, whatever could hold water was filled as high as I dared. Even the sink was filled with water. Some of it spilled as *Laiviņa* rolled, but I needed as much as I could carry.

I left with a bit over three hundred litres of water, enough for one hundred and fifty days of sailing using the very minimum ration of two litres a day. I would need to collect rainwater as I travelled. I had two one-hundred-litre built-in water tanks low in the hull on both the port and starboard side in the main saloon. This gave me two hundred litres. I also carried four plastic jerrycans that held about twenty-five litres each. This gave me another hundred litres. Now I carried three hundred litres. Additional jugs and containers added up to about twenty more litres.

Having entered the doldrums, I broke out some treats to celebrate passing another milestone. Now my job was to get us through the doldrums as quickly as possible.

Tue, Nov 20, 1984: 7°37′N 112°00′W, Previous Day's Run: 74

We were in the middle of the doldrums with funny, fickle winds alternating with calm. There was more wind than I would have expected and less sunshine. In fact, I hardly saw the sun. I also expected thunderstorms but hadn't seen any lightning or heard any thunder, just heavy, grey overcast and a wind that would spring up, last for a few minutes, die down to nothing, and then spring up again.

The wind was always blowing from the south, dead ahead. I had to set the sails close-hauled on one tack or the other, whichever tack gave me the advantage. We needed to go southward to pass through this band of turbulent weather.

I didn't get much sleep in the doldrums as I needed to be constantly adjusting sails. In the time of the sailing ships, traversing the doldrums was called "pulley-hauley" days because the sailors were forever changing the angle of the yards to catch every fleeting bit of wind.

Wed, Nov 21, 1984: 6°35′N 110°15′W, Previous Day's Run: 121

I worked *Laiviņa* through the night, catching forty winks on deck until the next time I needed to come about. I was tired when the grey dawn broke. We had made another degree southwards over the past twenty-four hours, so there was progress. I was becoming frustrated with the wind consistently from the south, and we were forced to beat into it.

For a while, I thought I was coming out of the doldrums as the wind was getting fresher, but unfortunately it was coming from the south and not from the east-southeast where it should be coming from had I reached the southeast trades. I was close-hauled and heading towards the west.

While provisioning *Laiviņa*, I purchased a large number of loaves of sliced bread on special in one of the local grocery stores. Penny and I dried the bread in her oven and then repackaged the dried slices back in their original plastic bags, sealed in more plastic bags and stowed in cardboard boxes. To reconstitute the dried slices of bread, I would fog them with a garden leaf spray mister filled with fresh water. It usually only took a couple of trigger squeezes for each side. I could spread up to four slices atop a flat camp toaster and put it over a slow flame from my kerosene pressure stove. The heat would steam the moistened surface of the slices, and the steam would soften the bread. It tasted as fresh as the day it was baked.

Figure 7.1: Fresh bread baked in the pressure cooker

Today I ran out of my dried bread so decided to bake the first loaf for the trip. I found remnants of three-year-old corn flour purchased in New Zealand in 1981 and the remains of some year-old yeast. After mixing and kneading the dough, I rose it in a lidless pressure cooker with a tea towel covering, beat it down, re-kneaded it, and rose it in the lidless pressure cooker again.

The dough didn't rise as much as it should have as the yeast had lost some of its potency, but it did rise, although quite slowly. As soon as it had risen high enough, I lit the stove, turned it down as low as I could, and then sat the pressure cooker atop my flat camp toaster to further reduce the heat. I took the rubber sealing ring out of the lid of the pressure cooker and clamped it in place without the pressure weight.

As the loaf cooked, steam escaped through the vent on top of the lid and out through the unsealed sides. Every now and then, I would whip off the lid to drain and dry the condensed moisture on the underside of the lid, so it wouldn't drain back onto the loaf and make it soggy.

Once the sides and bottom of the loaf had cooked and were firm, all that remained to be cooked was the centre and top of the loaf. With an oven mitt to catch the loaf, I tipped it out of the pressure cooker and inverted it, placing it back in the cooker upside down. After about an hour and a half, my loaf was done. It tasted nice and had a yellow colour from the corn flour.

Thu, Nov 22, 1984: 5°12′N 111°04′W, Previous Day's Run: 96

Even with a little more sun, there was a lot of cloud, so we were still in the doldrums. Winds were light and still coming from the south, dead ahead. Fortunately, being close-hauled all the time made it easy to work through the fickle winds. All I needed to do was occasionally change to the favoured tack to keep *Laiviņa* making the best southing possible.

To pass the time, I started working on an alternative solution to my Invisible Mountain navigational problem. How could I get a position line based on calculating the distance from a mountain that was over the horizon when I could only see the top portion? I knew the height of the mountain and could read an angle with my sextant from the top of the mountain to the sea horizon, but only the top portion of the mountain was visible. I just didn't know how much of the mountain I could see.

Two years before, I had worked out an iterative method, but I was sure that there was a more elegant way to solve the problem that was not repetitive. I decided to work on the math to find the solution.

Fri, Nov 23, 1984: 3°44′N 110°47′W, Previous Day's Run: 89

This day we were technically out of the doldrums, but it didn't look like it. There was still no sign of the southeast trades, the fickle wind continued to come from the south, and it was very cloudy. We were not too far from the equator, about two hundred and forty nautical miles, a couple of good days' sailing if we had wind.

Just after dawn, I started baking another loaf of bread as I had eaten all of the loaf I had baked two days earlier. This time I used fresh flour and fresh yeast, so it came out perfect. It had risen a lot and…mmm…it was good! What a pleasure it was to eat fresh bread, straight out of the oven...er...pressure cooker, thousands of miles away from land aboard a tiny floating home with barely enough room to swing a cat.

Sat, Nov 24, 1984: 3°05′N 111°37′W, Previous Day's Run: 63

Still the same weather. The wind kept coming from the south, rising and falling, and we kept getting becalmed. I suppose I really couldn't complain as my last day's run was still reasonable. The problem was that although I covered some sixty miles over the previous twenty-four hours, we only travelled forty miles south, the direction in which I wanted to head. It was very frustrating! We were a bit over three degrees or about two hundred miles north of the equator, and we should have been out of the doldrums.

Sun, Nov 25, 1984: 2°07′N 113°00′W, Previous Day's Run: 101

During the night we had good winds and made some significant progress. The morning dawned very differently to what I had been experiencing since entering the doldrums. It was a beautiful sunny day with clear blue skies and no clouds. The first such day since entering the doldrums. Unfortunately, there was no wind at all now.

As *Laiviņa* lay becalmed, I decided to go for a swim. While in the water, I checked the anodes and general hull condition. There were a few gooseneck barnacles attached to the hull, but everything looked in good condition. I swam around the new self-steering rudders. The replacement fittings I made and fitted on the bottom of the trim tab and auxiliary rudder looked good and were still in place.

After climbing back on board, I took advantage of the steady platform to work on other chores. I overhauled the sextant, cleaned it and greased it. I then checked and adjusted it for accuracy as I had a dead, straight horizon and a steady boat upon which to stand.

In anticipation of my journey around the stormy Cape Horn, I prepared *Laiviņa* for the worst possible conditions we might encounter. During the afternoon, I sealed the hatches by greasing the hatch base and then running a fat bead of silicon rubber around the inside of the hatch lid. I lowered the hatch lid onto matchsticks so it wouldn't completely close and the silicon took on the shape of the lower potion. I left it like that to allow the silicon to dry and cure properly, then took out the matches. Afterwards, the hatch closed and hermetically sealed itself once clamped from the inside.

It had been a very enjoyable and productive day, particularly since the seas were so flat and I had been able to move around *Laiviņa* effortlessly.

Mon, Nov 26, 1984: 1°19′N 113°40′W, Previous Day's Run: 63

I was becalmed during part of the night, but we made reasonable progress in the light airs. After the sun came up, I baked another loaf of bread. I was glad to have a lot of flour with me, some whole wheat, some white. It was a lazy day, though I spent some time boning up on math to help me solve my Invisible Mountain problem.

In the evening, I opened one of the many treat package that Penny had given me to while away my days at sea. I had a fresh set of batteries for the cassette player and a tape made up of selected music and poetry by Banjo Patterson, an Australian poet who was writing bush poetry a hundred years ago. He was famous for "Waltzing Matilda," "The Man from Snowy River," and "Clancy of the Overflow."

I lay on deck with the headphones in my ears, staring up at a star-filled sky and feeling warm wafting breezes brushing my face as *Laiviņa* gently rocked in the soft, low swells.

Tue, Nov 27, 1984: 0°20′N 114°30′W, Previous Day's Run: 77

The day started much the same as the previous day. The wind was light and still from the south, the sky clear, and I was beginning to wonder when we would reach the southeast trade winds. I knew we were getting close to the equator and yet there were still no winds to be had.

At noon, after I had worked out my sight, I found that we had a mere twenty miles to go before crossing the equator. I was excited. I did not expect King Neptune to come out of the depth and bestow his wishes upon me even if I gave libations to the god of the sea, but I was excited to soon be opening up my "crossing the equator" presents, cards from friends, and the bottle of Montecello sparkling apple juice I had been given to celebrate.

At 5 p.m. I took more sights and found that I still had another four miles to go. I kept taking sights every fifteen minutes and processing them as quickly as I could. At 6:30 p.m., I crossed the equator. I looked over the side of *Laiviņa* to see the line, but it was just a bit too dark and it was many fathoms below.

Quick, open the card! Open the bottle! Get out the treats! Yum! Celebrate! Sing some sea shanties! What would King Neptune think of me now? Had he poked his head above the water, he would have seen a young man, his hair long and wild, sporting a month-old beard, frolicking around on the deck, singing lustily at the top of his lungs with a half-emptied bottle in his hands, occasionally splattering some on the top of the dark, still, ever-so-deep water.

In among my gifts was a package with an attached card in which was written, "For the kid in all of us!" I carefully shook the box and heard something rattle around inside. I reread the card and shook the box again. I figured that some joker had wrapped up a baby rattle. Once I opened the box, I found to my delight that it contained a puzzle. I guessed that my cerebral nature had not escaped my friend's notice.

The wind also gave me something to celebrate. In the early evening, it finally, after nine days, went to the southeast. Hooray! The start of the southeast trades. King Neptune had smiled upon me.

Wed, Nov 28, 1984: 1°16′S 113°47′W, Previous Day's Run: 105

I slept well now that we were sailing in a steady breeze and *Laiviņa* was heading south. She was even making a little easting. I awoke refreshed to the familiar trade wind sky of puffy cumulus clouds dotting a soft blue. I had a relaxing day working on the next of Mhora's puzzles. She had provided me with cards and cryptograms to be opened at various milestones in my voyage. I found them a delightful interlude in my routine. Mhora had given me the sealed envelopes at a party a few days before I departed.

That evening, I had been working getting *Laiviņa* ready and was down below, when I was visited by my friend Fred, who lived about a kilometre and a half from Fisherman's Wharf. I had been mooring *Laiviņa* at Fisherman's Wharf for the last year or so.

"Ahoy, Matey!"

I came up from my lit cabin and poked my head out the companionway hatch.

"Hey Fred! What are you doing here?" I asked the man standing on the dock with a bemused smile on his face.

"Ahhh...I've ah...got to drop something off at Penny's, and I thought you might like a ride home," he said.

I hesitated. My brain scanned the various tasks I had planned to complete that day and quickly made decisions as to which ones could be put off until tomorrow. It was getting close to my departure date, only a few days left now, so I wanted to make sure I had them done. At the same time, the evening was drawing on, and although it was only a twenty-minute bicycle ride to Penny's house, I was getting tired and needed to get some food into me.

"Sure. Okay. Give me a few minutes to finish off here."

I completed what I had been doing and put away my tools in the locker under the settee berth. I came up on deck still in my overalls, my face dirty, wiping the grime off my hands with an old rag. I stuffed the rag in my overalls pocket and unlocked the old ten-speed Raleigh bicycle I had bought in Australia almost a decade before. I lifted it over the lifelines and onto the dock. Fred steadied it until I clambered onto the ancient dock boards.

"You have room to take my bike?" I asked him.

"Sure. I have the Kombi van."

As we headed out of the parking lot, I saw an opportunity to pick up some remaining provisions along the way, particularly since I could not have carried them on my bicycle.

"Hey, Fred. Do you mind if we stop at the supermarket? There's a special on porridge oats, and I'd like to pick them up if I could."

"Are you sure you need to pick them up now?"

"Oh... are you in a hurry to go someplace?"

"No, not really, but I think Penny probably has dinner waiting for you," he replied.

"Oh, no. I told her I would be working late and not to expect me for dinner. I was planning to make a couple of sandwiches when I get home," I assured him.

"All right then."

We diverted to the supermarket, and I went inside while Fred waited in his van. Grabbing a shopping cart, I went straight to the cereal aisle and filled the shopping cart with bags of oats. I virtually cleaned out their stock. I pushed the cart to the checkout and started unloading the bags onto the conveyor belt.

"You can leave them in the buggy, and... oh... wow! You have a lot!" the checkout clerk exclaimed.

"Yeah, true."

"Do you have a horse or something?"

I laughed. "No, I'm going sailing and stocking my boat for the trip."

"Oh...I see. How many bags do you have?"

"Forty. They're one-kilogram bags."

"That's a lot. I better count them," she said.

When I reached Fred's van, he helped me load the bags of oats. Off we went again, now heading for Penny's house. When we reached the house, Fred parked the van a bit up the street from the house. I was puzzled by his actions. In fact, he'd been acting strange from the moment he had arrived at Fisherman's Wharf. I would have to carry the bags some distance to the house.

"You can get your bike out, okay?" he said. "I'll be back in a minute to help you with your bags of oats."

As Fred walked back down the street, I wrestled my bicycle out of his van and started wheeling it to the door of the basement, where I normally stored it. I returned to the van, and we carried the oats to the front door.

"It's unlocked," Fred said.

I pushed open the door, and the house was in darkness. As I was fumbling for the light switch, the interior exploded into light.

"SURPRISE!"

I felt a shock of adrenaline course through my veins as I stared into the faces of about thirty people jammed into the hallway and the living room beyond. My knees sagged, and I dropped to the floor.

"Oh...my gosh. What's happening?" I asked weakly.

I got to my feet and looked at my dirty hands and down at my grimy overalls.

"Oh...I'm...I need to change..."

"C'mon, Pete. Don't worry about that for now, come and greet everybody. We've been waiting a while for you to get here. What took you so long?" Dug asked.

"He wanted to buy a ton of oats. I tried to dissuade him, but I couldn't talk him out of it without giving it all away," Fred explained.

"I'm glad you're here now," Penny beamed. "Come and say hi to everyone."

I walked into the living room and stood amid the large group of my friends and well-wishers. I was overwhelmed.

"I'm sorry. If I had known, I would have come better dressed," I said, holding my arms out to display my grimy overalls.

"Go and get changed, then please hurry back. You've got a lot of presents to open," said Leslie.

"Hurry up! We want to party!"

"You better get back here quick!"

"Okay, I'll be back soon," I said.

I changed out of my overalls, washed my face and arms, and combed my hair. The face that stared back at me from the mirror was tired. The days of intense activity were beginning to take their toll. I would be pleased when I was on my way and life settled down. I walked out of the bathroom and back into the living room.

The rest of evening was wonderful. I opened various gifts that would help me in my quest. Some were handed to me with strict instructions on their wrappings.

"FOR HALLOWEEN"

"OPEN ON XMAS DAY"

"OPEN AT THE EQUATOR—FIRST TIME"

"OPEN AT THE EQUATOR—SECOND TIME"

"FOR CAPE HORN"

"HAPPY BIRTHDAY! DO NOT OPEN PREMATURELY!!!"

"NO PEEKING UNTIL YOU ARE HALFWAY"

These gifts included Mhora's cryptograms.

A week or so before, Penny had asked me if I would like some books to take with me.

"Yes, books would be great to have. I know I read a lot at sea," I told her.

"What genres are you interested in?"

"All. I'd like a variety, you know, fiction, non-fiction, murder mysteries, adventure tales…anything you can spare, really," I suggested.

I was presented with a large cardboard box of about one hundred and fifty books. There were Zane Grey westerns, a French edition of *Madame Bovary*, Agatha Christie novels, *The Rise and Fall of the Third Reich*, and many other diverse titles. It was perfect. I could choose an author, style, or genre based on my mood.

I had been so focused on getting everything ready for my voyage and not disrupting other people's lives that I had not realized that my friends wanted to be part of the adventure. I came away from that party a richer person in many ways.

Thu, Nov 29, 1984: 3°10′S 113°56′W, Previous Day's Run: 114

Figure 7.2: Close-hauled in the southeast trades

Sailing is inherently a dangerous activity; as the saying goes, "He that would go to sea for pleasure would go to hell for a pastime."

I was never on deck without wearing my harness and clipped into one of the two running lifelines that went from stem to stern. I had rigged them to run down either side of the forward hatch, the mast, the companionway hatch, and the aft hatch. They ran free and clear of any obstruction, except for the need to pass the lazy genoa sheet, which I would lift over my head as I passed underneath. Before going on deck, I would slide open the companionway hatch, and by standing on the bottom step of the companionway, I would clip onto one or the other of these running lifelines. Only then would I climb the remaining treads and step out onto the deck.

When changing sails, sometimes I needed to move from the port to the starboard side or vice versa and then travel aft on a different side from the side I had travelled forward. At that point, I needed to transfer the harness carabiner from one lifeline to the other. Sometimes, I transferred my attachment and clipped into one of the lazy jack or spinnaker pole mast rings. Those were the moments that I was vulnerable. An unanticipated sea or swell could unbalance me or sweep me overboard, in spite of having a firm grip on a lifeline or stanchion.

On days when the seas were high and that risk existed, I wore two harnesses and would only unclip from one lifeline after I had clipped into the other. It was a good system and alleviated my greatest fear: that of being in the water and watching with horror as *Laiviņa* sailed away from me. This fear is important as it drives good discipline; it is very necessary for a solo sailor.

I found that sailing in the trades eased the fear of falling overboard as the consistency of the wind and waves made *Laiviņa*'s movement more predictable. I was sure-footed in moving around on deck.

It was another delightful day, so I spent it reading, studying mathematics, and baking another loaf of bread. I experimented with making two half-sized loaves, one whole wheat, the other made with white flour and containing chopped-up dried apricots. I rose the balls of dough side by side in the pressure cooker and cooked them together, giving me a Siamese twin loaf of bread. After tasting the apricot side, I decided I would use raisins next time. It was too tart.

Fri, Nov 30, 1984: 5°09′S 113°52′W, Previous Day's Run: 119

When I entered the trade winds, the wind was between force 2 and 3 on the Beaufort scale, about ten knots or twenty kilometres an hour. This day, the wind was slowly strengthening, and we were going faster as a result. In the sparkling wavelets, schools of flying fish were leaping out of the water to avoid being run down by *Laiviņa*'s hull.

I was reading a number of scientific magazines like *Discover* and *Scientific American*. Good intellectual fodder for my thirsty brain.

Sat, Dec 1, 1984: 7°21′S 113°54′W, Previous Day's Run: 132

I had been crossing out each day on a calendar pinned to the cork tiles glued to the main bulkhead. I tore off the page with the month of November, and I was now looking at the pristine page of December, a temporal milestone of sorts.

The trade wind was too strong to use the number one genoa as we were now heeled more sharply that I would have liked; the keel was starting to lose laminar flow, and the angle of heel was creating a lot of tip vortexes from the fin keel. I changed it for the number two genoa, and we sailed much better.

I dragged out my portable typewriter and resolved to improve my typing skills. I was not a "hunt-and-pecker"; I used all of my fingers, but in a non-traditional way, and I needed to look at the keyboard. I was not a touch typist. I wanted to change that. After an hour, my fingers got tired so I considered that to be enough athletic training for the day.

SUN, DEC 2, 1984: 9°30′S 113°30′W, PREVIOUS DAY'S RUN: 131

I noticed a few birds flying around. The beautiful and graceful albatrosses wouldn't be in evidence until we were at least forty degrees south, but I was looking forward to their companionship.

Each day, I conducted an examination of every fitting and line on the boat. I started at the bow, then worked aft along the starboard side and forward along the port side. I checked every fitting on the boom and the lower mast, then climbed the mast using the mast steps, checking the fittings at the spreader arms and finally the masthead. This was an important daily routine that prevented mere annoyances from developing into a serious problem or even a disaster.

All of *Laiviņa*'s shackles had their pin eyes wired to prevent them from vibrating undone. I had drilled holes in the pin flats of those shackles that had no pin eyes and wired them shut with stainless steel wire. In spite of that precaution, sometimes a shackle would rub heavily against another stainless steel component and the wire would break and unravel, allowing the pin to vibrate loose. I needed to regularly check the shackles for broken wire.

I looked for chafe in the lines, in particular where a line turned sharply around a block, completely reversing its direction. The mainsail, headsail, and spinnaker halyards at the top of the mast were particularly vulnerable to this problem. Once, I discovered that the mainsail headboard had almost sawed through the boom topping lift. I cut out the frayed section, re-spliced the line, and resolved to use a different tension on the boom topping lift.

Another time, the aluminum cheek plates at the masthead had almost cut through the mainsail halyard. It happened because I had hoisted it chock-a-block. I cut out the damaged end of the halyard and resecured it. To prevent it from occurring again, I resolved to fully hoist the mainsail and then lower it ten centimetres, adjusting the luff tension by using the gooseneck downhaul.

Mon, Dec 3, 1984: 11°41′S 113°03′W, Previous Day's Run: 134

I was enjoying life at sea. My day was spent reading and studying from whatever textbooks and magazines I had in my lockers. During the evening, a fishing vessel passed astern of us; it was the first one I had seen for a while. It looked like a squid boat with its bright lights, but I couldn't tell as it was too far away.

Tue, Dec 4, 1984: 13°52′S 113°00′W, Previous Day's Run: 131

My daily routine consisted of breakfast, reading, morning navigation, reading, noon navigation, lunch, reading, snoozing, many equipment checks, reading, evening meal, reading, and sleeping. I baked another loaf of bread as I loved having fresh bread on a regular basis. The time in the trades passed quickly as I didn't have to touch the sails or the self-steering, and all I seemed to do was read, eat, and sleep.

Wed, Dec 5, 1984: 15°57′S 112°35′W, Previous Day's Run: 127

I had come down from being aloft checking out the masthead fittings and was examining the lower mast fittings when I discovered that the gooseneck fitting was falling apart. I remembered that when I was preparing *Laiviņa* in Victoria, I greased the end of the boom. It was late in the evening, and I was working under the yellow sodium vapour lamp light coming from the parking lot at Fisherman's Wharf. Along with the dock lights, that provided enough illumination to do the job.

The original rig had a roller furling boom to reef the mainsail, but it was difficult to get a good sail shape when reefed. I mounted a jiffy or slab reefing system on the boom and was satisfied with the control I had over the shape of the reefed mainsail. The mainsail had three reef points, with the third or last reef, a deep reef. Although I never used the roller gear for reefing, it came in handy to create a gutter for catching rain.

When I examined the roller furling gear carefully, I noticed that the screws holding the gooseneck to the stationary roller plate had come loose. Each of the four large stainless steel screws was supposed to be secured by nuts inside the aluminum boom tube and out of reach. Those nuts were very loose, and there was no way I could get a wrench on them to tighten them as the nuts were inside the boom tube and completely out of reach.

Figure 7.3: Tightening the old roller furling gear

When I first tried to tighten the screws by turning them with a screwdriver, the screws went around and around without the nuts tightening onto the screws. I was finally able to tighten each screw by attempting to pull the fitting away from the boom, thus jamming the nut against the inside end plate of the boom. Now when I tightened the screw, the nut did not turn, and slowly I was able to resecure the fitting until each screw was as tight as I could get it.

Had a screw come out of the nut, I would have had to take the fitting out of the boom tube. It might have been very difficult as four years of sailing had almost fused the stainless fastening to the aluminum boom tube. It was always a problem when dissimilar metals were in contact in a saltwater environment.

The whole job took an hour, and I knew that I would have to pay particular attention to that fitting in the future.

Thu, Dec 6, 1984: 18°04′S 111°53′W, Previous Day's Run: 133

It was so nice to rest in preparation for the rigours of the Southern Ocean and Cape Horn. I spent the day reading magazines and eating popcorn that I made in the heavy aluminum pressure cooker, a great pot for so many purposes. What a life!

Fri, Dec 7, 1984: 20°00′S 110°40′W, Previous Day's Run: 135

The trades were really fresh today. With the increase in wind speed, the seas and swells were higher and more rambunctious. The advantage was that the sea pattern in the trades was nearly always a single wave train, uncluttered by swells coming from other directions. This made the motion more predictable. *Laiviņa* was again heeling too much, not pointing into the wind, and making more leeway. I went on deck and took down the number two genoa and in its place, hoisted the number one jib. After changing the headsail, I went from a full mainsail to a fully reefed mainsail, a big change, but it balanced *Laiviņa* better, and she drove to windward faster and more efficiently.

As I got closer to the western edge of the South Pacific high-pressure system, the trade winds were backing and coming from the east. Instead of barely being able to go south, I was getting a bit of easting in my course. When I projected my heading on the chart, I noticed that we were heading for Easter Island. This was exciting as I hoped to see the famous statues.

Sat, Dec 8, 1984: 22°09′S 109°42′W, Previous Day's Run: 140

The wind continued to back very slowly as I travelled south. I was able to go back to a full mainsail and the number two genoa, not because the wind was less strong, but because I was able to free the sheets and sail full and by, causing the speed of the apparent wind to drop. It was a beautiful point of sail, very stable, efficient, and fast.

Sailors need to thoroughly understand the difference between the true and apparent wind. They also need to understand the effect of changing course at different boat speeds on the apparent wind's speed and direction and how to balance the rig to make it easier for the self-steering to do its job under those conditions. It was particularly important for the self-steering system to be able to deal with these changes when broad reaching in light airs.

I now had about three hundred miles to go to Easter Island, and I was getting excited. It was the first land since leaving California. In preparation, I brought the chart tubes out of their locker, took out the next charts needed, and put away the ones used for the previous part of the journey. Before leaving Victoria, I purchased a large number of charts for the voyage. I already had charts for Canada, the North and South Pacific, New Zealand, and the east coast of Australia. For this voyage,

I now needed charts for South America and the Southern Ocean. For making emergency landfalls, I needed charts for places such as South Africa.

I organized the charts by putting them in a large pile with the first needed on top and the last to be used on the bottom. There was some overlap as I would be using charts of the North Pacific Ocean on my outbound part of the voyage and also on the homeward-bound section. I bought a long length of four-inch-diameter black ABS sewer pipe, cut it into three lengths that were longer than the widest chart, and bought two end caps for each pipe. I divided the charts into thirds and put them in the pipes, sealing the end caps on the outside with a bead of silicon rubber that could easily be broken when retrieving the charts. This would keep them dry in the worst of conditions.

I also made a chart holder for charts folded in two. It was made from two pieces of one-eighth-inch plywood joined on three sides by gluing a strip of waterproof sailcloth to each side. It made a large sleeve that could hold about ten folded charts lying flat. I used this for my immediate charts. After the voyage I built a new chart table that had a shallow bin under it to hold these folded charts. It had a section to hold my plotting instruments.

I spent the afternoon planning and plotting my route to Hobart.

Sun, Dec 9, 1984: 24°32′S 109°12′W, Previous Day's Run: 146

Today was a special day, as we passed under the sun. Now instead of the sun being south at noon, it was in the north at noon, or behind us. Little milestones such as these were very meaningful to me. I looked forward to such events with anticipation, and in my exuberance, I often celebrated the occasion with a lot of laughter and a couple of sea shanties.

Being close to the summer solstice, we also passed over the Tropic of Capricorn during the early morning, so I was now officially out of the tropics. As I left the tropics behind, the trade winds were dying down. I changed back to the number one genoa and folded and bagged the number two genoa.

The previous evening, I worked out a sight using a different set of navigational tables called HO 211. It was quite a neat method. I could now process a celestial sight using five different methods. I was getting close to Easter Island and calculated that I should sight it the next day around noon if the wind kept up.

Mon, Dec 10, 1984: 26°35′S 109°04′W, Previous Day's Run: 123

Astronomical twilight had come and gone, so just after dawn's nautical twilight, I took some early-morning sights of the stars to get a position before civil twilight made the sky too bright to see them easily. I wanted to correct my course early, if necessary, to pass to weather and east of Easter Island. From my plotted position on the chart, I knew where to look for Easter Island. While I could not see the actual island, a bank of cumulonimbus clouds hovered over it and gave its position away.

While waiting to sight land, I prepared the dinghy for an abandon-ship scenario. I lashed the oars, centreboard, and rudder to the thwarts. I wrapped the mast, sprit, and boom in the sail and covered and lashed it alongside the dinghy. In an immediate sinking, I planned to cut the life raft hold-down straps with the sharp knife taped to the side of the life raft. Next, I would cut the dinghy straps, and it would all float free should *Laiviņa* sink.

I had a grab bag that contained flares, a radar reflector, a plastic sextant, fishing gear, small-scale plasticized charts, and other essentials. This grab bag was always kept beside the companionway on the quarter berth for quick access.

I also tied the handles of the four twenty-five-litre plastic containers of fresh water together with a long line so each one could be brought up on deck independently. Being fresh water, the containers would all float free should *Laiviņa* sink. They could then be brought into the life raft.

My abandon-ship plan was, should I have to leave *Laiviņa*, I would deflate the life raft on good weather days, haul it into the dinghy, and make sail for the nearest land in a downwind direction. On bad-weather days, I would pump up the life raft again and tether the dinghy to the life raft. I would fill the dinghy with water knowing that it would still float because of the installed polystyrene buoyancy and would act as a drogue for the life raft. I hoped I would never have to put such a plan in action, but I regularly practised a simulated abandon ship.

I kept looking for the island in the direction that it should lie, but a lot of low cloud obscured it. I went out again about a half an hour before

Figure 7.4: Easter Island from the northeast

noon and looked. There it was! I jumped up and down and yelled out until I was hoarse.

"Land ho! Laaannnd hoooooo!!"

I climbed up and down the mast a few times to get rid of some excess energy. It was wonderful to sight land while at sea.

During the afternoon, as we closed the northeastern shoreline of Easter Island, I baked bread and came out on deck every half-hour to see the island getting bigger and bigger, with more land coming out of the sea. At first the two high points looked like islands, then other hills appeared as small islands, until I came over the horizon enough so that the lowland had filled in between the mountains and hills and it appeared as one island.

I searched it with the binoculars as we passed about five miles off its eastern shore, but could not see the famous statues, as they were on the western side. On the southeastern shore, there were six large tanks for an oil terminal. It would be interesting to visit Easter Island one day.

Just before sunset, when closest to the island, I could see that the soil was a rich red volcanic type with a lot of erosion. Most of the island was devoid of trees, with just a few groves here and there. Later that night I saw some lights. I was pleased to have seen Easter Island in daylight.

CHAPTER 8

Enter the Southern Ocean

Tue, Dec 11, 1984: 28°44′S 108°22′W, Previous Day's Run: 134

The day passed quickly as I relaxed and read my book. During the evening, I turned on the shortwave radio to calibrate the various time pieces to ensure the most accurate navigation. Time is critical for a sailor using a sextant to navigate. An error of four seconds can mean an error of up to a nautical mile depending on location and circumstances.

I had my original ship's chronometer, my wristwatch, which I never wore as it was now preserved as a backup chronometer, and about a half-dozen red LED watches given me by Barry, another sailor and a watchmaker. I received them about two weeks before departing Victoria; Barry had set them all to the correct time and had put in fresh batteries.

As soon as he gave them to me, I started logging their gain or loss each day, along with the average daily temperature. After a couple of weeks, I drew up a chart that allowed me to predict how much they would differ from Universal Coordinated Time in the future. Should I not be able to get the correct time from my shortwave radio, I could extrapolate it from my chart.

Once every few days or so, I would tune into the broadcast time signal and record the difference between each timepiece and the official time. I never adjusted the watches, just recorded their error. As the days went by, I had a more accurate figure for their gain or loss rate. It did vary depending on ambient temperature. When in colder waters, the watches that were slow lost time faster, and the watches that were fast gained it slower. The quartz crystal oscillations changed slightly with temperature changes. It was important to record the temperature each day so I could more accurately extrapolate the time should my radio fail.

Evening was a great time to listen to shortwave radio as the effect of ionospheric bounce can allow signals from very far away to be picked up by the receiver. I listened to Radio Australia on shortwave while the radio announcer in the Melbourne studios was reading out some interesting articles from the newspaper before the official news. It was wonderful to hear the news and the voices on the radio, as it made me feel connected to the people of the world who were so far away from me.

Wed, Dec 12, 1984: 30°56′S 107°46′W, Previous Day's Run: 136

Today the wind shifted so that it was abaft the beam. It was time to set the spinnaker. We were still getting a good day's run even though the wind was getting lighter and lighter. It was clear to see that we were getting closer and closer to the South Pacific high-pressure system. The pilot charts showed the centre of the high for the month of December, and I planned to pass about six hundred miles west of its centre to avoid being becalmed for days. I would encounter light winds at my closest approach. Soon we would be out of the trade winds and into the horse latitudes.

Thu, Dec 13, 1984: 32°58′S 107°14′W, Previous Day's Run: 125

We sneaked quietly past the high, hoping it wouldn't hear us, and come over to check us out. Our day's run was reduced in the ever-lightening wind. The direction of the wind stayed the same, still from the northeast but inexorably getting lighter.

Fri, Dec 14, 1984: 34°19′S 106°55′W, Previous Day's Run: 83

When I awoke in the morning, I found that the wind had died right down and we were cutting slowly through the still water. As there was less breeze, I felt the heat of the sun more, but the bonus was that the decks were staying dry now that no waves splashed them.

During the morning, I overhauled the self-steering system, greased all the bearings, and got it ready for the rigours of Cape Horn. There was still a lot of work to do, so I knew I would be busy. When the wind was light, it was so easy to work above and below decks.

The afternoon was a good time to get out a can of yellow deck paint and freshen up the deck where fittings had scratched away the paint. I managed to get a good bit of paint on the decks and some on the genoa when the sail flapped over on one occasion and hit the paintbrush in my hand. I quickly wiped the paint off the sail with a rag before it dried.

Sat, Dec 15, 1984: 35°37′S 106°14′W, Previous Day's Run: 85

During the night, the wind backed from the northeast through to the south-southeast, and we had ended up close-hauled on the starboard tack. I spent the day adjusting the sails and the self-steering as the wind continued to back. Between adjusting the rig, I experimented with a loaf of apple bread using dried apples, which was quite tasty.

The remainder of the day was spent mending the big rip in the old number one genoa. It took a lot of thread, and I had little thread left. I had to make sure I didn't push *Laiviņa* so hard, a difficult resolution for me to keep because I like going fast. Still, I couldn't afford another major sail blowout.

Sun, Dec 16, 1984: 36°10′S 106°47′W, Previous Day's Run: 42

I awoke to a dreary day. It was drizzling, and I was becalmed from time to time. When the wind blew, it was shifty and light. These were very frustrating conditions for a sailor as I tried to keep *Laiviņa* moving. It required a lot of attention and concentration. We were now officially in the "horse latitudes," but I didn't see any horses thrown overboard.

I finished sewing up the old number one genoa and then started insulating my sleeping berth. I had been sleeping exclusively on the starboard quarter berth which, because it was uninsulated, dripped condensation all over me and my blankets when I got into colder water.

I had purchased two-inch-thick foam insulation board before I left Victoria and cut it into pieces small enough to fit in the aft locker. When the sun came out and everything was warm and dry, I brought the foam out of the aft locker and started working. I now had time to finish the underside of the deck, which being relatively flat, was easy to do. After that was done, I started on the curved side of the hull. I first cut the foam into fifteen-by-fifteen-centimetre tiles, then, using foam adhesive, glued each tile to the inside of the curved hull leaving about a five-millimetre gap between each tile. Once the glue hardened sufficiently, I spray-foamed between the tiles.

There were two cans of spray foam, a half-empty one and a full one. Unfortunately, the half-empty one was jammed with old foam, so I used a drill bit to clean it out. Suddenly the valve opened wide and the foam started spraying out. At first I thought of letting it eject over the side and started to take it on deck, but the foam splattered everywhere. I rushed back down below and let it empty itself on my rubber collision mat, where I was able to scrape it up with a spatula and spread it into the joints without too much wastage.

What a mess! I had foam all through my hair, over various things inside the boat, on the lines and deck. It took some time to clean up. I found it was better to let it harden for a couple of days before scraping it off, particularly on fabrics and clothing. If I tried to scrape it off while it was still wet, it stuck more and was harder to get off when dry. I had a good laugh about the predicament in which I had placed myself.

I used the good spray can of expanding foam and ran the long, thin nozzle along the gap between the tiles. The spray foam also filled in the space behind the foam board tiles, and once the spray foam cured, it was a monolithic single piece of foam curved to match the inside of the hull. It was one of those chores that I hadn't completed before I left as there were many more important tasks to attend to. At last I had a warmer, drier bunk in which to sleep.

Mon, Dec 17, 1984: 36°55′S 106°54′W, Previous Day's Run: 45

It was another fine day, so I continued with my chores. I ran the motor for a while to charge the batteries and to keep the engine in good shape so it wouldn't seize up through lack of use. I spent a part of the day finishing foaming the insulation joints with good results. There was no mess this time. In anticipation of bad weather, I also packed clothes away into plastic bags to keep them dry for when I got nearer to Cape Horn.

Later I rigged the four-by-four piece of lumber I had shaped as a bowsprit and set the spinnaker out on its end. I was also able to set the number one genoa inside of it. I found some shackles that needed rewiring and scrutinized *Laiviņa* looking for anything that might require work or needed to be prepared for the rough seas ahead. Now was the time to do these chores as it was so much easier to work in calm conditions.

Tue, Dec 18, 1984: 38°19′S 106°09′W, Previous Day's Run: 91

After breakfast I continued preparing *Laiviņa* for Cape Horn. I noticed that the leather anti-chafing patch on the starboard side of the pulpit was worn through to the stainless steel. This leather patch was a form of baggywrinkle and stopped the tack of the sail from being worn through by the lifeline attachment point on the pulpit. The patch took the brunt of the wear instead of the sail. I sewed a new patch over the top of the existing piece of badly worn leather to prevent the sails chafing. I also overhauled my small flashlight and soldered all the battery connections, which had corroded and were making poor contact. I used a copper-headed soldering iron heated up on my kerosene pressure stove.

Figure 8.1: A genoa on the backstay to fly 1,775 square feet of sail

In the afternoon, I managed to set 1,775 square feet of sail for the first time. I had both big number one genoas set, the spinnaker and full mainsail up, and was drawing on a reach. It made a difference of about two knots. Under headsail and mainsail I would have only 585 square feet set but the conditions were right and I got a bit inventive. The spinnaker was out on the jury-rigged bowsprit, the new number one genoa on the forestay and the old number one genoa on the backstay, hoisted with the boom topping lift and poled out to windward. It looked odd, but it worked.

Later in the day, the wind increased and I had to take it all down. In doing so I discovered a good method for a solo sailor to get the spinnaker down in a blow. I used the same approach practised by sailors on a fully crewed boat. The mainsail created a pocket of dead air behind which the spinnaker was lowered. The difference was that each step could be performed independently, instead of trying to do two things at once.

I let the boom out fully until it was athwartship and touching the shrouds. Next, I set the self-steering for almost a dead run but with the wind coming over the weather quarter a bit. The spinnaker now collapsed easily. I next pulled the spinnaker sheet under the boom and sucked the sail hard up against the back side of the mainsail and attached the sheet to one of the cleats on the weather side of the companionway hatch. I went forward to the mast and uncleated the spinnaker halyard while keeping one turn around the cleat. I led the lazy end of the spinnaker halyard back to the companionway hatch and cleated it on the weather side of the companionway. Now I went into the cabin and positioned myself in the companionway.

If the wind was not strong, I could work both lines simultaneously. As I pulled the sheet, I eased the halyard. The spinnaker stayed sucked in against the back side of the mainsail so it was inactive as I gently eased it down. There was no need to hurry.

If the wind was very strong, I eased the halyard thirty centimetres or so with a safety turn around the cleat and then re-cleated it. Next, I pulled in the sheet the same amount. I continued this process, alternating between sheet and halyard, all the while keeping control of the lines by having a turn around the cleat. It was effective.

With the wind increasing, it looked like we were out of the horse latitudes. Having about fifty miles to go until the Roaring Forties, I had to start keeping my eye on the barometer and reading the weather signs in the clouds.

To make running wing and wing with two headsails easier to rig, I set up *Laiviņa* with twin forestays. Before leaving Victoria, I replaced all my rigging with new five-sixteenth-inch diameter stainless steel wire. Barry and I had split the cost of a drum of wire to save some money, and I had it cut and swaged by Paynes Marine in Victoria. The old rigging was coiled and stowed in my aft locker in case it was needed in an emergency. I brought the old stainless steel forestay up on deck, hauled it aloft with the spinnaker halyard, and shackled it to a spare pin on the starboard side of the masthead.

Back on deck, I shackled the tack end of the second forestay to a small piece of heavy chain, loosened the backstay turnbuckle a bit, and then, stretching the second forestay as tight as I could by hand, shackled the chain to the starboard side of the bow fitting. After retensioning the backstay and adjusting the turnbuckle on the port forestay, I was able to tension both forestays equally.

It made a difference as I could change the port sail independent of the starboard sail. Before, I needed to interleave the hanks on the forestay correctly and then hoist or lower both sails simultaneously. I had created a reference table showing the hank interleaving for all combinations of head sails. It was now no longer necessary to memorize the pattern from my table before running wing and wing. To hoist a sail on the port forestay, I used the spinnaker halyard; to hoist the starboard one, I used the jib halyard.

Now that the job was done, I set the two big number one genoas and lowered the mainsail to allow them to breath properly and pull the boat instead of being pushed by the mainsail. *Laiviņa* moved along nicely under 740 square feet of sail. I went to bed late and tried to get some sleep.

Wed, Dec 19, 1984: 40°43′S 104°50′W, Previous Day's Run: 156

The previous evening, we crossed over the forty-degree parallel of latitude and were now officially in the Roaring Forties. To celebrate, the weather presented me with a full-blown depression. The barometer began going down slowly at first, then dropped sharply. I didn't sleep much, as the wind was slowly increasing, but I was happy that we were moving fast. I figured that the rig I had up would last until first light.

Around 2 a.m. *Laiviņa* was flying. She was surfing down waves that were building bigger and bigger by the hour. The wind was dead aft, and the self-steering was handling the conditions better than a lot of helmspersons could. The log showed a steady nine knots climbing to ten knots on occasion, and the noise was like an express train. Occasionally we would broach and one of the big genoas would back with a thump that shook the rigging, but nothing like the explosion of sound that shook the boat when the sail filled again with an almighty bang. It was as if a whale had struck *Laiviņa*. I knew that I should reef down and put smaller headsails up, but I wanted to push her to the limit and see if I could break the voyage distance record for a noon-to-noon run of 150 miles that I had set a few days before the self-steering rudder broke.

By first light I had to reef. We were broaching about once every two minutes and skimming across the water all other times. I dressed and went on deck. What an experience! The biggest seas were five metres in height. As they approached *Laiviņa* from behind, the seas would lift the stern and tip the bow down, and we would start rushing down the face. Just as *Laiviņa* was going the fastest, the wave would pass under us and for a second would be like a see-saw with a scary five-metre drop-off at the bow. Then *Laiviņa* would slow down and slide down the back face of the wave only to repeat the process again and again. I believe that it was the fastest I have sailed *Laiviņa* and the hardest I have driven her. It was hard to tell how quick she was going as the needle of the electronic log was often stuck hard against the end stop at ten knots. She was really strong and tough.

Unfortunately, the force of the broaches was peeling the spinnaker pole track off the mast. I knew that I wouldn't be able to push that hard again without strengthening the track attachment to the mast. I dropped the genoas and replaced them with twin number one jibs, which gave me 476 square feet instead of 740 square feet. Things were more controlled now. It took two hours to change the rig from the big genoas to big jibs as I was tired from lack of sleep. I went below, got out of my wet-weather gear, and crawled into my bunk.

How could I think that I was going to be able to sleep? The wind kept increasing, and within an hour of changing from genoas to jibs, *Laiviņa* was rocketing along banging and crashing as she had done before. I climbed back into my wet-weather gear, went on deck where I replaced the twin number one jibs with twin number two jibs, bringing the sail area down to 260 square feet. It also took two hours to change the rig from the number one jibs to number two jibs. I went below... again, got out of my wet-weather gear... again, and crawled into my bunk... again.

Bang! Crash! Roar! Swish! I climbed back into my very wet wet-weather gear, went on deck for the third time, where I changed the rig for twin storm jibs, giving me 140 square feet of sail. I went down below and got ready to rest as sleep was now out of the question. It was about 2 p.m. and I could see the signs in the clouds of a cold front moving in. A lowering layer of scudding clouds was moving fast from the southwest while the surface wind was still blowing from the northwest. From the speed and the direction of the new wind, I could tell that we would get a violent shift to the southwest in a very short time. I waited.

Just before the cold front passed our location, there came a hard blast of wind that lasted about ten minutes, blowing at storm force. The wind shifted from the northwest to the southwest instantly. The self-steering turned *Laiviņa* to follow the wind, and off we went, scooting towards the northeast instead of southeast. I went up on deck again and set the single storm jib of seventy square feet. As I was too tired to set the trysail to balance it, I set a reaching course, crashed on the bunk, and slept. Based on my previous experience with violent shifts of wind at the bottom of the barometer, coupled with such a strong blast for a short time, I believed that the wind would get less and less. I slept easy knowing that the worst was over. Later that evening I awoke, and the wind had died down a little. I set a fully reefed mainsail to balance the storm jib and went back to bed.

Behind me lay the trade winds and Canada and my friends. Ahead lurked Cape Horn, the object of my growing fears. As *Laiviņa* cut away the miles that separated me from the place that had claimed many lives and many ships, my state of mind changed slowly from cheerful optimism to fearful dread. The barometer appeared to me as a vulture forecasting my possible demise. If it dropped, intense fear cut into me; if it rose, I relaxed a little and dared to hope that we would round the terrible cape unscathed.

CHAPTER 9

Approach to Cape Horn

Thu, Dec 20, 1984: 40°50′S 102°54′W, Previous Day's Run: 88

I awoke after a solid night's sleep, and although I was still exhausted and felt very groggy, I was alert. The wind had gone right down, so I dressed and went on deck to set the full mainsail. I hoisted the number two genoa instead of the number one genoa as there were still a few gusts and I was a bit leery of the weather being unpredictable. Later, when there were no more gusts and I felt more confident of my weather predictions, I changed the number two genoa for the number one genoa.

During the day, I carefully planned a course that would first get me to the latitude of Cape Horn while I was far to the west and away from the western shores of South America. Should I become disabled by a bad storm, I wanted to make sure that we would not be in any immediate danger of being driven onto the continental rocks of Chile. By getting to the latitude of Cape Horn early, should *Laiviņa* be disabled, we might safely drift past the cape to its south.

After checking over the storm jib, I noticed a bit of damage that needed repairing. I also noticed that a grommet on the luff of the number one genoa had torn out, so I carefully repaired it. I was still exhausted and couldn't do much else under the now dark night sky, so went to bed early and slept another long night.

Fri, Dec 21, 1984: 41°17′S 103°02′W, Previous Day's Run: 28

While sleeping through the night, *Laiviņa* had also slept, lying becalmed on a still ocean. It was as if she were also resting and recovering her strength, just idly swaying from side to side in the swell, recuperating from the gale. When I awoke, I dressed and went on deck to discover that there was a little zephyr so I trimmed the sails and adjusted the self-steering, coaxing *Laiviņa* along like a tired old horse.

I spent the morning tidying up and doing odd jobs. Later that afternoon, a light breeze sprang up, and we started moving better under the spinnaker, mainsail, and genoa. During the late afternoon, I came across an albatross floating on the surface, pecking at something. It was directly ahead and in our path, so the bird took to the air when we came uncomfortably close to it. Looking down at the water, I saw a dead octopus. Strangely, the albatross didn't bother to come back. Perhaps it didn't have any reference to where it was two minutes before.

Today was the summer solstice. From now on, the sun would start heading north from the Tropic of Capricorn towards the equator. This was another event to celebrate and to mark the passage of time as I sailed the many miles of deep, dark ocean.

Sat, Dec 22, 1984: 43°20′S 101°50′W, Previous Day's Run: 134

The weather settled down a bit, and we were getting steady winds. I wondered when the next blow would come. I was also excited as there were only three days to go until Christmas, when I would get to open more presents.

I spent the day overhauling the tool box and greasing up all the tools. I also screwed down one of the pieces of plywood that form the cabin sole. Under it, 120 kilograms of anchor chain was stored. If we were rolled over, I would not want that weight to come hurtling out onto the underside of the deck! I did the same for the locker that held all my tools. I put many screws in the lid, hoping the tools would stay put in a capsize.

Later I went on deck and set twin number one genoas, wing and wing. The wind had veered back to the northwest and was right behind us. The wing and wing rig was an easy rig to set up and manage, and it made the self-steering's job easier. One of the headsails was poled out with the spinnaker pole, and for the other headsail, I ran the sheet through a carabiner acting as a fairlead and attached to the end of the boom. I took down the mainsail completely and secured it to the boom so the two headsails could breathe freely without getting stale air from a set mainsail. The boom was fully extended out to one side and locked in place by pulling it forward towards the bow with the boom foreguy. These boom foreguys went through turning blocks attached to the bow fitting and then led back to a cleat on either side of the companionway hatch. I tightened the mainsheet a bit so the boom stayed snug in its outboard position.

Sun, Dec 23, 1984: 45°41′S 101°03′W, Previous Day's Run: 145

I woke up to find *Laiviņa* roaring along and the wind getting fresher. To ease the damaged spinnaker pole track, I changed the twin genoas for twin number one jibs.

Now that we were in the Roaring Forties, the sea was rough most of the time. I relaxed when possible during strong wind to conserve my energy as so much gets expended in changing sails.

I had been reading a book by the author Joseph Wambaugh called *The Black Marble* and finished it before noon. I had enjoyed it so much that at times I was laughing so hard, I ended up on the cabin sole rolling around and holding my sides while gasping for breath.

It was only two days until Christmas, and I was looking forward to it, anxious to see what I would get when I opened the presents that my friends had given me.

Mon, Dec 24, 1984: 47°53′S 100°11′W, Previous Day's Run: 137

It was Christmas Eve here and Christmas Day in New Zealand.

We were sailing in fog with a lot of drizzle, and *Laiviņa* was going well. This morning, I went on deck with some tools and moved the jockey pole rings up the mast until they were a bit over a metre off the deck. I drilled and tapped fresh holes in the mast and screwed them in place. I would use them instead of the spinnaker pole rings on the track. The force from the pole would push into the side of the mast, rather than trying to peel the spinnaker pole track off the front of the mast. Now I could drive *Laiviņa* hard again.

The water was getting very cold now, and consequently so was the air. I was wearing a woollen undershirt, a woollen sweater, a woollen shirt, a woollen vest, a second woollen sweater, a woollen jacket, a woollen balaclava hat, woollen long johns, woollen trousers, and corduroy trousers. Before the trip, I had soaked all my woollen clothes with a mixture of raw anhydrous lanolin dissolved in white gasoline. The clothes were hung on a line in the outside air until the gasoline evaporated and left them evenly infused with lanolin. It stopped the wool from absorbing water and thus drier and warmer…though I smelled like a sheep!

Now in the westerlies, there was more variability in the weather. I could not trust the wind to stay consistent for more than a short time, so I always set the alarm to give me a maximum of two hours' sleep. I did fall asleep quickly though.

I stayed completely dressed all the time so that when the alarm went, I just needed to throw on wet-weather gear and my harness and I was ready to go on deck. Sometimes, it was just a matter of climbing out of the bunk, quickly sliding open the companionway hatch, and shining a flashlight on the compass and the wind indicator at the top of the mast. If the wind strength was the same and we were still sailing a good course, I would crawl right back into my bunk.

If I needed to go on deck to adjust the course, I would go to the stern, pull the little wooden shear peg out of the hole in the vane tiller that lined up with the hole in the course selector disc and slide it into an adjacent hole. Just inside of the circumference of the course selector disc were thirty-six holes drilled ten degrees apart. I could adjust the course in ten-degree increments.

To allow for finer adjustments of five degrees, the vane tiller had two holes drilled fifteen degrees apart that lined up with holes in the course selector disc. I would clamp the vane tiller to the course selector disc with my hand to stop relative movement between the two, shift the wooden peg from one hole to the other in the vane tiller and rotate the course selector disk five degrees until I was able to push the wooden peg into a hole of the course selector disc directly below. To prevent damage to the wind vane gear, the wooden shear pegs were quarter inch pieces of dowels and would break if excessive force was suddenly applied to the self-steering wind vane. In a pinch I could also use a pencil if I ran out of dowel.

Occasionally it was necessary to tweak the sail trim a bit, or even change a sail if the wind strength varied. Every two hours, I had a chance to sniff the wind, check the cloud cover and the sea state, tap and record the barometer, and feel the boat's movement, sensing the rightness or wrongness in my environment.

Tue, Dec 25, 1984: 49°09′S 99°12′W, Previous Day's Run: 85

It was Christmas Day! I awoke to find it foggy and the winds light, so I set full sail again. Later in the day it drizzled and it looked like it was going to be a bleak Christmas. By noon, we had a clear blue sky, a warm sun, and light breezes.

First, I opened Dug's Christmas box. This took me quite a while as he had nailed it up and sealed it well. Not wanting to damage the contents, I pried off the lid carefully. Inside there were books, cards, a packet of wild rice, and more wrapped gifts. I decided to save them for later in the voyage as a reward for reaching various milestones. I made a note in the ship's log as to when I would open which gift.

Next, I opened Mhora's gift. It was a small jigsaw puzzle, which I promptly sat down and put together. It was fun and I loved it. Inside the gift wrapping was a card and a sealed envelope containing the third of her series of cryptograms.

After crossing the equator, I had taken out a similar sealed envelope containing the second cryptogram and put it aside to open on Christmas Eve. I thought "I'm not going to open Mhora's third sealed envelope until I solve the second cryptogram." It took two hours. I had given myself some incentive. The first cryptogram took three weeks!

Finally, I opened Penny's gift and her card to me. I guessed that she must have read my mind. Inside the card was a photograph. It was something I needed as I had no photograph of her to take with me on the voyage. I regretted that I didn't ask her for one before I left. This one was of her and the children, Patrick, Christy, and Robert. Saving the rest of the presents, I planned to open them at a rate of one per week to extend Christmas.

I spent the afternoon getting rid of cabin fever by sunbathing in all my woollens atop the dinghy as we slid along the ocean.

Since the start of the voyage I had been recording the barometric pressure as often as I could. I plotted the results on graph paper that I had pinned up on the corkboard below the barometer. Today I noticed that the barometer had jumped up sharply and there were signs of an approaching depression or at least a front. I was curious as to what we would get.

Wed, Dec 26, 1984: 50°50′S 96°17′W, Previous Day's Run: 151

We were now in the Furious Fifties. Because I suspected another serious blow was coming, I spent the morning screwing down more cabin sole boards where I had more chain, (another 120 kilograms) and a spare

Figure 9.1: Sunbathing in woollens on Christmas Day

anchor, which I secured to the base of the mast support with some lashings.

I started work on Mhora's third puzzle and solved it in a couple of hours. Either they were getting easier, or I was getting better at solving cryptograms.

Thu, Dec 27, 1984: 52°05′S 92°53′W, Previous Day's Run: 148

Today, I got a bit of a shock as I was lowering one of the genoas. When it was about halfway down, a gust of wind blew the belly of the sail into the water, and the force broke the spinnaker pole topping lift wire. The pole then dropped its end into the water and, with the other end still attached to the mast, bent the jockey pole ring and pressed hard against the cap shroud holding the mast up.

I was very concerned. I thought the mast was going to come down about my ears. A second later, I knew what had to be done. I grabbed the water filled genoa and hauled it out of the water and up on deck. This eased some of the pressure on the shroud. With considerable effort, I managed to get the pole up and out of the water. I lashed the pole securely and went below. I was shaking with shock because I realized how close we had come to a disaster. It was my own fault as I hadn't lowered the sail onto the deck properly, thinking that in the light wind it wouldn't matter.

Once in the cabin, my shaking hands fetched a large spoon out of the drawer, and I had myself a spoonful of sugar. After I sat down for a minute or two, the sugar settled my hands, and I went on deck and finished doing the sail change.

Fri, Dec 28, 1984: 53°06′S 89°10′W, Previous Day's Run: 149

We were getting closer to Cape Horn now and still experiencing excellent weather. I hoped to make it there without any more storms, but one never knows. The only means at my disposal to predict the future were the barometer, the thermometer, and the old standby of casting a jaundiced eye at the clouds. I could usually predict with some certainty events a half day away.

Sat, Dec 29, 1984: 54°00′S 86°17′W, Previous Day's Run: 116

Today was another beautiful, warm day, relatively speaking. I got rid of some more cabin fever by sitting up on deck and feeling the sun soak

Figure 9.2: Southern Ocean squalls

through my thick layer of clothes. Later in the day, a cold front moved in with squalls and hailstorms coating the decks with ice. I was taking down the spinnaker at the time, and it was cold. Brrrr! In the period between squalls, I managed to photograph a beautiful rainbow.

We were far enough south that now that it was close to the summer solstice, it didn't get dark. The sun rose in the southeast and moved around the horizon, climbing steadily as the day went on until it was high in the sky in the north. Then it descended while moving around to the southwest, where it set. Ever so slowly, the twilight came on until only the brighter stars came out at midnight. The sky in the south was still light with the red and yellow colours of sunset. At midnight, the sun was only ten degrees or so below the horizon. There was plenty of light from the time the sun set at 10 p.m. until it rose again at 2 a.m. It was so exciting to experience this for the first time.

Sun, Dec 30, 1984: 54°52′S 82°33′W, Previous Day's Run: 140

This morning, my brain wasn't in tune with my body. First, I spilled powdered milk all over the place, then after carefully mixing the milk with water in a shaker, I broke the jar, and milk went everywhere. I was very clumsy and didn't seem to have my sea legs or sea arms. It made me angry, and I became even clumsier. By noon, my mood had improved, and I was moving around *Laiviņa* as graceful as a dancer on a dance hall floor.

During the afternoon, the sky clouded over except for a perfectly formed blue sky ring. It was a strange thing, which I had never seen before. I took a photo of it, and after my voyage, I showed the photo to a meteorologist. He told me it was a rarely seen vortex. It was quite stable, lasting the entire time I sailed past, and it continued to move with the cloud mass. It functioned like a smoke ring that was blown out of a smoker's mouth and appeared to be a rotating doughnut-shaped mass of air. It may have been caused by a column of warm air rising from below that started the air mass rotating.

Another possibility was that the phenomenon was fallstreak holes or cavum. This appeared less likely because cavum is usually a hole in the cloud mass, not a ring.

Figure 9.3: Vortex formed in the clouds

Lots of black-browed albatrosses were around now, and the water appeared to be rich in plankton, with many jelly-like organisms. I noticed how the colder waters here in the Southern Ocean supported more life than the hot waters of the tropics. I had read that upwellings from the ocean bottom brought nutrients to the surface which allowed plankton to flourish.

Mon, Dec 31, 1984: 55°16′S 79°27′W, Previous Day's Run: 109

It was New Year's Eve here and New Year's Day in New Zealand and Australia. Ever since gale number two when I had just entered the Roaring Forties I had experienced really mild winds, and I now had only about four days of sailing to reach Cape Horn.

Tue, Jan 1, 1985: 56°12′S 76°26′W, Previous Day's Run: 116

On the western horizon, I saw the signs of an approaching depression. It also signalled my approaching depression. I was worried. *Laiviņa* was still three hundred miles from Cape Horn, and I knew that I would not get around Cape Horn before it struck. I thought that it would be a bad storm. By noon the barometer was dropping fast and the wind had risen accordingly. I was reacting to the effects of my troubled state of mind. I cursed and grumbled and felt helpless in the face of the oncoming depression.

To prepare for it, I had rigged the storm jib and the trysail, secured everything above decks and most things below decks, and settled down to read to stop my mind preying on itself. The wind never reached gale force, and by midnight it had dropped to a steady breeze.

However, I didn't trust it as the barometer went up a bit and levelled off. I expected the cold front to move in with its associated rise in barometric pressure, but it didn't come. Something was wrong.

Wed, Jan 2, 1985: 56°51′S 74°00′W, Previous Day's Run: 89

Around midnight, it started raining, but there was still very little wind. I set full sail again so I could collect water off the mainsail, but was ready to drop it at a moment's notice. It was mainly light rain, and I was able to collect only a few litres. I was suspicious as I just knew that the barometer had to go further down and felt I had only experienced part of the drop with a halt in between. I also remembered the old sailor's adage: "Wind before rain, topsails remain; rain before wind, topsails take in."

Sure enough, by 6 a.m. the barometer dropped quickly and eventually reached 982 millibars, the lowest I had experienced so far on this voyage. With the drop in barometric pressure, the wind increased very rapidly. There was only enough time to get the number one genoa down and the mainsail dropped. By the time I set the storm jib and trysail, it was blowing a near gale.

I must have torn a tendon in my left shoulder, for now it was giving me a lot of trouble. Massaging it didn't ease the pain, and I had little strength in my left arm. With the preparations I must do before any gale, it left me exhausted. I wondered if I would be able to use my arm in the critical hours to come. It had taken me three hours to set the storm sails, a job that in good weather would take ten minutes.

A problem cropped up when I was about to hoist the trysail. The main halyard had become wrapped up with the flag halyard, which ran from the base of the mast to the cap shroud near the top of the mast. I could not free it from the deck, so there was no solution other than to climb the mast.

With only one arm working properly, I struggled my way slowly upward as *Laiviņa* kicked and bucked in the waves. At the masthead I attempted to unwrap the light line and untie the bowline knot that secured it. I was using fingers that were numb from the biting cold winds. With three frozen fingers, I clung to the mast step as I forced my index and middle fingers to undo a knot they couldn't feel. Slowly, the knot loosed as I strained my wind-torn, watery eyes, forcing the stiff fingers to work. It came free. Back down the mast I clambered slowly, every metre gained at the expense of my shoulder already inflamed with a sharp lancing pain.

The rest of the day, I came on deck every hour to check the ocean for potential rogue seas that could capsize the boat. There was nothing in the wave train that indicated that potential.

Later the barometer reached its lowest point and then started to rise. I was relieved as I knew that the gale had reached its worst and the wind could only get lighter. The wind shifted from the northwest to the west, and it started to die down. I went below after a final check on deck, set the alarm for 1 a.m. to check on the weather, and crashed on my bunk to sleep.

Thu, Jan 3, 1985: 56°20′S 70°10′W, Previous Day's Run: 130

When I awoke the wind had died sufficiently so I put on more sail. I went back to bed but lay awake awhile before I finally dropped off to sleep. How I slept! I awoke at 9 a.m. feeling fully recharged. After heavy weather, I always seem to sleep deeply, and when I wake, I feel restored but groggy. For the first hour or so, I had lost my sea legs and had to be careful not to fall over.

Figure 9.4: Gale from the spreaders

The wind had gone down even more, so I set full sail. I wanted to set the spinnaker, but I had to first fix a small hole I had noticed earlier. It only took about a quarter of an hour. Soon the spinnaker was set, and while it was pulling *Laiviņa* along, I brought in the mainsail to repair a small hole, torn while reefing it the day before.

If I had more money before I left on my voyage, I would have bought a new mainsail as the existing one was getting rotten. The sunlight had deteriorated the eight-ounce cloth to the point where I could tear it with my hands. A feat quite impossible with new cloth. I was careful with the mainsail and kept pressure off it by reefing early. I couldn't afford to blow it out. I also repaired some tears in my wet-weather gear as my left knee was always getting a soaking.

Later in the day, I saw a flock (or was it a school?) of penguins leaping out of the water ten metres away. An hour later I heard the resonant tone of a whale sounding. I rushed on deck to see a school of killer whales. They were likely hunting the penguins.

At sunset I was treated to a beautiful red sky, which persisted all through the night. Being only about six hundred miles from the Antarctic Circle and a couple of weeks past the summer solstice, it never became dark. At midnight, sunset blended into sunrise.

Figure 9.5: Midnight sunset

CHAPTER 10

Rounding Cape Horn

Fri, Jan 4, 1985: 56°07′S 67°49′W, Previous Day's Run: 79

I set the alarm for 3 a.m. When I awoke, I dressed and went on deck to scan the dawn horizon. There in the distance was land.

As I jumped up and down on the deck, I yelled out the call that many sailors have shouted from the masthead in this place for centuries before.

"Laaannnd hoooooo!"

There was Islas Diego Ramírez in the distance, about twenty miles away. These islets were further south than Cape Horn and belonged to Chile. I would pass to the north of them and not see them up close, but it was great to spot my first land since Easter Island.

The weariness of the last week was still affecting me, so I made my way to my bunk for some more sleep and set the alarm for 7 a.m. It would give me another four hours' sleep yet ensure that I didn't run into my first landfall.

It was just as well, because the wind had shifted again, and at 7 a.m. I woke to find that instead of passing the islets, we had swung in towards them and were now fifteen miles away. There was still plenty of room, but I was annoyed that I had been fooled by my trust in the wind.

It was a special day. I started a day-long celebration of my thirty-third birthday, opening my gifts to find a tiny but rich fruit cake and a box of twenty-four candles in a special waterproof container. I cut the long thin candles in two with a pair of scissors, and into the cake I poked thirty-three of the candle halves. It took a while to light all the candles, and as they were so closely spaced, the heat became intense. The candles started to melt. While the huge bonfire of blazing candles belched up towards the cabin top, I took a photograph and then blew out the fire in a single, strong breath. A wish came easily to mind. Half an hour later, Cape Horn reared its awesome visage above the horizon.

This was an important milestone for which I had been headed these long and solitary months.

The overcast morning had given way to a bright blue sky and warm sunshine. When the final clouds over the land cleared around noon, I could see Mount Darwin and the Pyramids, which struck me as an excellent name for a rock group.

Mount Darwin stood 2,438 metres high and was about eighty-four miles away, tinged with the golden yellow of distance. In the cabin, I plotted our noon position and measured the distance to Cape Horn. Twenty miles. At our present speed of four knots assisted by a knot of current, we would soon be there.

The day turned out to be perfect. The shallow dark green water and the nearby land had blocked the heavy swell coming from the north, and conditions were similar to sailing outside of Victoria Harbour. Up went the spinnaker, and *Laiviņa* started surging along in ideal sailing conditions. Closer and closer we sailed, with Cape Horn getting bigger and more awe inspiring than before.

When we were a mile off, I climbed the mast to look out for rocks below the surface of the water. I arrived at the top of the mast and was overcome by the power and beauty of the place. The wind had died down, but I could still hear the air whispering as it flowed across the sails, and below, the soft swoosh as the hull gently spread the water like the legs of a lover. All around, albatrosses hugged the air currents on the surface, climbing and diving, flattening out centimetres from the water, their wing tips caressing the wave tops, then banking hard and lifting for yet another search for food.

I stood there on the topmost step, overcome with emotion as Cape Horn loomed high above me, under a mile away. My body quivered with passion, and my mind effervesced with feelings I had not experienced in a long time. The power of that place, and above all the sense of age, history, and permanence, struck me. It was as though I had come across the ancient ruins of a temple in a desert. I had met the object of my most intense fears and found it benevolent.

It was time to climb down from the mast as the distance to the cape was closing rapidly. When about half a mile away, the breeze started to fade away and *Laiviņa* slowed down. Four cables to go, three, two, and finally at one cable distance, I turned *Laiviņa* and we veered away a little. There it was. I could see the cracks in the rocks, the tough grasses and lichens, the small waves washing the barnacles between the tide lines. Cape Horn. I made it. Never again would I have misty imaginings of this place. Like a lover wanting more intimacy, I longed to feel the hard rock under my hands; I wanted to mount the rock and climb to the top of the cape in ecstasy. I felt as Odysseus would have felt with the Gods controlling the winds to bring me to this place and then allowing the wind to fade to a faint zephyr, leaving me gliding gently past its bold visage.

Figure 10.1: The mighty Cape Horn up close

Slowly my mood softened and I looked around me. Ahead at the eastern end of the island stood a couple of buildings, which my binoculars revealed to be either a weather station or another government outpost. I broke out the ship's flag, unfurled it, and sailed on past.

Idly *Laiviņa* rotated in the still air and strong current. The horizon ahead ruffled with the incoming new wind, which was just beginning to reach us. I dropped the spinnaker and set *Laiviņa* for a close-hauled course. Within ten minutes we were driving at maximum speed in a freshening northeasterly away from the coast. What a remarkable event. To be at Cape Horn at such a calm time. The gods had smiled on me. What a day! What a birthday!

CHAPTER 11

To the Falkland Islands

Sat, Jan 5, 1985: 55°30′S 64°04′W, Previous Day's Run: 132

After I had passed Cape Horn, I set the alarm for midnight. The breeze had freshened, and I needed to reef the mainsail and set the number two genoa.

I awoke at midnight to find the wind had backed, so I eased the sheets and *Laiviņa* drove faster. I set the alarm again, this time for 2:30 a.m. Upon wakening, I found that the wind had veered and I had to sheet in again. After *Laiviņa* was sailing on course, I stood at the backstay, watching the weather, the waves, and the way *Laiviņa* was moving.

Suddenly I heard a roaring noise behind me. Turning quickly and looking over the stern, I saw a sight that transfixed me with horror. *Laiviņa* was about ten metres away from the lip of what appeared to be a whirlpool twenty metres in diameter. It wasn't really a whirlpool, but a hole in the water as if an invisible giant had pushed a smooth fist into the sea. The water was rushing down the sides of this hole into the centre, but it wasn't spinning like a whirlpool.

I suddenly thought that my navigation was incorrect and I was in a tidal race, but no, I was on the edge of the continental shelf. This phenomenon lasted about eight seconds, and then it was gone. I was left shaking, with my stomach in my mouth. Gripping the handrail, I staggered forward to the companionway and went below to collapse on the bunk. After eating a cookie, my nerves settled and I realized what I had just seen. It was a "rogue trough." And just as "rogue waves" were caused by the occasional linking of the crests of three or more large waves, the antithesis was the linking of three or more large troughs. Just as a rogue wave was forced to break and the water cascaded down to a lower level, a rogue trough was so steep that the water was forced to flow into the centre. It was probably caused by multiple wave trains coming from both the Pacific and Atlantic Oceans.

The rest of the day, I navigated past Isla de los Estados. In between obtaining fixes, I relaxed and spent the time reading *Aztec* by Gary Jennings.

Sun, Jan 6, 1985: 54°40′S 60°40′W, Previous Day's Run: 127

Bright green streaks of the southern aurora stretched high into the Antarctic sky as *Laiviņa* close-reached her way through Drake Passage. The soft twilight refused to give in to the dark of night and cast its glow upon the grey, turbulent water. I woke just before dawn, dressed for the elements, and came on deck for my regular weather check. I stood up against the backstay, my hands sheltering behind my back from the cold wind, and scanned the sky and sea looking for a change in the weather. Fifty miles behind us lay Cape Horn, successfully rounded in perfect conditions the day before. I reflected upon my good luck so far on this voyage and *Laiviņa*'s fast progress.

I had a rough night of wind shifts. At one time, I woke to find us ninety degrees off course. By noon, the wind had settled down and I was on a close-hauled course for Port Stanley.

Today I brought some more rations of food out of my stores. I had a jar of jam, peanut butter, honey, flour, and some Velveeta cheese. It was ecstasy to taste foods that were so rich in flavour when I had been eating mostly tuna, brown rice, porridge, raisins, and homemade bread.

Whenever I depleted a substantial amount of my immediate supplies, I would to restock the locker at the back of the galley sink. I had organized my food in such a way that I kept a record of every cardboard box and every wrapped package of groups of food in those boxes. I used codes to identify the locker in which the cardboard boxes were stored and their location in that locker. I also used codes to identify where in the cardboard box an item was placed.

As I took an item out of a cardboard box, I would subtract the amount from the remainder and update the record in my notebook. At all times, I knew how much water, flour, rice, porridge, tuna, raisins, peanut butter, jam, and even treat foods I had left.

There might be an entry for rice that said "RICE—SAB3—18 kg" when decoded meant "RICE—starboard aft berth—box number three—18 kg remaining."

When I needed to replenish my immediate stores, I did an inventory to see what was getting low in my immediate stores locker. If I needed to get more rice, I would fetch other foods at the same time I had the locker open and boxes unpacked. After getting more supplies, I would reseal all the plastic bags and carefully restow the cardboard boxes. I usually did this chore when the winds were light and motion was minimal.

Mon, Jan 7, 1985: 52°26′S 59°00′W, Previous Day's Run: 147

When I awoke for my night check of the weather, the wind had gotten up again and I had to reef the mainsail. It was biting cold as the wind was coming from the southwest and Antarctica. I went back to sleep and set the alarm for 4 a.m. I would be getting into the vicinity of Beauchêne Island, a small island lying south of the Falkland Islands about forty miles or so.

During my sleep, I accidentally pushed in the stop-alarm button and slept through to 7 a.m. When I awoke, I rushed on deck in a panic to find that we were just passing the island, which was now ten miles abeam. Although our course took us safely past the island, I was annoyed that the alarm didn't go off. I don't like running that sort of risk. I decided to reverse the position of the alarm clock over my head to avoid inadvertently pushing in the button.

I used a bearing to Beauchêne Island and found the distance off using my Invisible Mountain formula to obtain a position. As soon as I had plotted the fix on the chart, I set a course for the Sea Lion Islands, another group of islands that lie south of the Falkland Islands by only fifteen miles. At noon they hove into view, flat and barren save for tough, salt loving bushes that covered them like the head of a crewcut sailor.

It was a beautiful sunny day, and with a brisk following wind we made good mileage. This was mainly due to the strong current that flows from west to east through Drake Passage, the narrow gap between Cape Horn and Antarctica. Now that we were in shallow coastal waters, the tide was helping as well. We soon left the island behind and sped up the coast.

At 9 p.m. I could see the Falkland Islands through the mist and coastal fog. I managed to get a rough fix and later could see the town of Stanley when their lights came on. There was something puzzling me. I could not spot the lighthouse, which I should have seen by this time. It was possible that my rough fix was more inexact than I had thought, so I moved back out to sea and sailed north to make my approach to Stanley from the east. This way, I would avoid the reefs and rocks to the south of the harbour entrance. As I approached the lights of the town I could see aircraft constantly taking off and landing.

Tue, Jan 8, 1985: 51°42′S 57°51′W, Previous Day's Run: 62

When I had sailed sufficiently north for safety, I altered course to the west and approached the visible lights where I guessed the harbour entrance should be. I was wary because my dead reckoning navigation could be many miles out. The lights may not have been the lights of Stanley, but those of another settlement. I was really puzzled. Although my charts were of the latest edition, the war in the Falkland Islands two years prior must have made some changes to what was charted. The other possibility was that lighthouses were not working so as not to provide the Argentinians with a navigational advantage. Unfortunately they were not providing me with any advantage either.

I heard an airplane in the sky above and looked around for it. Coming towards me at a slow speed was a Sea Harrier, the main fighting aircraft of the Falkland Islands War. I watched it approach me slowly and was amazed as it hovered above like a giant preying mantis, its jets screaming in my ears. After a while, it lifted away and went back to land on the dark mass of island to my north.

I moved in to the land on a close-hauled course in the cold night wind. I stood right up at the bow, well rugged up in warm clothing, with my eyes wide open peering into the gloom around the bright yellow lights. It was just as well I took care, as suddenly I began to sense the jet blackness of land coming closer and closer.

"Oh no! Bloody land!" I exclaimed.

I raced aft and feverishly swung the tiller hard over until we were hove to. After my heart quieted its mad beating, I checked our steady drift. The wind coming off the land was pressing us slowly away from the black horror of hard substance. There was nothing to do now but wait for the dawn, which was about three hours away.

I kept myself awake by munching bits of food at intervals while keeping a good lookout. After a couple of hours, we drifted out to sea a mile or so and I decided to rest for an hour. I set the alarm for 4 a.m., when it would be sufficiently light, and fell asleep.

CHAPTER 12

Port Stanley

The soft, warm sunlight pouring through the portholes awakened me at once with the realization that I had overslept.

"Damn!" I exclaimed.

I looked at the hour hand and the figure seven directly behind it. I had pushed the clock against the side of the cockpit and pressed in the stop button again. Something had to be done about that button before it wrecked me. Once on deck, I could see that we were at least five miles away from the nearest land. As we lay hove to during the early-morning hours, the land breeze had carried us far enough out to sea and safety, but again I didn't like the loss of control caused by that button.

After setting a course as close to the wind as practicable, I unreefed the mainsail and changed to my biggest genoa. We tacked in towards the harbour entrance, and I went below to fix the alarm clock. I took a cap from a tube of toothpaste and fitted it over the alarm shutoff button. Using some insulation tape, I fixed the cap in place. Now I had to shut the alarm off by changing the alarm setting time. At least it would always go off, provided I remembered to wind the alarm spring.

I took out the sextant and obtained a position line of the sun coupled with the calculated distance off from various mountains and hills of known height and plotted them on the chart. My navigation had been correct, and the lighthouse had been switched off. I worked my way in towards the coast as a seagoing tug came out of the harbour towing a barge. I guessed that it was heading for South Georgia six hundred miles or so away, or that it was just going to sea to dump garbage.

Closer and closer I worked in towards the land as more detail became obvious. I spotted the black and white banded tower of the Cape Pembroke lighthouse and the harbour entrance. Seal Rocks soon showed up with the waves crashing around their edge. I climbed the mast with my camera and photographed the barren yet beautiful landscape. Amid rolling plains of low, hardy bushes, arose mountains, weathered and bare of vegetation. It reminded me so much of Stewart Island to the south of New Zealand, which I remembered with feeling.

Figure 12.1: Cape Pembroke lighthouse

Our tacks became shorter and shorter until we reached the point where I could choose a route between some middle islets and the southern boundary of the harbour. I freed the sheets a little and slid into the calm waters. What a joy it was to slide slowly past those islets while the wind ushered me gently towards Stanley further up at the head of the sound.

It was then that I noticed the paraphernalia of war. On the southern peninsula stood rocket launchers, command posts, and soldiers moving about the barbed wire enclosures. Earlier I had seen a Sea Harrier land behind the peninsula, and after sighting a rotating radar antenna, I guessed that there was a major airstrip just out of view.

Further in, a tanker of the Cunard Line lay at its mooring. Beyond it, lying at anchor, were two naval vessels; *Sir Percival* was one of them.

We slid past the ships while sailors working on the hull of one ship gave me a wave. A greeting between men of the sea. There was a lot of activity in the inner harbour as I entered it. Barges were transporting army vehicles across the harbour, and various work boats were moving around. Ahead in the distance lay Stanley, a large group of homes nestled on the slope of the hills and sheltered from the prevailing winds.

I steered for what appeared to be the main wharf and noticed some people standing there. I hoped that they would not leave so that I could give them my mail. When I was still some distance away, I dropped the genoa onto the deck and moved in at a slower pace under mainsail alone. Once I was within hailing distance, I announced my request.

Figure 12.2: Stanley

"Ahoy! I am circumnavigating the globe, and I wish to drop off mail. I shan't be stopping. Would you be able to take my mail from me?"

"Yes, certainly," one said, "but come alongside here and we can sort it out."

I noticed that both men were well-dressed and one was in uniform. I figured that they were government officials, perhaps customs and immigration.

"I would prefer to come alongside the front of the wharf as there are good fenders alongside," I returned.

"No, you must come alongside here, as that area is reserved for the boats which are docking here all the time," he answered.

I checked the strength of the wind and figuring on a little current. I calculated my approach and decided to work up to windward. I had lost too much speed so I set the genoa again. About a hundred metres to windward I dropped the genoa again and turned downwind, running under mainsail alone.

With about three knots of speed, I approached and headed up into the wind and for the jetty. The mainsail fluttered idly, and I watched my progress towards the jetty. Still a bit fast. I sawed the tiller back and forth to create fluid friction from the turbulence to take some of the speed off *Laiviņa*. She came alongside gently, and I passed a mooring line to one of the men who dropped it over the bollard for me. It was a good berthing but not perfect. I dropped the mainsail as the two climbed down from the dock onto the foredeck.

"I'm Frazer Wallace, the chief police officer, and I also handle immigration affairs. I wear a couple of hats. This gentleman here is William Richards, the customs officer, but you can call him Bill," he said.

"I'm Peter Freeman, and I'm doing a non-stop circumnavigation. I called in for a couple of reasons. I wanted to drop off my mail, but I also wanted to have proof that I actually rounded the Horn. Would it be possible for you to put a stamp in my passport?" I asked him.

"We can certainly do that."

"I noticed that you were expecting me," I said.

"Of course. You would never have come in here without us knowing."

I had guessed right. In a place such as the Falkland Islands they must have been monitoring my approach from the night before, when I would have been picked up by radar.

While Bill, the customs officer, looked through my ship's papers and clearances, I chatted with Frazer.

"Have you had any news about Chay Blyth? Did he call in here?" I asked.

"Oh, yes. He was here all right, but the last we heard was that he was belly up at the Horn."

"He was rescued all right?" I asked.

"Oh sure, they picked him up."

I had read of Chay Blyth's attempt to beat the record set by a clipper ship that sailed from New York to San Francisco in some incredible time, around Cape Horn. Chay was going to beat it in a fast trimaran. Unfortunately, the subsequent capsize put paid to that attempt. His capsize would certainly provide more ammunition for the anti-multihull faction.

"I see the army is still very much in evidence here; I had thought that it would have been toned down a bit more," I ventured.

"It has toned down; you should have seen things a couple of years ago!" the police chief replied. "Although a lot of these boys will be going home once the airstrip is finished," he added.

Apparently they were building an airstrip large enough to land the big cargo carriers so that with the possibility of war breaking out again, the heavy gear could be moved in quickly.

"I should mention that there is a harbour fee you'll need to pay," Frazer informed me.

"How much?" I asked.

He told me. Although it was a small fee, I knew that I didn't have the money.

"I don't have any cash as I had to purchase hardwood in Santa Barbara to rebuild my self-steering rudder," I told him. But suddenly I had an idea. "I can pay you in cans of ham!" I said.

"Since you're only here for such a short time, I think we can waive the fee," he said. "Besides, I'd hate to leave you hungry at the end of your voyage."

"Thank you!" I was relieved.

We finished the paperwork. I had my passport stamped as proof that I had rounded the Horn, and I passed over my mail, which consisted of two postcards, a bundle of letters, and two rolls of film.

Figure 12.3: Falkland Islands stamp

"Thank you, Frazer... Bill. I best get out to sea before the wind picks up," I said.

I prepared *Laiviņa* and, after the mainsail was hoisted, slipped the mooring line and sailed out into the harbour leaving behind a group of soldiers struggling to secure the lines of a little sailing boat they had sailed across the harbour in the freshening winds.

The sky was ominous and threatening, and I remembered the words of Frazer Wallace as he pointed out the great petrel cartwheeling along the banks of the shoreline.

"See that!" he exclaimed. "See! When they do that, it's going to blow."

I didn't doubt it. Earlier, I had noticed a sharp drop in the barometer, and I figured as much. How much of a blow, I was yet to find out. I wanted to get away from the land and into deep water for safety.

Once I reached the outer harbour, I exchanged the number one genoa for a number one jib as *Laiviņa* was getting too hard pressed by the wind, and I knew it would continue to freshen. I set a course to pass astern of the naval vessels and ahead of the tanker. Once clear of the anchored ships, I looked astern to see *Sir Percival* steaming up fast behind me and getting ready to put to sea. I was a bit worried because

Figure 12.4: Sir Percival putting to sea

when big ships put to sea, little ships should put into port. How much of a blow was this going to be?

I thought about reefing the mainsail, but although it was a bit gusty, it was still a light wind and I needed a bit of a push to get out to sea.

Just as I reached the harbour entrance, the wind increased suddenly. As quickly as I could, I reefed the mainsail right down. Even with it fully reefed and with only a number one jib hanked on to the forestay, we were flying.

I was pretty tired, but we were still too close to land for me to sleep, so I wrote up the log and had a bowl of rice for dinner. After three hours of sailing out to sea, I set the alarm to go off in a couple of hours and fell quickly into a deep sleep.

This time I was awakened faithfully by the alarm. I noticed that the wind had shifted from the north to the northwest so I could free *Laiviņa* off a bit and get some more speed. I adjusted the sheets and went back to bed after repairing a small tear in the number two genoa.

CHAPTER 13

Lonely Southern Ocean

Wed, Jan 9, 1985: 50°19′S 54°50′W, Previous Day's Run: 141

After the stimulating days I had been experiencing, I awoke feeling very refreshed from a good night's sleep. The wind had died down, so I was able to set the full mainsail and number one genoa. It was a beautiful day for drying things out and relaxing in the warm sun. Later, the wind backed a bit, and I was able to set the spinnaker. That's when we really got moving.

I felt pleased that I was leaving the Cape Horn region behind. When I had studied the pilot charts in choosing the best time to round Cape Horn, there were two periods during the year when the weather was more benign: around Christmas Day and around the winter solstice which occurs in June in the Southern Hemisphere. I did not want to be sailing these waters in winter, so I targeted New Year's Day as the date for passing through Drake Passage. I was not out of danger yet. I had the vast Southern Ocean ahead of me, and that would take a couple of months.

The closer I dared sail to the Antarctic ice shelf, the shorter that distance would be, but the closer I sailed to the pack ice, the higher the probability was that I would hit an iceberg. I was deep in the iceberg zone already, a zone whose northern limit was the farthest point where all large icebergs can reach before the warmer waters from the north would melt them into non-existence. The other concern I had was that if I went too deep into the iceberg zone, I might encounter small chunks of ice that had broken off icebergs. These pieces of growler ice would be invisible, rolling in the waves and I would likely not see them.

Thu, Jan 10, 1985: 49°45′S 51°50′W, Previous Day's Run: 120

Today another milestone was reached. I crossed the zero variation line. From where I was now located, my compass pointed to both the

Figure 13.1: Broad reaching with a balanced set of sails

magnetic north pole and the true north pole. I did not need to add or subtract degrees to convert a true course to a magnetic one or vice versa. One less calculation to perform for the day.

I still had to check the compass for the effects of the steel that was throughout *Laiviņa*'s ferro-cement core. I had "swung" compass before I left and built a deviation card for the main compass that allowed me to perform that correction. Regardless, I often checked the compass by momentarily steering towards the sun or a star when it was close to my course and whose bearing I had calculated when performing celestial navigation. I compared that bearing with the course I was steering when pointing at the celestial object. This was important as the magnetic orientation of steel in *Laiviņa*'s hull, deck, and cabin change over time, particularly when sailing on the same course for a long time.

Before I crossed the zero variation line, the compass was deflected to the east. From now on until I got near Australia, where there was another zero variation line, the compass would be deflected to the west in varying amounts, reaching a maximum of fifty-four degrees just past Île Kerguélen.

In celebration, I opened the next treats box and found a cassette tape. It was Christmas music. A bit late, but I was happy to listen to Christmas music anytime. In fact, I often found myself humming Christmas songs in July. When I played the Christmas tape, there was a live recording from all of my friends. Now that was a surprise! It was incredible to hear everyone's voice again. It went a long way toward dispelling the feelings of loneliness I sometimes had when I was beset by fears in this wild place.

In general, I did not feel lonely as I sailed these waters. I felt the separation from my friends more acutely at moments when I was troubled by approaching storms. I found the Southern Ocean a truly beautiful place. It was rich in life and ever changing in its moods.

Later in the day, I looked up into the sky and saw a jet coming from South Africa and bound either for the Falkland Islands or beyond, following a great-circle course.

Fri, Jan 11, 1985: 48°52′S 48°44′W, Previous Day's Run: 132

The wind had freshened. With the wind behind, I ran under the twin genoas and then later under the twin number one jibs. I had a good day's run and decided not to go all the way north up to the latitude of forty-five south but to run along the fifty south parallel. This decision involved a greater risk of encountering icebergs and storms, but it was the best time of the year to travel this course. As the distance was much shorter, it would mean a quicker trip in these dangerous latitudes. I would be spending less time in the violent Southern Ocean, something that would help to mitigate the risks.

Sat, Jan 12, 1985: 49°01′S 45°21′W, Previous Day's Run: 134

The wind was holding well, and we were moving fast now on a beam reach. I had a lazy day continuing to read *Aztec* and was enjoying the book.

Sun, Jan 13, 1985: 48°46′S 41°07′W, Previous Day's Run: 168

I had a great previous day's run, breaking all records on this trip with a run of 168 miles. This averages seven knots exactly. The wind was a lot stronger, and I was reaching with just a single sail, my number one jib on a beam reaching course in heavy seas. It balanced the boat better by having all of the sail area put into a "pulling" headsail instead of being split between the headsail and a "pushing" mainsail.

I spotted a pod of orcas swimming very close to *Laiviņa* and managed to photograph them. There were sounding lazily, probably to check me out.

I also finished reading *Aztec*. What a great book; it had a profound effect on me. I wondered if reading books in such a powerful and dramatic environment as I was in, boosted my emotional reaction to what I was reading.

I was now getting close to the forty-degree-west meridian of longitude, which I had chosen as an occasion to open another present, and I was looking forward to tomorrow!

Mon, Jan 14, 1985: 48°25′S 36°35′W, Previous Day's Run: 181

I knew that I had had a good day's run before I worked out my sight, but 181 nautical miles! This broke all records for this trip and all other trips I have ever done in *Laiviņa*. It was her best! This was an average of seven and a half knots, which was the hull speed of *Laiviņa*. Beyond this speed we were surfing, and since it was an average, we were surfing most of the time.

As we sailed hard, close to *Laiviņa*'s maximum hull speed, the water level at the bow was right up to the bow fitting. When I looked over the stern, the water level was right at the deck level. When we exceeded the speed of seven and a half knots, the stern wave would move aft of the stern, and now *Laiviņa*'s stern would drop down into the trough and she would be forced to sail uphill. She would slow down, until the stern wave retreated and go back under her, supporting her stern once again and putting her back on a level keel.

I have seen this delicate balance in operation when sailing in very sheltered waters and driving *Laiviņa* hard under a spinnaker. I have watched the top of the bow wave reach higher than the deck and start spilling over the bow fitting and running down the side decks and out the scuppers. I have seen the stern wave rise higher than the stern, flow over the aft deck, and spill into the cockpit. I have seen her settle into that state of balance where the wind pressure on the sails balances the angle at which she was climbing up the back of the bow wave. In sheltered waters, it was impossible to go much beyond this maximum hull speed. *Laiviņa*'s speed was limited by having to climb uphill in sheltered waters.

In the Southern Ocean, the situation changed when the steep front face of a large swell caught up to her from behind. Then she was pointing downhill and could easily leave her stern wave behind. Her speed would pick up, until for many seconds, the electronic log needle was jammed hard against the maximum stop. Although it showed ten knots, she was probably doing fifteen. At that point, she was surfing the face of a large, steep wave. Strangely, *Laiviņa* was not surfing down the face of a wave; rather, she was moving up the face of the wave, even though she was pointed down the wave. This all stopped when she reached the crest of the wave; then the stern fell down over the back of the wave, and her speed would almost instantly drop to just a few knots. The wind then allowed her to accelerate back to her maximum hull speed. When the next swell came, this process was repeated.

When she was surfing down a wave, the pressure of water supporting the bow was immense. There was little chance that the bow would dig in and pitchpole *Laiviņa*. It was this effect that I believe made it safer for me to keep the boat driving hard with pulling sails rather than pushing sails. For this reason, I chose running wing and wing with no mainsail and driving her hard so that when she was sailing in level water she was close to her maximum hull speed. As soon as the initial gentle slope of a large wave reached *Laiviņa*, she would exceed her maximum hull speed and the water pressure at the bow would increase significantly. By the time the steepest part of the wave face reached *Laiviņa*, her bow was high out of the water and far less likely to dig in and start a very dangerous pitchpole.

I don't believe in trailing lines to slow down her speed. I consider it an erroneous and dangerous method for displacement hulls. I have read of many boats that pitchpole in spite of trailing lines. I believe the reason is that the trailing lines are in the region at the back of the wave where the surface water is moving very fast towards the vessel. At the critical moment when the trailing lines need to apply a force to stop the stern lifting and the bow digging in, they provide no restraining force at all.

For a sailor with a displacement-hulled vessel, it is a simple matter to test. In heavy but not dangerous weather, take down all sails and run dead downwind under bare poles. The vessel will not be surfing, but going at a speed similar to trailing lines in a bight in a much stronger wind. Trail a light line behind the boat with a monkey's fist on the end. Feel the tension on the line at different times, particularly when the vessel is pointing downhill at the steepest angle.

Conduct the test when the monkey's fist is at different distances beyond the stern and at different fractions of the wavelength. The location of surface water where a bight of a trailing line would apply the greatest restraining force, is so far astern that it is unlikely a small vessel would be able to carry enough line to have the bight in the right place. I believe it's safer to rely on the bow wave pressure to keep from pitchpoling.

I used my fishing line and the lure to get a sense of when the greatest pressure and the least pressure was on the trailing line. It was very interesting to sit up on deck watching the way *Laiviņa* surfed down a wave, supported almost entirely at the bow.

Later I started playing with numbers. It was three months since I left Victoria and I had so far travelled 9,069 course miles, plus 282 miles to detour to Santa Barbara, making a total of 9,351 miles so far.

I started reading the *Dune* trilogy by Frank Herbert again. I read it many years before when I was a lot younger with less experience and a shorter attention span. I enjoyed it more this time.

I opened my present, a pair of lovely, thick, warm socks. I didn't dare wear them regularly on this trip as I would wreck them. I wrapped them in plastic and stored them in my grab bag for emergencies.

TUE, JAN 15, 1985: 48°30′S 33°30′W, PREVIOUS DAY'S RUN: 123

Cabin fever was reigning supreme! I decided to bake some pancakes to relieve it. The weather had been cloudy, drizzle or fog, but always with plenty of wind. I made lots of miles, but I was cooped up in the damp cabin except for the times when I had to make sail or course changes. Then I was cooped up in damp wet-weather gear. The cabin temperature was around eight degrees Celsius, just cold enough to make things uncomfortable as my trousers and socks were always damp from the salt encrustation.

Sailing in the Southern Ocean was a repetitive life with some variations. Starting with a high barometer, the wind was weak or non-existent and the sky clear. The barometer started to drop. A light wind started up in the north and brought with it warm, moist air. When this warm air reached the colder water, it condensed the moisture into a thick fog that could last for hours and even days. Then the wind backed to the northwest and freshened to a near gale while the fog and drizzle persisted.

To travel east, I could sail on the port tack and have the wind coming over the port quarter, but it was harder to self-steer, because *Laiviņa* wanted to broach from the unbalanced forces on her sails and hull. Sailing with only a headsail and no mainsail improved the balance, but it worked better to use the mainsail and free fly an unhanked headsail off the spinnaker pole set on the port side. I adjusted the pole so the centre of effort on the sail was right on the vertical projection of the average position of centre of lateral resistance. I could tell when the forces were balanced as the tiller should be close to amidships.

I learned this technique from a schoolmate of mine. Don Reed invited me to be the navigator on *Cadence*, a thirty-foot Spencer design sloop in the Brisbane-to-Gladstone yacht race in 1982. *Cadence* was the winner of the Sydney-to-Brisbane yacht race in 1964. It was a great race, and *Cadence* did exceptionally well, arriving in Gladstone soon after the maxi-yachts. Don is an exceptionally talented yachtsman and a brilliant tactician, having successfully competed in major offshore races.

In this race, with a cyclone coming down the east coast of Queensland, we sailed through the night, planing at extreme speeds and creating a wall of water running down both sides of the boat. We overtook nearly all of the fleet to arrive in Gladstone just behind the maxi-yachts that were twice our size. While we were free-flying big genoas as a spinnaker in perfect balance, the rest of the fleet were down to their storm sails and trying to control their vessels from perpetually broaching. I took what Don had shown me very much to heart and applied it successfully on *Laiviņa* and other sailing craft.

In the Southern Ocean, as the barometer dropped, the wind continued to come from the northwest until the barometer bottomed out. Then the wind backed to the west. Now I could run wing and wing for a while. Soon after the barometer started to rise, the wind backed to the southwest, bringing cold, dry air up from Antarctica. Visibility improved as the fog dissipated, and there was often hail or snow squalls. I picked my course carefully now as there were two or more wave trains, an established swell coming from the northwest, a new swell coming from the southwest, and a smaller swell from the west. The seas were quite irregular at this time.

I set a course so that *Laiviņa* was travelling on the line of bisection between the two main wave trains. If a rogue wave peak formed just behind *Laiviņa*, we would not broach badly. Sometimes the building southwest swells presaged the new wind from the southwest.

Eventually, as the barometer came close to the top of its rise, the wind backed to the south, directly from Antarctica, and the cold became extreme. After a while, the wind weakened until we were becalmed for a few hours. I knew that the cycle I had just experienced would continue to repeat itself.

I went on deck to change the North number one genoa, the new one I had bought for this voyage. I noticed that all the hanks had come off the forestay. The rapid vibration had caused the piston to open up against its spring. All opened that way except one hank, which had torn out of the sail. It was probably because this hank was the only one left holding the luff to the forestay. It was the same hank that had torn out a month previously.

Wed, Jan 16, 1985: 49°40′S 30°30′W, Previous Day's Run: 137

It was another cloudy day. To get a sun sight with the sextant, I had to stand on deck for up to an hour, cradling the sextant carefully in my arms and protecting it from wind-driven spray. Eventually I was rewarded with a brightening patch of thinner cloud. I got ready and brought the brightening patch down to the horizon, waiting for a momentary glimpse of the lower limb of the sun. I was in luck. It appeared faintly for a few moments, and I was able to align it with the image of the horizon. As soon as I got the sight, I worked my way forward.

"One thousand and one, one thousand and two, one thousand and three, one thousand and four…"

I slid open the companionway hatch and climbed over the storm board.

"One thousand and five, one thousand and six…"

I worked my way down the companionway treads.

"One thousand and seven, one thousand and eight…"

I worked my way carefully forward to the bulkhead on which the ship's chronometer was mounted.

"One thousand and nine, one thousand and ten…"

I read the chronometer and subtracted ten seconds. I wasn't wearing my wristwatch as I didn't want to damage it in rough weather.

I had been getting my position by snatching the sun when it peeped feebly through the clouds a half a dozen times through the day. Besides these brief moments, I hadn't seen the sun for days.

We passed through large patches of brown water with a flock of birds hovering overhead and swooping down onto the patch. I think it was a school of krill.

There were four different kinds of birds here. Beside the albatrosses and the great petrels, there was a small bird with silver grey wings. Later research indicated that this was a grey-backed storm petrel. I called them "water runners" as they swooped down to the water, and with their wings still outstretched, ran along the water as they examined the surface closely. Occasionally they dove under after something. They were quite funny to watch.

The other bird that caused me to laugh at its antics was even smaller, the size of a sparrow. I later learned that this was the white-faced storm petrel. I named them "water hoppers" as they fly at the water banked over to the right, and before hitting the water, put out one or both feet to the side nearest the water and hop back up into the air, repeating this process every few seconds.

Thu, Jan 17, 1985: 50°06′S 26°26′W, Previous Day's Run: 159

Today was a nice day with sunshine, although the wind was quite cold as it was the last wind of the depression, which usually blew from the south or southwest.

The weather was basically a never-ending sequence of depressions, which travelled from west to east, overtaking me as they did so. The barometer dropped with the approach, and rose again as the depression left me behind. After the barometer had risen as far as it would go for the prevailing system, there was usually a period when I could dry out gear and get some work done as the seas were a lot calmer. Sometimes this calm period lasted about twelve hours and other times only an hour or so. When it came, I put in a feverish burst of activity, focusing on urgent jobs such as sail and gear repairs.

I sewed up the patches on my wet-weather gear as I had only glued them on and they kept peeling off. The trouble with sewing on a patch was that the water came through at the stitch holes. I used a fine needle and fine thread to reduce the amount of water coming through.

Fri, Jan 18, 1985: 50°12′S 23°15′W, Previous Day's Run: 123

Another depression was on its way as the barometer was dropping. After the calm period with its attendant sunshine, the first sign of the next depression was the high cirrus cloud, and the wind started to blow very gently from the north. Because it was from the north, this wind was bringing warmer, moist air south across water that was about five degrees Celsius. This caused fog or drizzle, so that when the warmer wind came, the sun disappeared, and the sails and sheets started dripping with moisture.

Later, when the wind increased more and the sails shortened, the fog was replaced by rain and cloud. The wind continued to increase until about a day or a day and a half later, when gale or near-gale conditions prevailed and the wind came more from the northwest.

When the barometer read its lowest, it was a lot colder, around freezing and sometimes below zero Celsius. The wind blew from the southwest, and the barometer started rising. The weather was more squally with the wind suddenly increasing to gale force and then dying down. The sun started to peek through the clouds as they were broken up into cumulonimbus squall clouds. Sometimes I got sleet, sometimes hard snow. Changing sail in those conditions froze my fingers as the wind chill effect was at least ten degrees below freezing.

The barometer continued to rise, and the wind and squalls diminished until the next fine period. This whole process repeated itself every three or four days.

Sat, Jan 19, 1985: 49°35′S 20°20′W, Previous Day's Run: 119

Gale number five had arrived. It was a cold southwest gale as the barometer jumped up very fast. As a general rule, the faster the barometer moved up or down, the stronger the wind would blow. This gale wouldn't last long.

I was getting tired of eating pancakes, which I had been making to get rid of my recurring cabin fever, so I made popcorn for a refreshing change. Later that evening, I worked out the program steps based on the formula for the sun's position to put into my programmable calculator. I succeeded, but the program was too large for my calculator's memory.

Sun, Jan 20, 1985: 49°22′S 16°54′W, Previous Day's Run: 134

Today we passed the twenty-degree meridian of longitude, so to celebrate, I opened another present. A beautiful sweater! I put it into a plastic bag and hung it up, saving it for emergencies. I was wearing all my ragged clothes as the conditions in the Southern Ocean were quite harsh. When I got back to Victoria, my clothes would be ready to be burnt. The next milestone was a major one, the prime meridian.

Later, Penny told me how sad she was that I had not worn the clothes she had wrapped up as presents. She wanted me to be warm and comfortable. I knew that they would not be in good shape after months at sea, so I kept the good clothes for when I was in port meeting people.

Mon, Jan 21, 1985: 49°27′S 13°13′W, Previous Day's Run: 144

It was a nice day again. The seas had gone down as it was a break between depressions. I spent the day practising my typing skills. Unfortunately, my fingers were cold and hurt when striking the keys. I also tried to work out a simpler formula for the sun's position with no success. Later I studied more mathematics. Quiet times are very good for mental exercises as it is hard to concentrate when one is being flung across the cabin during a gale.

Tue, Jan 22, 1985: 49°41′S 9°30′W, Previous Day's Run: 145

Yesterday, while I was baking bread, I happened to glance out the porthole to see a log floating by, all encrusted with goose barnacles. It was the sort of thing I would expect to see in the Juan de Fuca Strait, not here. Here I expected to see icebergs.

I spent the morning trying to collect water from the many snow flurries. No success. I decided to wear my new mitts in the cabin to keep my fingers warm, but I could only find one even after spending a lot of time thoroughly searching the forward section of the boat.

I very rarely wear gloves, so I was not that concerned. I had sailed across the Tasman Sea in the winter of 1975 with Max Dorfliger when I was twenty-three years old. Max's boat was also the same class as *Laiviņa*, a Hartley 32. Max is an accomplished and famous mountaineer who has a number of extreme ascents to his credit. He has soloed the north face of the Matterhorn in winter, soloed the Caroline Face of Mount Cook, and climbed the north face of the Eiger in winter. Max taught me that it was better to not wear gloves to condition my hands to withstand the cold. Since that time, I have sailed without using gloves and have been able to use my hands in cold conditions.

While I was searching for the mitt, I noticed that *Laiviņa*'s motion had chafed through the various plastic barriers that protected one of the boxes of tuna and the cans had become wet with salt water. I dried and wiped the tins with an oily rag and repacked them in fresh plastic bags. I had caught it just in time as the tins were still shiny, with no traces of rust.

Wed, Jan 23, 1985: 50°40′S 8°30′W, Previous Day's Run: 82

We were a bit south of the fiftieth parallel, so I decided to work north again the first chance I got. It was a busy day. First I re-spliced the topping lift, which had been cut through by the flapping headboard of the mainsail. I climbed the mast to re-rove it through the block at the top of the mast just as the wind decided to get up and *Laiviņa* started bashing to windward. Although I was secured by my harness and hanging on tight, I was flung around a bit.

Next, I seized and re-spliced the frayed lifeline. This was an important piece of line that acted as a running leash system that I used to clip myself onto it when I went forward to change sails. I couldn't afford to have this line break if I were ever hit by a large wave and washed overboard.

It began to rain, so I started collecting water. It was a light rain or heavy drizzle, so I could leave the bucket and come back five or ten minutes later to find it half full. I collected water all day while the drizzle continued and the wind stayed light. However, the barometer was dropping and dropping and dropping. I was getting worried. As a rule, a very low barometer meant a full gale, and when the barometer dropped without much wind it was usually a strong blow when it rose.

By nightfall, I had collected a hundred litres of water. I was ecstatic. I had not only filled up the plastic bottles, the starboard tank, and all available containers, including my belly, but I had water stored in plastic bags in my kitchen tidy bin and washtub!

The weather was worrying me. Still no wind, and still the barometer dropped. As a precaution, I set the number one jib with the fully reefed mainsail and went to bed an hour past midnight.

Thu, Jan 24, 1985: 51°08′S 5°35′W, Previous Day's Run: 96

The alarm woke me a couple of hours later, and the wind had dropped completely. Now I was really worried. The barometer was down to 982 millibars and still dropping. As a precaution, I changed the number one jib for the storm jib and lowered and furled the mainsail. Now it was just a matter of waiting for the wind and hoping it wouldn't be a storm. A half an hour later, the wind started to blow. By daybreak it was blowing stronger but only about force 6, less than a near gale. I was still suspicious as I expected a lot more wind so I monitored the barometer frequently.

All day, the conditions stayed the same, we made good mileage, and the barometer stayed at 982 millibars. A couple of hours before sunset it all happened. The wind shifted to the southwest and the barometer dropped to 980 millibars, the lowest so far. In the space of an hour, the wind rose to gale force and stronger. I quickly changed down to a storm jib from the larger headsails, and even with a mere seventy square feet of sail, *Laiviņa* was blown side-on to the seas. I could not control the course. So I set a near downwind course and went below to secure any loose objects.

Suddenly, a wave broke on *Laiviņa*, slamming her sideways and tearing the jib sheet off the winch. What a noise! Books had burst out of the bookshelf, and the storm jib was cracking like a machine gun as it flogged itself loose of the constraining sheet. I dressed in my wet-weather gear as quickly as I could, which was about five minutes, and went up on deck to secure the flogging sail and check for damage.

What a scene! The top of the water was smoking with wind-driven spray, and big waves were breaking their tops. I reset the storm jib, but *Laiviņa* kept slamming sideways into the wind, so I lowered it and stowed it below.

Things were a bit quieter now as we lay ahull. I was scared of capsizing, as every now and then a wave would break on *Laiviņa*, throwing her sideways. I stowed all my books in plastic bags and screwed down the bunk tops with the gear under them. It was now midnight, and I was exhausted from trying to work as *Laiviņa* was regularly dropped on her beam ends. I went to bed, set the alarm, and managed to sleep for a couple of hours.

Fri, Jan 25, 1985: 50°45′S 3°30′W, Previous Day's Run: 82

The alarm woke me at 4 a.m. The wind had abated a bit, so I set the storm jib and went back to bed. I slept well, as I always did when the wind was dying down. At 9 a.m. I was able to set more sail by putting up the number one jib and full mainsail. A couple of hours later, I was under full sail with sunny skies and my gear drying out.

I had to re-splice the topping lift again as it had sawed through at the same spot. I decided to hoist the mainsail a bit lower still as the headboard came in contact with the topping lift and was the cause of the topping lift being frayed through.

I had about six hours of calm before the next depression was on its way. I hoped it would not be as bad as the one I had just been through. It had been the worst conditions I had ever experienced at sea in my entire sailing career.

Sat, Jan 26, 1985: 51°26′S 2°07′W, Previous Day's Run: 67

The wind was blowing from the east! This was from dead ahead, which was very unusual. I set a southeast course and hoped that when the wind changed, I could work back to the fifty-degree parallel. By midnight the wind had died away to nothing.

Sun, Jan 27, 1985: 51°21′S 0°32′W, Previous Day's Run: 59

A bit before noon, a very light wind started. We had been becalmed the previous twelve hours, so we didn't make much mileage. An hour after sunset the wind freshened, very cold, and from the southeast. These easterly winds were driving me crazy. The cabin temperature was about one degree Celsius, and my feet were numb. At this temperature nothing was dry, and the salt in my clothing was absorbing moisture.

I was getting too far south and sailing below the depressions. Unfortunately, I wasn't getting the winds to work north again. It was taking me forever to get to the prime meridian although my noon shot showed me to be twenty miles away.

I managed to bake bread and dry clothes, which at that temperature, I considered a real success. When the wind was blowing hard at sub-zero temperatures, I couldn't complete a sail change in one go, as I had to go below to warm my hands up again. Once on deck, I worked as fast as possible before they froze up. The problem was that the spray wet them and the sub-zero wind froze the water very quickly. I was still able to operate my hands to some extent. I couldn't use gloves as finger work was needed to open the piston hanks and snap shackles.

To work the deck in very cold conditions, I would first have something to eat. With all my clothes on and dressed to go on deck, I would hold one of the bulkhead posts and run up and down on the spot until I was overheated. Only then was I ready to go on deck to change a sail.

Mon, Jan 28, 1985: 50°34′S 1°50′E, Previous Day's Run: 101

During the night, I had gotten up to check the course and conditions and noticed the jib halyard had come uncoiled and was dragging in the water. As I hauled it inboard, it glowed with phosphorescence. When I shook the halyard, a spray of phosphorescence flew through the air, creating a beautiful display of light.

After sunrise, the winds abated, so I set more sail. My noon position had shown me to be well past the prime meridian, which I celebrated by having a can of ham, a can of corn, and one of Dug's peanut butter cups. Boy, what luxury! I also opened a present. It was the book *Shoeless Joe* by W. P. Kinsella. I planned to read it next. At the time, I was reading *Mountain Man* by Vardis Fisher, which I was enjoying but finding terribly sad.

I managed to repair the luff of the number one genoa, and before going to bed, I lowered the spinnaker anticipating a wind change during the night.

Tue, Jan 29, 1985: 50°00′S 5°18′E, Previous Day's Run: 137

At last we were getting westerly winds again so we would be able to work north to get out of this cold weather. My noon position showed me to be exactly fifty degrees south.

Although the seas were rough, I managed to repair my wet-weather trousers as they had ripped again. I finished reading *Mountain Man* which I really enjoyed. Now I was starting on *Shoeless Joe.*

Wed, Jan 30, 1985: 49°12′S 8°27′E, Previous Day's Run: 132

It was warmer again. The cabin temperature was back up to eight degrees Celsius, and the wind was steady. I was now sailing north of the Antarctic Convergence, the place where the cold Antarctic water slides under warmer water coming down from the north. I decided to try to stay just north of the convergence to get warmer weather. Just sailing a degree south would put me in water that was close to zero Celsius.

I managed to replace some broken mainsail slides and fixed the salt-water pump, which had failed a few days previously. It had caused a backup of dirty dishes. Not that I minded, as washing dishes in that freezing water I was sailing in a few days ago would not have been pleasant.

Thu, Jan 31, 1985: 49°12′S 11°10′E, Previous Day's Run: 107

I had a lazy day reading and making pancakes. I changed over to the Indian Ocean pilot charts as these charts start at ten degrees east longitude.

During the night, I witnessed a beautiful and wondrous display of bio-luminescence coming from a sea full of jelly-like organisms. The creatures were shaped like footballs about thirty centimetres along the long axis and were suspended in the ocean at different depths. They were spaced about four metres apart, some close to the surface, others deep in the water so they were barely visible. The sea was not rough and *Laiviņa* was sailing easily along so the extensive field of organisms was sharply in focus. It was a surreal sight sailing above these glowing footballs, almost an alien experience. It reminded me of a cover of a science fiction novel.

Fri, Feb 1, 1985: 49°26′S 14°43′E, Previous Day's Run: 140

During the afternoon, the sky showed signs of a good hard blow coming up very fast. With my heart in my mouth, I got things ready for it. Although the wind shifted and increased a bit, it didn't blow up to even a near gale.

It's funny, but I always relaxed when the barometer was rising again as I knew that the worst was over. I felt anxious when it was falling because I never knew the severity of the blow to come.

Sat, Feb 2, 1985: 48°20′S 17°52′E, Previous Day's Run: 141

I spent the day reading as the seas were too rough to do any work. I had a surprise when a large wave broke over *Laiviņa* from astern and spun her around. It was the largest wave to break on us so far this trip. It must have been a rogue or freak wave as the seas weren't really that big.

Sun, Feb 3, 1985: 47°57′S 21°07′E, Previous Day's Run: 132

The wind was easing with the depression going away, and later in the day it was calm. The seas had gone down, the sun was shining, and I was feeling great. I spent the day busily repacking the food and getting out the rest of the February rations. I had emptied out three lockers, so the food that was still left, occupied only three bins, with six boxes in each bin. The food for this trip had worked out very well. The only thing I could have used more of was flour, as I enjoyed my boat-baked bread.

My noon shot showed us in the Indian Ocean with the South Atlantic Ocean behind us. To celebrate, I got out my rewards, which consisted of a fruit leather, a can of peanuts, and a Pink Panther stuffed toy from Penny's daughter, Christy. By 10 p.m. the wind dropped away to nothing, but there were signs in the clouds and the dropping barometer that showed the next depression was on its way.

Mon, Feb 4, 1985: 48°00′S 23°40′E, Previous Day's Run: 102

By noon the wind had gotten up to a near gale for a while, and I ended up on deck to change sails. Once *Laiviņa* had settled down to her new rig, we were close reaching under a storm jib and trysail while I read in the cabin below.

Tue, Feb 5, 1985: 48°17′S 26°52′E, Previous Day's Run: 129

The barometer was slowly rising as this depression was taking its time leaving. The wind was strong but less than a near gale, and we were going well. I was reading *Dear and Glorious Physician* by Taylor Caldwell.

Wed, Feb 6, 1985: 48°27′S 30°41′E, Previous Day's Run: 152

Today I celebrated crossing the thirty-degree east meridian by eating a half a can of chicken. My next goal was the forty-degree east meridian. These mini-goals helped me push *Laiviņa* harder so I could have a treat earlier.

The wind stayed strong most of the day until around sunset, when it unexpectedly blew up to a near gale. A thirty-centimetre tear appeared in the number one jib near the tack. As the sail tore, it also tore out the hank. I was below when it happened. *Laiviņa* broached, and with the extra wind pressure, the self-steering couldn't get back on course. The sail flogged and flogged with such a hard shaking that it started to tear before I could get to it in time.

I had almost dressed in my wet-weather gear to take it in when the wind flogging the sail did it for me. It caused the halyard to chafe through. All the hanks had been blown off the forestay with the result that the sail went into the water and under the boat. By the time I brought it inboard, the head of the sail was red with antifouling paint. I wasn't pleased as it would be more work.

As soon as the halyard chafed through, the rest of the halyard had fallen back inside the hollow mast. I used the spinnaker halyard to set the number two jib to get moving again. I now had to thread a new halyard down the mast and pull it out the bottom, not an easy job at sea. There was also a big tear in the mainsail.

Thu, Feb 7, 1985: 48°02′S 33°43′E, Previous Day's Run: 124

When I awoke at dawn, I found that *Laiviņa* wasn't steering properly. Looking over the stern at the self-steering, I discovered that the trim tab had come off and was trailing behind on its safety line. It appeared that the bottom bearing system I had devised in Santa Barbara had failed. Fortunately, the safety line saved the trim tab from being lost.

I was getting despondent. First the torn jib and cut halyard, and now this. To fix it would mean that I would have to pull out the rudder pintle and bring the rudder inboard. I needed reasonably calm conditions to do that. In the meantime, I connected the wind vane to the rudder direct. It steered *Laiviņa*, but the response was sluggish, and I could not carry much sail. The winds were strong, just a bit below a near gale, so I was still making reasonable mileage. I spent the rest of the day repairing the tear in the mainsail near the bottom batten pocket, and finishing reading *Dear and Glorious Physician.* I started reading *Rags of Glory* by Stuart Cloete. It's about the Boer War in South Africa.

Fri, Feb 8, 1985: 48°00′S 37°00′E, Previous Day's Run: 132

The barometer was slowly rising and the wind dropping, but it was still too rough to remove the self-steering rudder.

Sat, Feb 9, 1985: 47°58′S 39°50′E, Previous Day's Run: 114

The alarm was set for first light, and I awoke to find still a bit of wind, but the seas were a bit calmer. I had wanted the surface to be more placid, but I was afraid that if I waited too long it would get rough again.

I decided I had to go for it. After securing lines to all the parts so I wouldn't lose them overboard, I used the mainsail halyard to hoist the self-steering rudder up and onto the deck. As I was removing the long stainless steel rudder pintle, one of the thrust washers fell into the water. It was a part that I could not secure, and I would have to make another.

It took an hour before I had the rudder up from the transom and down below in the cabin. I rested it on the chart table and got my tools ready. The task of getting the rudder off the transom had gone well, but it had cost me some bruised and bleeding knuckles.

The stainless steel straps holding the bottom bearing had fatigued, and the rod bearing was missing. Oh, it wasn't really missing; I knew roughly where it was. A mile and a half below me on the bottom of the sea! I had a bit of rod left over, so I bent it into shape, but this time I doubled up on the straps holding it.

I made a new thrust washer using a bit of plexiglass in my material spares, which I shaped to fit the pintle. It would not be as friction free as the original nylon one, but it should do the job if I kept it well-greased.

The whole job, including refitting the rudder over the side, took four hours while I lay hove to. Not long after I had fitted the rudder, the wind came up again. I had completed the job just in time!

Next, I tackled the problem of the jib halyard. After climbing to the top of the mast with a coil of fishing line, I lowered a lead sinker down the inside of the mast until it was at the bottom. The fishing line was white braided nylon, so I could see it through the exit box at the base of the mast. Taking a hook made from old coat hanger wire, the universal tool, I fished it out through the exit box. I then sewed the end onto the new halyard and pulled it up through the mast. Voila! A clean, white, new halyard.

My spirits high with two successes, I set twin genoas to get *Laiviņa* really flying and also fixed the feedback mechanism on the self-steering. It had broken some time back, and I hadn't bothered to fix it. I could get by without the feedback system, but it would improve the response under certain difficult sailing conditions, such as running with the wind behind. I was now firing on all eight cylinders. I repaired the jib and was then caught up on the necessary jobs.

It was now dark, and I was exhausted from working hard all day. The barometer threatened to drop fast, and the wind would probably increase. I set only a small amount of sail for the night, so I could get a good night's sleep.

Sun, Feb 10, 1985: 48°03′S 43°12′E, Previous Day's Run: 135

The wind didn't eventuate, so I wished that I had driven *Laiviņa* hard all night. Oh well, win some, lose some. I set plenty of sail and got us surfing again. I was still groggy from the twelve hours of sleep, but I was feeling great.

It was getting near February 14, St. Valentine's Day, and I had to finish Mhora's puzzle. I hadn't had time to work it out as the Southern Ocean had demanded much of my free time. I wanted to finish this puzzle before opening her next card on that day.

I baked a loaf of rich sultana bread, which was too delicious. The trouble was that I was rationed only one loaf of bread per week, but I would eat it in two days because half was gone before it cooled!

I crossed the forty-degree east meridian and opened my present, a globe pencil sharpener. I was looking forward to the antipodes, where I expect to be on St. Valentine's Day.

Mon, Feb 11, 1985: 48°13′S 46°43′E, Previous Day's Run: 141

Today was sunny, and the seas had gone down. I busied myself by repairing the head (ship's toilet). It had broken a couple of weeks before, but as I had other, more important jobs to do, it stayed unfixed. It meant that I had to urinate in a can during rough weather and quickly tip it out an opened hatch before a wave broke over the boat. Having the head repaired gave me a little more comfort. After noon, I got out a fresh batch of books and tidied up the boat.

TUE, FEB 12, 1985: 49°00′S 49°35′E, PREVIOUS DAY'S RUN: 123

It started raining in the morning, so I spent the day collecting water off the mainsail. I managed to collect nineteen litres before the rain stopped and had all of my containers filled up again. The barometer had dropped considerably, and because of the rain, I suspected some strong wind. I was still reading *Rags of Glory.*

WED, FEB 13, 1985: 49°17′S 52°53′E, PREVIOUS DAY'S RUN: 131

Sure enough, the wind did increase, but only to force 6 and not even a near gale. I finished reading *Rags of Glory* and found it sad. Tomorrow I would be halfway around the world. I was getting excited.

THU, FEB 14, 1985: 49°40′S 56°37′E, PREVIOUS DAY'S RUN: 147

St. Valentine's Day. Rather ironic, as I was on the opposite side of the earth from the people I love! It was exciting to know that I was coming home instead of going away. I was 10,800 great-circle miles, or half a circumference, away from Victoria. Sailors use nautical miles instead of statute miles for a very good reason. A statute mile is simply an arbitrarily chosen distance. A nautical mile has a special significance. It is exactly one minute of arc at the earth's surface.

Let the professor explain. We know that 360 degrees makes a circle, right? This means that 180 degrees makes a half-circle and 90 degrees makes a quarter-circle. So, from the north pole to the south pole (or vice versa) is 180 degrees, and from either of the poles to the equator is 90 degrees. Still with me? Okay. So, if I were to journey from the equator to the north pole, I would travel 90 degrees. If I wanted to go from the equator to Victoria (which I would soon), I would travel 48 degrees 25 minutes, which is also 2,905 minutes (48 x 60 + 25), or as we say, 2,905 minutes of arc, which is 2,905 nautical miles. Simple!

Of course this presumes that we would travel straight north along the meridian of longitude 123 degrees 22 minutes west, which is Victoria's longitude. Also, 360 degrees equals 21,600 nautical miles (360 x 60), and 180 degrees equals 10,800 nautical miles (180 x 60). I was now 180 degrees away from Victoria, or straight downward. Not literally in hell, although conditions on *Laiviņa* those days sometimes made me wonder...

Now the final piece of explanation: great-circle miles. The shortest distance between two points on the earth's surface is a great circle joining those two points, or if you will, a piece of string stretched between two points on the globe. This means that I had a minimum of 10,800 miles to go because I couldn't actually sail along the great circle to Victoria due to the intervening land masses and weather and current conditions. In fact, to get to this spot, I actually travelled 12,859 miles—an extra 2,000 miles or so—to avoid the intervening land masses. It was likely that I would travel a similar distance on my return.

I celebrated this momentous occasion by reading *Himalayan Assignment* by F. van Wyck Mason, eating a Reese's Peanut Butter Cup, green apple candies, and Ovaltine, while listening to James Galway. I was in heaven! Such luxury! I still had some cabin fever as the wind had not abated and it was rough on deck. But I was on my way home.

Fri, Feb 15, 1985: 48°15′S 59°50′E, Previous Day's Run: 128

I was now reading *Fifty Ghost Stories*, which was not as exciting as the other books but provided variety. The wind had eased a bit, though it was still foggy and cloudy. I crossed the sixty-degree meridian a little after noon, so I rewarded myself by opening a can of ham and another gift, which turned out to be a Cookie Monster doll. I didn't dare put him in the drawer with the cookies. I was getting excited as I was now looking forward to arriving at Île Kerguélen in a few days' time. I made a note in the ship's log: "Yay! Much excitement among the crew."

Sat, Feb 16, 1985: 49°15′S 63°20′E, Previous Day's Run: 137

We were getting closer to Île Kerguélen. It might be possible to sight the island sometime tomorrow or the next day if I was lucky. This was the fourth day of foggy weather, and as I had not been able to get a sight, I had been navigating by dead reckoning.

I spent the day reading and calculating my estimated time of arrival at Hobart. I put this ETA into a postcard to be sent to my friends in Hobart. When they received the postcard, they would have a reasonable idea as to when I would reach Tasmania. I planned to drop off the postcard at Île Kerguélen.

CHAPTER 14

Île Kerguélen Storm

Sun, Feb 17, 1985: 49°10′S 66°50′E Days Run 137

Daylight slowly slid into my world, revealing yet another day of grey mist and clouds, the fifth such day in succession. I roused myself, pulled on my oil skins and harness, and went on deck for the routine weather check. I peered into the gloom, feeling the presence of Île Kerguélen a hundred miles ahead. I sniffed the wind and wondered if the sun would show itself and enable me to get a reliable position fix, instead of the haphazard and inaccurate sights I had obtained the days before. I was concerned as I could easily be sixty miles off course and not know it.

The sun stayed hidden from view as *Laiviņa* forged ahead into the world of grey. Mile after mile slid under the keel as we reached along in the steady northwest wind, cutting through the seas and rolling in an easy slow motion. It wasn't until mid-afternoon that the fog started to thin a little and I could see where the sun was by the bright glowing mass of mist and clouds among the grey.

I clambered on deck and rested against the backstay, cradling the sextant close to my body to protect it from the spray. My eyes grew tired from watching and waiting for the blob of white sky to turn into the ball of the sun. I shivered and tensed as the cool wind and damp started penetrating the many layers of wool clothing I was wearing.

A thinning in the clouds moved closer to the sun, and the light intensified. I put the cold brass eyepiece of the sextant up to my eye and started swinging the image of the sun along the choppy horizon. As I quickly dropped a filter into place and waited until we rose on a larger swell, the sharply defined edge of the sun brushed the image of the horizon. I had it! The sight I had been waiting for since we ran into the fog five days before.

In the slightly warmer cabin, I processed the information and found us to be still sixty miles away from Île Kerguélen. It looked as though I wouldn't sight land until the next morning. I had only one position line that ran mostly north-south, so I still didn't know how far I had meandered to the north or south of my planned track.

Abruptly, the mist disappeared, and I saw, to my consternation, a spectacular cloud pattern displayed right across the sky. There were mare's tails that were twisted and torn, showing the massive violence being wrought high aloft. I was concerned, as spectacular cloud patterns were usually caused by severe weather. Soon afterwards, low cloud covered up my view.

To confirm my suspicions, the wind freshened at sunset, and I noticed that the barometer had dropped quite a bit. I was getting worried as I still needed another position line to cross my earlier one, before I could get a fix.

In a rare stroke of luck, a large hole opened in the clouds just after civil twilight, enabling me to see Rigel Kentaurus and the Southern Cross. With my heart pounding, I rushed below, grabbed the sextant, clambered back on deck, and managed to get a couple of readings of these southern stars.

It was after I processed the results and started plotting the position lines on the chart that I recognized the dangerous predicament in which I found myself. We were forty miles to the north of our dead reckoning position and heading straight for the centre of Île Kerguélen. I had to get away.

Originally I had wanted to close the coast of Île Kerguélen on the southwestern shore, weather permitting, but with a dropping barometer, it would eventually make it a lee shore when the wind shifted to the southwest. It was a sailor's nightmare.

I changed course and headed southeast instead of east in order to get some more sea room. I figured that the wind would first blow northwest for perhaps twelve hours before blowing from the southwest and we could run easily towards the south of the island.

Up on deck in the fading light and increasing wind, I prepared to gybe the mainsail. After securing the boom foreguys to ease the strain on the sail, I altered course. The wind swirled around the leech of the mainsail, and the sail filled on the other side with a sharp crack followed by a horrible tearing sound. I stared in disbelief at the two halves of the sail flogging in the stiff wind. In an instant, the sail had split from luff to leech.

I was shocked by this unexpected event, but it was no time to puzzle over why the sail had torn. I hauled down the top half of the sail and carefully manhandled it to the main hatch, where I dumped it onto the cabin sole below, and then with wrench in hand, I unshackled the tack and clew of the bottom half, tossed it down below, and secured the boom.

By this time it was blowing a near gale, so I lowered the number two genoa and replaced it with the number one jib. The speed at which the wind was increasing was disturbing me, and I now wanted to get even more sea room. Instead of sailing on a southeasterly course, I set a southerly course and trimmed the jib for a reach. I wanted to get out of there and away from the land, although fifty miles away was too close for my liking.

In the dark of the night, the wind increased to a full gale, and waves lashed *Laiviņa*. We were tossed about at whim as I further reduced sail until we were trying to hold our course under just a storm jib. Hunger gnawed at me as I staggered below from the effort of changing sails in the rough conditions and fixed myself a meal of soup and rice. While I ate the rice, I scrutinized the chart and worked out a plan of action.

My main concern was a rock, aptly named Île Solitaire, lying about thirty miles off the southwest corner of Île Kerguélen. This rock was sixteen metres high and probably about fifty metres in diameter at the base. I had to avoid it at all costs. Although I hoped that I would clear it to the south, I was already sailing as close-hauled as I could under the storm jib, and I could not be certain of the amount of leeway I was making. I calculated that I would be the closest to the islet sometime around midnight, which meant that from 11 p.m. I would have to stay on deck to keep a lookout.

By 11 p.m. the wind had increased to storm force, force 10 on the Beaufort scale. I had to do something about the wild broaching as the self-steering was having difficulty keeping us on course. Even with only a storm jib, the wind was heeling *Laiviņa* right over on her beam end, and she was having trouble recovering. After getting dressed in my cruiser suit and oilskins, I went up on deck, carefully lowered the storm jib, and managed to get the sail safely down below. Although I could see very little now in the pitch black of the night, I could sense that it was getting very rough by the violent motion and the number of times that waves broke over us.

I went down below, tidied up the cabin, and screwed down the locker lids in case of a capsize. Next, I dressed myself as warmly as I could and put on my cruiser suit over all of my clothes. Up on deck, the shrieking wind lashed the halyards against the mast in a machine-gun staccato of sound, adding to the already ear-piercing sound of the wind. I carefully crawled to the stern and lashed myself to the pushpit rails, settling down for a long watch. To keep my spirits up and to help me stay awake, I started singing the sea shanty "South Australia." In spite of my lusty singing, I could barely hear myself above the noise of the storm.

South Australia

In South Australia I was born
Heave away, haul away
In South Australia round Cape Horn
We're bound for South Australia

Haul away you rolling kings
Heave away, haul away
Haul away, you'll hear me sing
We're bound for South Australia

As I walked out one morning fair
'Twas there I met Miss Nancy Blair

I shook her up and I shook her down
I shook her round and round the town

I run her all night and I run her all day
And I run her until we sailed away

There ain't but one thing grieves me mind
To leave Miss Nancy Blair behind

And as we wallop around Cape Horn
You'll wish to God you'd never been born

In South Australia my native land
Full of rocks and thieves and fleas and sand

I wish I was on Australia's strand
With a bottle of whiskey in my hand

Anon

Mon, Feb 18, 1985: 50°05′S 68°27′E Days Run 84

By 1 a.m. I was starting to feel the effects of such intense physical punishment. For two hours I had been stung and slapped by spray and water whipped off the tops of waves by the shrieking wind, and my cramped and aching body was bruised by *Laiviņa*'s violent jerking in the turbulent seas. The cold, cold water had numbed my face and frozen my lips so that I could only mumble the words of the sea shanty I was attempting to sing. Hypothermia caused me to forget verses and repeat lines. The combination of storm-force sub-zero wind, icy water, and the pounding of waves had nearly exhausted my strength. The wind chill factor of minus eleven degrees Celsius was causing me to lose my concentration.

"I will sing this song two more times," I thought. "Then I'll go below, cook up a meal, and get warmed up."

Suddenly, I heard a loud hissing sound, followed a second later by a huge explosion of noise and water. Time seemed to be frozen as I felt *Laiviņa* instantly punched sideways a good six metres. I was covered in thick foam. I held my breath as I felt solid water enclose me in its icy grip. Clipped and tied securely to the pushpit, I was unable to move as we began to fall down the face of a wall of water invisible in the darkness. *Laiviņa* surfed on her side down this monstrous wave, bouncing over smaller waves and rolling over as she fell.

"Oh no! Don't go over! Don't go over!" my mind screamed.

She rolled until her mast pierced the water like a spear and was now deep underwater. For what seemed ages, I held my breath under the mass of churned up water. Time stood still. I wondered if I would be trapped forever, tied to the pushpit rails, unable to breath.

"I need air!" my lungs screamed.

As if in answer, *Laiviņa* stopped rolling, paused for a moment and then slowly rotated back until her mast broke surface. With a shrug, she shook off the confining ocean and swiftly righted herself. As soon as I felt the water leave my face, I forced the stale air out my mouth and sucked the icy wind into my raw lungs.

Except for the sound of the breaking wave expending its fury downwind, there was a brief moment of silence as *Laiviņa* descended into the deep trough behind the wave. I lay against the rails, stunned by what had happened. The hollow mast had taken in a lot of water, which was now pouring out of the exit blocks at its base. Water cascaded from the mast, dinghy, and deck, and gurgled out the drains of the water-filled cockpit. The screaming wind soon returned, thrumming the halyards against the mast and heeling *Laiviņa* over again as if nothing had ever happened.

A knockdown. It was almost a complete rollover. I untied myself and crawled forward to the hatch. After judging the waves as best as I could in the dark, I quickly slid open the main hatch. I clambered below, unclipped and closed the hatch before a wave broke through the opening.

In the pitch-black cabin, I felt the cabin sole strewn with objects. I found a spare lighter in one of the lockers and surveyed the shambles by the tiny flickering light. Books everywhere! In spite of the heavy line holding them in place and the fact that they were tightly wedged together, the force of the initial punch had stretched the line and burst the books from the shelf. I tidied up and stowed everything away again, lit the stove, and heated up the remnants of the evening meal still sitting on the gimballed stove.

I pumped the bilge and found that only a half a bucket of water had squeezed past the tightly fitted storm board and sliding hatch while we were overturned.

After the food began to take effect and I felt my energy returning, I began to understand the seriousness of the situation. With such a strong wind, driving spray, and heavy overcast conditions, I could just discern the sea and the sky. Although I would probably pass Île Solitaire safely, I couldn't be sure, and I doubted I would survive if we hit the rock in such conditions. My morale was at a low ebb.

"Well, I can't complain. I've had a good life so far, but what a pity that it should end now," I thought.

I sat in the cabin, feeling cold, exhausted, and frightened, while outside the slightly muted shriek of the wind competed against the heavy thumping of waves against the hull and deck. Eventually I managed to reassert myself, and although I was still afraid, I knew in my heart that I would make it.

"I'm going to survive this one, mate!" I said to myself. "There is no way this is going to beat me! Come on, *Laiviņa*! I know you won't let me down."

With my resolution fortified, I spent the rest of the night up on deck among fierce winds and crashing waves while the halyards continued their machine-gun drumming against the mast. This time, I secured myself against the pushpit rails with my harness so that I could still free myself should we capsize again. Amid this confusion, minute after minute passed ever so slowly as I peered hopelessly into the gloom for the sign of spray being kicked skyward by a semi-submerged islet.

The hours crept by, and slowly the dawn enabled me to see five metres, twenty metres, a hundred metres, and finally the whole ocean. I was exhausted from my night of keeping watch and was pleased that morning had finally come.

Although the increasing visibility assuaged my fear of blindly running into Île Solitaire, it was replaced by horror at the sight that dawn had brought. To windward, when I managed to see against the slashing spray, watery mountains were approaching us. Up, up, up we went, and at the top I looked down into a valley of white froth. Except for the thin, grey clouds racing overhead, everywhere I looked was white. White water, white spray, and white foam. I stared in disbelief at the gigantic heaps of water rushing towards me at speeds closely approaching the scudding clouds.

Occasionally, the top five metres of a wave would break with a long, drawn-out roar that lasted for fifteen seconds. Sometimes *Laiviņa* was struck by the edge of one of these breaking waves and spun around like a doll in a dog's mouth. I never knew when or where the next breaking wave would strike.

After watching this amazing world of violence, I began to grow accustomed to it, and my fears subsided a little. I wondered how large the seas were, and I decided to measure them as accurately as possible. During gales I had experienced previously, I climbed the mast until I was at a position where I could just see the horizon over the top of the next largest wave. My height above the water was the height of the seas. Dare I climb the mast in these terrible conditions?

After putting on a sit harness and a chest harness, I groped my way carefully forward until I reached the mast. I clipped onto a mast step and started to climb slowly, keeping at least one harness clipped to a step at all times. I managed to get a third of the way up the mast before I rested back on my sit harness and wrapped the line from the chest harness around the mast to stop my body's violent swinging.

In spite of being secured to the mast, I still had to grab the cold steel steps with my bare hands to stop me from being bashed against the wildly swaying mast. I rested as best I could and looked up at the top of the mast, still eight metres and twelve steps away. The cutting spray lashed my hands, and I could feel them going numb. If I wanted to get to the top of the mast and down while my hands could still function, I had to get a move on. I unclipped the chest harness, waited for a small break in the motion of the mast, and quickly stepped upwards. Another step and yet another until I had reached the spreaders. After a rest, I waited for a brief quieting of the whipping mast and hoisted myself up and onto the spreaders until I was sitting astride the mast with one leg over each spreader.

I was now at a spot where the motion of the mast was at its worst. I was high enough to feel the extra distance the middle of the mast was swinging through, but not high enough so that my body weight would dampen the whiplash as the mast swung back to the upright position. My muscles ached, and I wondered whether I would make it down again, let alone get to the top. The fingers of both my hands had lost their ability to work, and I had to hold on with my bent arms through the mast step and the inside of the elbow joint against the cold stainless steel.

Up or down? I stared at the top of the mast now only four metres away and then looked at the deck awash with water below me. At least I wasn't getting as wet now, as only the occasional spray reached this high. I stared at the bent wind indicator on the top of the mast, held my breath, moved up into a standing position, and started to climb again. It was getting easier to move now, but my arms were being drained of their strength, and I found myself resting more frequently. Three steps to go, two, and at last I hauled myself up until my head was level with the masthead fittings. With what felt like the end of the strength in my fingers, I fumbled the carabiner of the sit harness open and snapped it onto an eye on the masthead fitting.

My breath, ragged and hoarse, burst from my lungs as I eased back on my sit harness and rested my shaking legs. With weary eyes, I looked around me. At one moment I was atop a tower on a white moving hill, and the next I was in a seething chasm of madly churning foam. Where was the horizon? From my lookout twelve metres above the water, I stared at the approaching swells still towering above me a similar distance. How could I measure the waves with a measuring stick that was only half the size. How could I call these massive mountains of water "waves"?

I looked at the surreal landscape around me and felt microscopic. *Laiviņa* was a toothpick floating on an alien ocean made of seething marshmallow. I shuddered, partly from cold and cramp and partly from fear, as I grasped the predicament I was in. What if we were to capsize while I was tied to the top of the mast?

"Get down, you fool!" I called to myself.

I looked at the eighteen steps below me and started to unclip. With my arms wrapped around the steps, I slowly lowered myself step by step. Finally, I reached the spreaders, where I rested before going on. I looked at the deck below me and at the bleeding cuts on my frozen hands. I wasn't going to stay there forever, so, by wrapping my arms through the mast steps, I carefully descended the remaining steps.

After an age, I reached the deck and crawled along it to the hatch. Down below in the cabin, I nursed my painful hands as the blood returned to warm my frozen flesh. I leaned back against the settee cushions and rested my bruised arms. It was an extraordinary experience to see such conditions from the masthead. This is what the old Cape Horners had endured and what they had seen when high aloft taking in a topsail.

At 9 a.m. the wind blew its strongest, the barometer started to rise, and the sun burst out through racing clouds. Overjoyed with this chance to fix my position, as rough as it would likely be, I brought the sextant up on deck and crawled to the backstay, cradling the instrument to protect it from spray and water. At my usual sighting position, I tried to use the sextant, but the mirrors were covered with water and I found it impossible to hang on and sight anything.

I went below and dried the mirrors. On my next attempt, I tried taking a sight from the companionway. Accuracy was out of the question now, but I would do my best to get a number of sights. After closing the sliding hatch against my chest, I found that I could use both hands to swing the sextant. Unfortunately, as I brought the telescope up to my eye, the rushing wind whistled between the eyepiece and my eye, and tears flooded across my vision. I could not see a thing. I tried holding the sextant away from my eye, but I could not see the sun. Finally I used one hand to shield my eye from the wind, and ever so slowly and painstakingly I managed to get the sun down to the horizon. What horizon? Surely that bouncing, buckled line couldn't be the horizon.

I took sight after sight, never really knowing whether or not I had the sun resting on the horizon, and then in the shelter of a kicking and bucking cabin, I prodded my flagging brain into action. By noon I had plotted our rough position and found that we were ten miles past Île Solitaire. My plot showed that we had passed within three miles of it.

At last I could safely rest now that the wind was likely to ease and there were no more dangers ahead. I collapsed onto my bunk. In spite of the deafening sounds and violent motion, I fell asleep almost instantly and slept, oblivious to all noises for three hours.

I awoke feeling much better and found the wind had died down enough to set a storm jib. Up on deck, I checked the gear for damage and discovered a link arm on the self-steering had broken. Beside the bent wind indicator at the top of the mast, this was the only damage *Laiviņa* had sustained. Soon it was fixed, and I was elated to be sailing again. I had come through this storm alive.

An hour or so later, the wind eased further, and I managed to take down the storm jib and set the number one jib in its place. After dragging the storm jib below, I fixed myself something to eat and crawled into my wet bunk. Just before I closed my eyes, I looked around the tiny cabin at the charts, books, and objects that had decorated my little home for the last four months and smiled. Before I fell into a deep sleep, I had one last thought.

"*Laiviņa*, you and I are going to see this voyage through!"

Southern Ocean

It was such a state, when I tempted fate
The year I sought to roam.
I was in a place, so full of grace
That had now become my home.

My little boat, so strong and blessed,
Had taken me so far south.
The wind blew hard from the nor'west,
The sails so tight in its mouth.

Near the ice and through the fog
For days we surged along.
No sun to sight, no track to log.
Just the albatross, with wings so strong.

The pressure dropped, the wind backed nigh,
The fog it thinned to show.
A tortured sky, the mare's tails high,
And it really began to blow.

The night came on, the stars they shone,
And my sextant snatched a sight.
Up ahead, to my dread,
Lay an island, with ice so white.

I changed my course, to open sea;
Southward I would go.
There lay a rock, in my lee,
That added to my woe.

The main it tore, from luff to leech,
The remnants flogging hard.
I took it in, less some of my skin
Yard by weary yard.

Without a sail, bare poles to the sky,
I lashed the tiller down.
My boat would drift, by and by,
And I hoped I would not drown.

The water cold, the ice so near,
The dark, a funeral gown.
The rigging screamed as if to fear
The mast would crash on down.

I lashed my body to rails so hard
The cold cut to my core.
Sea shanties I did sing;
My spirits would raise, I swore.

Midnight came, and an hour went;
The cold was so intense.
I'd go below, some food I meant
To help me make some sense.

Before I moved, a roar so loud
Behind me it came.
I clung in dread, my body cowed,
As I braced against the frame.

A watery punch, like a pile,
Knocked us in a heap.
My little boat, it fell a mile
Till the mast had buried deep.

I held my breath in waters greyed
My lungs so ached for air.
Upside down, my boat it stayed
Until I coaxed a prayer.

A shudder felt, an unseen hand
Had turned us from our tomb.
The mast rose up and pointed high
A first cold gasp, outside a womb.

The hollow mast drained its load
Of ocean so very deep.
The fluorescent glow, away it flowed
Until the dark was complete.

The hours crept by until I spied

A grey dawn easing sweet.
At first ten yards, then a mile,
An alien world I did greet.

The sea I saw was covered wide
With white foam a metre thick.
The wind it plowed through the froth
Leaving furrows long and slick.

Between the swells, quiet for a spell
Until a hill came near.
I lifted up and from high aloft
I came to see my fear.

Far away and below my feet
Lay a valley so deep and wide.
The rolling hills so swift and fleet
Took it in its stride.

The sun came down, and the wind it slowed,
And I felt my spirits leap.
I took the sign to be benign
And fell into a blissful sleep.

When I awoke, the day was new;
The sun it kissed the sea.
I set some sail and headed east.
I once again was free.

Peter Freeman (April 2, 2015)

CHAPTER 15

Île Kerguélen

Tue, Feb 19, 1985: 49°39′S 70°25′E, Previous Day's Run: 80

Twelve hours later, I woke feeling groggy but relaxed. The sun was just rising into a clear, cold sky with *Laiviņa* moving slowly in the light breeze. The seas of yesterday had flattened to a lumpy six-metre swell, rolling and pitching *Laiviņa* around. I set my number one genoa and, in place of the torn mainsail, hoisted the number one jib using the mainsail halyard, ran the sheets through the spinnaker turning blocks, and secured the lines to spare cleats. It was loose footed, but I had a working substitute for my mainsail.

As soon as it was set up, I steered north to close the southern shore of Île Kerguélen. When the sun was above the horizon a bit, I started taking sights every half-hour to establish my position. Good! I was just where I wanted to be. At 8 a.m. I sighted mountains. I felt so excited and alive.

"Land ho!" I yelled. "Land ho!"

By noon, we were just off the coast, and the wind dropped away almost to nothing. I decided that this was a good opportunity to start the motor and warm it up. It hadn't run in two months and I didn't want it seizing up through lack of use. There was a furious burst of activity on deck as I hung out the bedding and clothes to dry. In the light winds, I carefully navigated towards the entrance of the Baie du Morbihan that houses the tiny French settlement of Port-aux-Français. Île Kerguélen is a treeless island very much like the Falkland Islands, except the mountains are much higher and glaciated. The highest mountain has a glacier running right down into the sea. I loved what I saw and hoped to return one day to explore the inlets and fjords and climb the mountains.

We passed a submerged rock over which waves occasionally broke. The swell was being bent around to the sheltered side of the island and coming in to the shore in an even pattern, only a metre high. What a change from yesterday. After a while the wind came up from the north, and I worked into the bay, eventually setting the spinnaker and running fast on the smooth, still water.

What a luxury after weeks of tossing and rolling. I could see the buildings of Port-aux-Français, and when we were about two miles from the village, the wind dropped. I was becalmed. After a short while it came up again, and over the next half an hour I was nearly driven mad by the ever-changing wind. It would blow for five seconds from one direction then ten seconds from the opposite direction, and then no wind at all for a while, only to repeat its fitful efforts. I would never have enough time to get *Laiviņa* pointed in the right direction and have the sails set and drawing before the wind changed again and again. It was particularly difficult as it took much longer to change the sheets of my jury-rigged mainsail than had I been using my regular mainsail attached to the now unused boom.

Someone on shore must have noticed my plight. As I looked at the tantalizingly close village, I saw a boat set out to meet me. As it got closer, it appeared to be a landing barge with an aft wheelhouse. There were two men standing on the foredeck waving. I waved back. Now would come my big moment. For weeks I had been studying the French from the recipes on the backs of the labels of the various food packages in order to brush up on my high school language skills.

"Bonjour, monsieur," I called.

"Are you English?" he asked in return. "I can only speak a little English."

By this time they were alongside, and the conversation started in earnest. He was trying to impress me by speaking the English he knew while I was doing the same with the French I had learned from the labels of soup cans. It must have appeared quite strange to hear a Frenchman speaking English to an Australian living in Canada speaking French in culinary terms.

At first he was explaining the route through the kelp beds to the docks, but as I only wanted to give them two postcards, I tried to explain that I wasn't going to enjoy their hospitality. An idea struck me. I raced below, grabbed the globe, and came on deck. I circled it with my fingers.

"No stop, no stop."

Eventually, he understood, and I then held up my postcards.

"Poste? Poste?"

They edged the barge in closer to my leeward side, and as a gust of wind blew *Laiviņa*'s bow towards the barge, I quickly passed the two postcards and a one-dollar note to the short, quiet Frenchman. There was a danger of the boats hitting, so I jumped onto the barge and pushed *Laiviņa*'s bow away. I then had to run all the way along the barge's deck while the taller Frenchman clutched at my many layers of clothing to prevent me from falling between the two boats. There was only a light bumping and no damage. I leaped aboard before the two vessels separated, and we continued our sporadic conversation. Eventually he asked my name.

"Je m'appelle Peter Freeman," I replied.

As the boats moved apart, I prepared for the sea again.

"Au revoir! Merci beaucoup!" I called.

"Goodbye! Goodbye!" they replied.

The short Frenchman was getting quite excited. He wrung his hands together, which I took to be the French symbol for "Good luck." After we parted, I felt sad that I wasn't going to spend some more time with them. By now the wind had gotten up a bit, so I hoisted the number one genoa and the number one jib, which I was using instead of the mainsail. The mainsail that had torn from luff to leech at the beginning of the storm was lying up in the forepeak, and I hadn't had time to mend it. My sewing machine was not stitching properly, and I needed to repair it.

Away we went, sailing quite fast out of the inlet. It was now just past sunset, and I was in a hurry as I had to clear a couple of rocks before it got too dark. An hour later I spotted them, and it seemed as though it would be a race to get there before it became too dark to see them. I won. I sailed closer and closer, and I could still see the now jet-black rock against the dark grey sky. We passed them safely, and I went below for a meal.

I ended up staying awake until 2 a.m. The wind kept increasing until it was blowing a gale, and I reefed down to the storm jib. What weather! First a storm, and a day later, a gale. I saw the lights of a foreign fishing vessel, which had previously been anchored in the bay. He must have come out of the harbour after I did.

CHAPTER 16

Île Kerguélen to Australia

Wed, Feb 20, 1985: 49°40′S 72°24′E, Previous Day's Run: 77

At 2 a.m. I allowed myself a couple of hours' sleep. After waking, I checked the course and the wind. As it seemed okay, I allowed myself four hours' sleep. When I awoke at dawn, the wind had died a bit, so I went on deck, checked my course, changed sail, and went back to sleep. Later in the day, I awoke refreshed but feeling a bit despondent because I had just been talking with people and now I was back by myself. The next time I would see people was when I reached Tasmania. Hobart, here we come!

At dusk, the sky cleared, and the wind died down. I took a few star sights but didn't process them as I wanted to program the calculator later in the morning to handle star sights.

Thu, Feb 21, 1985: 49°26′S 75°37′E, Previous Day's Run: 126

When I was sailing on the open ocean, far from land, it was only necessary to obtain one position fix each day, preferably at noon so I could accurately establish my noon-to-noon run. I achieved this by taking a morning sight of the sun and a noon sight at the sun's meridian passage and combining the two into what is called a "running fix."

The noon sight was the easiest one to process, as the time I took the sight only needed to be accurate within minutes, not seconds. I looked up the sun's declination, that is, how far north or south of the equator it was at the approximate time of the sight, and corrected the measured angle for various errors and adjustments. These adjustments were: my eye height above the water, the air temperature, barometric pressure, refraction, the sun's apparent diameter, and the sextant error. After that, it was just a case of addition or subtraction between the corrected sextant angle and the declination, and I had my latitude.

If the sun was not visible during the morning, I took an afternoon sight and combined it with the noon sight to get my noon position. If it was cloudy all day, I then needed to measure the angle between catalogued stars and the horizon. If the sun was visible near sunrise or sunset, I didn't use it for a sight as the refraction error became too large and the resultant position line too inaccurate. I sometimes used the moon when the sun was low on the horizon, provided that the moon was high enough in the sky to not also suffer from the same extreme refraction errors and not too thin of a crescent to have no upper or lower limb (top or bottom of the sphere) easily visible. When I was near land I took star sights to ensure I had the most up-to-date position.

I had already programmed the calculator to perform sun sights, but I wanted to include star sights in the program. There was a limited amount of memory in the calculator and only 203 program steps available. I reorganized my routines and subroutines and spent most of the day devising a way of fitting all of the code into those 203 program steps and then building the new program.

To test it, I plugged in the data from the previous evening's star sights and today's sun sights and compared it to my manual calculations. It worked well, and the program fitted into the calculator's memory with not a single program step to spare. This would enable me to process sights very quickly, particularly when I was making a landfall and needed to have our position fixed every hour.

It had been a bright sunny day with little cloud, but the barometer was low. It didn't make sense to me, so I felt that the weather would get rougher sooner or later.

I was still listening to tapes on the Sony Walkman I had received as a gift, but the batteries were getting weaker. Half the problem was that everything was so cold that the batteries didn't deliver enough power. I solved this problem by taking out the cold batteries and dropping them down my shirt front. Brrrr!

After a while, the cold batteries against my skin warmed up, and I could listen to music for an hour or so before they got too cold and didn't deliver power.

I had a funny incident when I retrieved three batteries from the inside of my shirt but couldn't find the fourth in spite of my groping around the dozen layers of clothing. I ended up completely naked and searching through everything carefully while I alternately cursed and laughed at the situation. I found the battery on the settee, as I hadn't even put it down my shirt in the first place!

Fri, Feb 22, 1985: 48°36′S 78°24′E, Previous Day's Run: 120

In general, I was enjoying the voyage. I didn't feel lonely because this solo sailing lifestyle became normal after a while as I was not experiencing any other. When I had a brief encounter with people, it affected me. But on this day, I was quite despondent. I knew it was a reaction to meeting people and then being back on my own again. It was something of a tease.

The other reason for my despondency was that I had just read *On the Beach* by Nevil Shute. It was a depressing account of life in Australia after a nuclear war in the northern hemisphere. Total destruction of this world was not an improbable scenario. I loved this beautiful place in which I was sailing, and such an event was a terrible thing to imagine.

Later in the afternoon, I started overhauling the bobbin mechanism of the sewing machine so I could repair the mainsail. It was frustrating trying to manipulate the delicate parts while a heavy southwest swell rolled under us. I managed to bake a beautiful loaf of bread in spite of my mood!

Sat, Feb 23, 1985: 49°00′S 81°10′E, Previous Day's Run: 112

I spent the morning getting the sewing machine working properly and then started on the mainsail. By noon I had joined the two halves together and hoisted the repaired mainsail. Although the jib was about the same area and it worked well, it was good to take it down and put up the proper sail.

My noon position showed that we had reached eighty degrees east longitude and the position of maximum variation (fifty-two degrees west). The magnetic lines of force here were not parallel to the earth's surface. The magnetized compass card that floats in oil was deflected so much downward that it jammed and did not turn. I had to turn the compass on its gimbals until the compass was not level but at a forty-five degree angle. Only then was the compass card parallel to the compass base and turned freely. Now I could see the course we were on.

It was also time to open another present. I celebrated with a can of peanuts, a trail mix bar, and potato flakes. I then opened the most important present.

Wow! Whoopee! I jumped up and shouted with joy. *The Rime of the Ancient Mariner.* I sat down and read it right through aloud. I now had quite the task, to memorize that poem. I hadn't realized it was so long!

Sun, Feb 24, 1985: 48°47′S 84°00′E, Previous Day's Run: 113

I spent the day reading as it was rough and overcast. I was finding that it was getting light too late in the morning, so I changed the ship's time to only one hour of daylight savings instead of the two hours I had been enjoying. It would mean more candle consumption as I liked to read before retiring to my bunk. It's wonderful to be able to make these arbitrary decisions when you're the emperor of your own little world.

Mon, Feb 25, 1985: 48°39′S 87°10′E, Previous Day's Run: 126

It was still rough, and I was still reading books, mainly by the author Robert Ludlum. They held my attention, but this type of novel is just a mind filler, something akin to television's sitcoms. The selection of books I had been given by my friends provided me with quite a contrast in my reading.

Tue, Feb 26, 1985: 49°32′S 90°40′E, Previous Day's Run: 147

My noon position showed that I had crossed the ninety-degree east meridian, so I opened a can of chicken to celebrate. The next goal was one hundred degrees east and the reward of another present. Our track on the chart was slowly creeping eastward. I spent the afternoon repairing the hanks and grommets on the number one jib.

Wed, Feb 27, 1985: 49°30′S 94°00′E, Previous Day's Run: 130

I finished processing my noon sight and went on deck to change sails. After lowering the number two genoa, I was getting ready to hoist the number one jib when I saw what appeared to be bright orange seaweed dead to leeward of me. At this stage *Laiviņa* was without sail and just drifting at about one and a half knots. It was a ship's hawser. I grabbed the boat hook, and as it came alongside, I started to bring it aboard. After hooking it, I threw a loop over the winch and caught my breath. As soon as the rope caught, *Laiviņa* almost stopped dead in the water from the drag. If I hadn't been able to throw the loop over the winch, I wouldn't have been able to hold it, and it would have drifted past.

Figure 16.1: Retrieving a ship's hawser

It was about fifty metres long and forty-five centimetres in circumference, quite large and heavy. Although it was encrusted with goose barnacles, it was in fairly good condition. I decided to hang on to it as it might be useful if we were lying ahull during a storm and needed to slow *Laiviņa*'s sideways drift.

Usually when a rope has been floating at sea for some time, it is in a tangled heap as the waves virtually tie it in knots. This time was no exception, and I had to spend the whole afternoon winching the mess of rope over the side.

Thu, Feb 28, 1985: 49°14′S 97°25′E, Previous Day's Run: 134

Today was another important milestone for me. I was on the great-circle track to Hobart with a vertex north of fifty degrees south.

To sail a great circle from the Falkland Islands to Hobart would require us to go across the Antarctic continent. This is impossible to sail. The shortest navigationally possible distance was to sail as far south as I could, or dared, avoiding icebergs, and follow that parallel of latitude until I reached a great-circle course to Hobart which did not go further south.

In my voyage plan I originally chose forty-five degrees south as my most southern limit. I decided to risk going to fifty degrees south. I even went to fifty-two degrees south, but found that I was meeting easterly winds and the intense cold, wind, and water predicted the presence of icebergs. I found that, by staying just north of the Antarctic Convergence where the icy Antarctic waters slide under the warmer waters, the temperature shot up to between five to eight degrees Celsius with good westerly winds. Generally I sailed between fifty and forty-eight degrees south.

I kept sailing east between these parallels, and even at Île Kerguélen, a great-circle route would take me down to fifty-two degrees south before coming back up to Hobart. Eventually, if I continued eastward, I would be on a great circle that was tangential to or just skimmed the latitude of fifty degrees south and went no further south.

Today I was on it. What that means was that I now followed the great circle, and in a few days I would start heading slowly northward along such a track. Northward to warmer weather!

Fri, Mar 1, 1985: 48°54′S 101°00′E, Previous Day's Run: 142

A new month! I flipped over the calendar page, bare of the usual red crosses that I drew as I marked off each day with a thick red felt pen. We also crossed the one-hundred-degree-east meridian, so I opened the next present from Penny, *A Sailor's Dictionary* by Henry Beard and Roy McKie. I had plenty of laughs reading it. The next goal was the zero variation line, which was around 130 degrees east.

Today the last burner of the stove gave out. The right-hand one had corroded some months back, and I was using the left-hand one. The pricker had broken and was jammed in the jet. I spent the afternoon stripping the stove down and putting a spare burner in place of the corroded one and repairing the other by scavenging parts from the corroded burner.

Sat, Mar 2, 1985: 48°30′S 104°30′E, Previous Day's Run: 141

What a day! I awoke early and baked bread amid snow showers and gale-force squalls, one of which laid us over and sent all of the books flying. I had left the hatch open on one occasion when I went on deck to adjust the self-steering. A wave broke over *Laiviņa* and filled the locker under the port quarter berth with saltwater. I was annoyed with my forgetfulness, but luckily I only had things such as sails and sail covers stowed in that locker. The only casualty was the top of the loaf of bread that had been splashed.

Early in the morning, while I changed sail, I witnessed a beautiful display of the southern aurora.

Sun, Mar 3, 1985: 48°28′S 107°32′E, Previous Day's Run: 121

It was another busy day. In spite of the rough conditions, I got out the next month's supply of food. I unscrewed the locker tops and spent most of the day bringing out rice, sugar, oats, milk powder, the staples, and the treats, and storing them in the galley locker above the sink.

I got a bit of a shock when I went to process the morning sight and found that water had gotten into the calculator. It was going berserk. I was concerned as it saved a lot of time in processing sights, and it was worth $120. I took it apart. As methanol dissolves water, I immersed it in a container of methanol to flush out the water, carefully dried it out, and tested it. It worked. What a relief!

Mon, Mar 4, 1985: 48°30′S 111°40′E, Previous Day's Run: 164

Today I had to strip down the radio, as it wasn't working. I soon found the problem. It was a wire on the circuit board that had broken free of the solder. I heated up the soldering iron and re-soldered the wire back in place. To test it, I tuned it into Radio Australia for the first time since I left Easter Island, got a time check, and listened to Australian accents. It was a nostalgic time for me!

Tue, Mar 5, 1985: 48°43′S 115°15′E, Previous Day's Run: 143

I spent the day just reading. I was becoming quite excited now as Hobart was getting closer and closer.

Wed, Mar 6, 1985: 48°00′S 118°00′E, Previous Day's Run: 118

During the night, I saw another beautiful display of the southern aurora, with lovely green-white pulsating streamers. We were pooped when a wave broke over *Laiviņa*'s stern and squirted through the gap between the storm board and the sliding hatch. The foot of my sleeping berth was all drenched. I would be sleeping curled up in a ball at the head of the bunk tonight. I was getting weary of the constant rough weather as we hadn't had a break since Île Kerguélen.

Thu, Mar 7, 1985: 47°12′S 121°20′E, Previous Day's Run: 143

I awoke to a beautiful sunny day so I dragged out all the wet mattresses, blankets, socks, towels, and other clothes to dry and busied myself with folding sails. I also cut the ship's hawser in half and discarded one piece as I only had room for the other piece. I baked a loaf of bread and cured my cabin fever. As my noon position showed me to be past 120 degrees east longitude, I opened another present. It was a jumping kangaroo toy. With the motion of the boat, the kangaroo only occasionally landed on his feet.

A heavy southwest swell came rolling in from a storm far away in that direction. I climbed the mast to measure the height of the waves and found the largest swells to be twelve metres high. What a beautiful day. I was changing sail after the sun had set, when out of the corner of my eye, I saw what looked like a blood-red ship. It was the moon rising into a cloud bank, and its colour and shape were extraordinary.

Fri, Mar 8, 1985: 46°50′S 124°40′E, Previous Day's Run: 138

During the night, I changed sail under a full moon on a beautiful sea. I was so happy. By day the wind had risen, and I was confined to the cabin again, but it wasn't so bad as the temperature was up to twelve degrees Celsius, lovely and warm. My feet weren't cold for the first time in ages. I was reading *The Rise and Fall of the Third Reich* by William L. Shirer. It was a fascinating book and I had discovered a love of history that I didn't feel when I was in high school.

I could already recite part one of *The Rime of the Ancient Mariner* and was now working on part two. During the evening, I started planning the Pacific crossing in fine detail, experimenting with different routes, and calculating potential speeds to find the optimum route.

As I would be mostly close-hauled during my transit across the Pacific Ocean from New Zealand to California, I wanted to determine the best meridian from which to enter the southeast trades in the southern hemisphere so that I could reach Santa Barbara without unnecessary tacking.

I used the pilot charts and averaged the winds from the wind rose in each sector. Having the average wind direction and strength, and knowing *Laiviņa*'s pointing performance, I projected the close-hauled course on the port tack back from Santa Barbara until *Laiviņa* would be pointing more than fifty degrees away from Santa Barbara. This was the place at which I would change tack.

From this point, I used the average wind direction and strength for each sector with *Laiviņa*'s pointing performance to project the close-hauled course on the starboard tack to reach the northern boundary of the doldrums. I assumed that I could probably average a northerly course through the doldrums, so I projected a southerly course through the doldrums to reach the southern boundary.

From that point, I continued plotting backwards using the average wind direction and strength for each sector to find the meridian at which I should enter the southeast trades at their southern boundary.

I knew that once *Laiviņa* emerged from the doldrums on the northern boundary, we would likely be in a different position from the one I had calculated, so would need to plot north from that position on the starboard tack until I met my plot south on the port tack from Santa Barbara. This would establish the new change-tack place.

Sat, Mar 9, 1985: 46°20′S 127°41′E, Previous Day's Run: 128

Today was a rare day of light winds and smooth seas. I spent the day organizing my charts and doing some more course planning.

Sun, Mar 10, 1985: 46°54′S 130°00′E, Previous Day's Run: 101

I celebrated crossing the zero variation line by eating a fruit leather and opening a jar of Marmite. The next goal was 140 degrees east longitude where I would open another present. I was really looking forward to reaching Hobart, as I had under eight hundred miles left to go now.

I spent the day baking bread and doing some preparatory navigation on the chart of Tasmania. This was the third day of beautiful weather, and I was really soaking it up as it was such a rare phenomenon. The temperature reached an all-time high of seventeen degrees Celsius. Impressive! A heat wave!

At 3 a.m. I brought the radio out on deck and tuned in to the Tasmanian radio stations. I started dancing to the music. Yes, madness, I know. Of course, I was tied to the lifeline with my dog's lead. I often wonder what the captain of a submarine would think if he saw me under such circumstances through his periscope!

Mon, Mar 11, 1985: 46°27′S 132°17′E, Previous Day's Run: 98

Just after midnight, the wind suddenly increased and blew a four metre tear in the spinnaker. Damn! I was taking it down when it happened, and if I had taken it down a few minutes earlier, it would not have torn. Ah, well, repairing it would keep me out of mischief.

Another beautiful day, the fifth in a row. I dried the spinnaker and also had a squab (boat talk for mattress) drying on top of the dinghy. I hadn't tied down the squab, so it inevitably blew overboard when *Laiviņa* broached in a gust of wind. I was running under twin genoas at the time, and there was a frantic rush to take down the one with the pole so I could tack back and retrieve it.

I used my man-overboard technique and, although I had sailed for ten minutes past the mattress, ended up sailing right back to it when I returned. I had gone up the mast to look for the squab, a difficult job with its dark green colour. After ten minutes I spotted it dead ahead. I managed to pick it up on the first try, although I nearly broke my back getting it inboard. It was full of water and felt like it weighed a ton. So much for drying out a squab. Now it would take weeks to dry out.

I noticed that there was green slime growing on the decks as they were constantly awash and had never dried out. I hoped that this good weather would kill it.

I managed to sew up half of the spinnaker, but I had almost run out of thread.

Tue, Mar 12, 1985: 44°58′S 134°40′E, Previous Day's Run: 134

I started work on the spinnaker again. When I ran out of the thread, I used dental floss. It didn't work. The bobbin just got gummed up with the wax from the floss, and because the fibres were not twisted together into yarns, the bobbin picked up only half of the strand and it became jammed. Next, I tried the coil of whipping twine, but it also jammed up the machine. So I left it for a while to see if I could dream up a solution.

Wed, Mar 13, 1985: 43°18′S 135°55′E, Previous Day's Run: 114

The wind moved around until it blew hard, a near gale, from the east. Dead ahead. I spent the day changing sails and reefing. While I was hoisting the number one genoa, I tore out the bottom hank. More work!

Thu, Mar 14, 1985: 43°07′S 136°55′E, Previous Day's Run: 45

I was exhausted today. After the easterly blew out, there was a lightning storm. I shackled a four metre piece of chain to the base of the mast and tossed the end of the chain overboard so that a lightning strike would go into the water over the side instead of blowing the bottom out of *Laiviņa* if the electricity ran down the mast. I did very poor mileage due to the lack of wind and low morale. It was frustrating getting headwinds where there shouldn't be any.

Fri, Mar 15, 1985: 42°35′S 139°12′E, Previous Day's Run: 105

More damn easterlies! I was being driven north towards the west coast of Tasmania. I hoped this would stop because I was eager to get to Hobart, and such contrary winds played havoc with my morale. I spent the day reading to put it out of my mind.

Sat, Mar 16, 1985: 42°55′S 141°22′E, Previous Day's Run: 98

It was a better day, so I baked a loaf of bread. I was still getting easterly winds, southeast to be precise, so I couldn't get back south again and was still heading for the west coast of Tasmania instead of the south coast. If the wind held we might sight Tasmania tomorrow. Whoopee! I changed to a larger-scale chart as I was getting closer and closer.

Sun, Mar 17, 1985: 42°48′S 143°38′E, Previous Day's Run: 100

The wind was still blowing from the southeast. I was just about going crazy with frustration from being driven more and more off my course. To really make me happy, the weather gods split the mainsail in half. That meant more sewing, and I still didn't have any thread that the machine wouldn't chew up. This weather was very unseasonable as normally the wind was mostly westerly and only very rarely easterly. The gods must have been testing my resolution, as this was the seventh day of headwinds. Still no sign of Tasmania.

CHAPTER 17

Tasmanian Coast

Mon, Mar 18, 1985: 42°55′S 145°16′E, Previous Day's Run: 72

Figure 17.1: Landfall on the west coast of Tasmania

During the night, we were still getting southeasterlies and it was tough going. Finally, I was able to see the tops of mountains in the east. I had sighted Tasmania.

"Land ho," I announced with little enthusiasm as I was exhausted from the weather we had experienced of the last few days.

Dawn was just breaking, and I could make out the mountains from forty to fifty miles away. I perked up when I saw Frenchman's Cap, a mountain I had wanted to climb when I lived in Hobart but never had the opportunity.

The wind became fresher and fresher as we approached the coast. At 3 p.m. I was a mile off the coast and had to change tack to work southward a bit. While I was in the smooth water to leeward of a reef, I changed down to a number two jib. On the tack heading back out to sea, I managed to get an hour of sleep before tacking back towards the shore. I wanted to be in range of a faint lighthouse on the point to help navigate through the night. This would enable me to get a fix of my position. The wind increased to a near gale, and then in under a half an hour, it dropped to almost nothing. We were left wallowing in the clapotic, disorganized swell.

Tue, Mar 19, 1985: 43°17′S 145°40′E, Previous Day's Run: 28

All through the night, *Laiviņa* barely moved in the faint, fitful airs. I slept an hour at a time, getting a position from the lighthouse to check my drift each hour. It was a broken sleep yet better than nothing. By dawn we had drifted out to sea a bit and I was still snatching sleep when I was awoken by the sound of a large fishing vessel. It was the *Cape Don* of Fremantle in Western Australia. The noise of the motor woke me with a start, and I rushed on deck to make sure we were not being run down. They passed a fair distance away.

All day we crawled south, pushed gently by the occasional light breeze. I basked in beautiful warm sunshine, hot enough so that for the first time in ages I stripped off all my sweaters and got to see my body. I was shocked to see that I had quite a bit of fat around my stomach. It was something I never expected, as I thought that my activity would burn all the food I was eating. Then again, it could be my bread... naw! It couldn't be my bread. Perhaps I grew the spare tire as insulation against the cold. Yes, that was it. It was definitely not my bread!

Figure 17.2: Close to the west coast of Tasmania

By evening, I lay becalmed at the entrance to Port Davey. A fishing boat chugged into a bay, past beautiful high granite cliffs being smashed by the heavy southeast swell. I had a lovely day in spite of the light wind.

I was lucky to find a whole ball of heavy whipping twine in a locker I rarely used. After I separated the four yarns, I was able to use it in the sewing machine without it jamming up and managed to finish repairing the spinnaker. I was very tired and hoped I would get to Hobart within a couple of days. Perhaps I would be there on the first day of spring, when I would open the next card.

During the evening, I listened to the radio. I could receive Sydney stations due to "ionospheric bounce," but I couldn't get Hobart from just over the hills and mountains. Just after dark, faint zephyrs started, and I managed to get a little further to reach South West Cape, where I was becalmed around midnight.

Wed, Mar 20, 1985: 43°36′S 146°02′E, Previous Day's Run: 25

Unfortunately, I was too close to South West Cape to risk sleeping. There was no wind, and I could not sail away from the cape, so I stuck it out. I was very tired. Over the last twenty-four hours, I had only four hours of sleep in one-hour increments, and in the twenty-four hours before that, I had only three hours of sleep. I was losing physical coordination after being deprived of so much sleep. It made me quite clumsy and a little vague. I would have to be extra careful.

At sometime during the morning, I staggered down below to check the chart. A quarter of an hour must have passed before I realized that I had been standing looking at the chart in a dream state. The strain of the whole trip was beginning to tell, as I didn't have quite the physical and mental stamina that I normally had.

Some time after a beautiful dawn, I got a bit of wind and proceeded to tack against an easterly wind away from South West Cape. Unfortunately, the tide had turned, and by noon I was still beside the cape and the wind again dropped to nothing.

The section of orange ship's hawser I had picked up started to stink as the embedded gooseneck barnacles began to rot. I consigned it to the deep... er... surface. It floated away. It would likely end up on a nearby beach.

Around 3 p.m. I saw a sailboat approaching, so I hoisted the "K" flag, which means "I want to communicate with you." The boat motored over to see me. Unfortunately, the skipper did not have a radio, so he couldn't get a message to Hobart for me. I believed the vessel was *La Belle* from Melbourne.

When I spoke with him, I was having difficulty constructing my sentences. I was fatigued and hadn't spoken English to anyone since the

Figure 17.3: South West Cape of Tasmania

Falkland Islands, so I must have sounded like a drunk. I was mixing up my verbs, subjects, and objects and throwing adjectives in the wrong place! We take speech so much for granted. While we were speaking, he spotted a fishing vessel rounding the cape so motored over to the other fishing vessel to ask the skipper to come and see me.

It was the vessel *Investigator UK1.* We chatted for a while, and the skipper agreed to radio my message on his 4 p.m. "sked" or radio schedule. I could relax now. In my postcard that I dropped off at Île Kerguélen, I had written that I would be in Hobart on the 19th, give or take a couple of days. With the headwinds and light winds, I might not get there until the 22nd. Whoever was there to meet me might have packed up and gone home.

After the fishermen left, the wind came up lightly and I was able to get a few miles away from the cape, where I intended to sleep for only one hour. I set the alarm and fell asleep. In my exhausted state, when the alarm sounded, I turned it off, put it back, and fell back asleep, oblivious to what I had just done. Three hours later I awoke in a panic. Fortunately we had drifted further away from the cape.

I realized that I would have to be careful in deciding when to sleep because in an overtired state it was so easy to make mistake. I might not even set the alarm properly. It is dangerous to sleep while on a course heading for land, and at times may be better to heave to instead of sailing a course. A change of wind coupled with oversleeping could land us on the rocks.

Thu, Mar 21, 1985: 43°32′S 147°00′E, Previous Day's Run: 42

Around midnight, a breeze came up allowing me to sail a few miles further to Maatsuyker Isles with its outcrop of rocks and lighthouse. Once I was past it and in clear water, I hoped to get an hour or two of sleep. Unfortunately, the wind dropped just as I was among the black pinnacles of rocks, and I had to keep my eyes open. Around dawn the wind came up again, and a couple of hours later we were really flying along under the newly mended spinnaker. By the time I reached South East Cape, I had to drop the spinnaker. Soon afterwards, I lowered the number one genoa, yet we were still hurtling along under mainsail alone in the near-gale winds.

I entered the D'Entrecasteaux Channel and saw what appeared to be a shipwreck. Just as I looked through the binoculars, I saw a sudden spray of water heave into the sky. Next came the sound of an explosion. I guessed it to be a salvage team blasting the wreck to remove equipment. A little later I saw another sailboat ahead. As the wind had eased, I hoisted the spinnaker again and tried to catch up to him. I was gaining on him slowly but surely and was about to catch him, when unfortunately he turned up into the mouth of the Huon River.

Sailing up the D'Entrecasteaux Channel was one of the most beautiful moments in my sailing career. I can't say the best, as I would have said that a dozen times already. It was a beautiful place. On either side of the channel were lovely hills covered with gum trees, and I could hear the Australian birds. I hadn't heard those sounds for a long time.

The wind dropped a bit after sunset just as I tacked into Perch Bay, past an old wrecked boat. It was so peaceful. I dropped anchor, lowered sail, and after wolfing down some bread collapsed on the bunk, exhausted but supremely happy.

CHAPTER 18

Hobart

Fri, Mar 22, 1985: 43°07′S 147°18′E, Previous Day's Run: 28

Twelve hours of sleep later, I awoke feeling great, my mind and body very relaxed. I had vivid recollections of my dreams in the morning. Outside, it was foggy with not a breath of wind. I tidied up *Laiviņa* and had breakfast. After breakfast, I noticed some cat's paws of wind, so I hoisted the mainsail and weighed anchor. All the morning and part of the afternoon, we tacked in a light breeze against a one-knot tide, so we didn't get very far. During the morning, I encountered a powerboat, and we chatted for a bit. He agreed to phone the yacht club and let them know my estimated time of arrival at Hobart. Tonight!

I tacked slowly in light breezes until I entered a large open piece of water a bit after noon. At 3 p.m. the breeze freshened, and we started to make good headway. Hobart was only ten miles away up the River Derwent. Far up ahead, I spotted two people in a dinghy rowing across the channel. I thought they were crazy as they had quite as distance to row in the choppy water. My tacks would enable me to pass quite close to them, so I thought I could offer them a tow. As I got closer, they started yelling and frantically waving their arms. At first, I took it to be a signal of distress. Next, I thought that it was someone who had heard of my being in the vicinity. Perhaps it was my father and my brother, Carl.

I got out the binoculars. It looked like my father rowing and Carl as passenger. I soon discarded that idea because if there were two persons in a dinghy and one of them was my father, he wouldn't be rowing; he would be sitting in the stern like Captain Bligh giving orders.

Then I heard a voice, a Scottish voice. It was my friends Rose and Tony. I was ecstatic. I dropped the sails, drifted alongside, and greeted them. We ended up spending a couple of hours talking our mouths off while *Laiviņa* lay ahull. Well, Rose and I did. I don't think Tony got a word in edgewise. As we talked, our two boats drifted some distance downwind. When we had finished talking, I gave them a tow back to the spot where they had launched their dinghy. We arranged to meet later near the Royal Yacht Club of Tasmania.

In a light to medium breeze, I tacked the remaining ten miles, finally dropping anchor a bit after 10 p.m.

Figure 18.1: Hobart with Mount Wellington in the background

Once *Laiviņa* was tidied up, I took the securing straps off her dinghy, launched it over the side, and rowed over to the jetty, where I met Tony and Rose again. I sat in the dinghy and talked to Rose until 4 a.m. Tony gave up and went home to sleep hours before. After we agreed that we should get some sleep, I rowed back to *Laiviņa*, tied up the dinghy, went below, and set the alarm to wake a bit after dawn.

Sat, Mar 23, 1985: 42°54′S 147°20′E, Previous Day's Run: 13

I awoke around 7 a.m., washed, and put on clean clothes. I felt good. I climbed down into the dinghy with a plasterer's float, scraped off some of the easy-to-reach gooseneck barnacles near the waterline, climbed back onto the deck, and readied *Laiviņa* for sea again.

I sealed up all the letters I had been writing, and along with my rolls of exposed slide film, secured them in a plastic bag. I was just about to go up on deck to row over to the yacht club when I heard someone hail me.

I came up on deck to find Tony and my brother, Carl, in the same dinghy as Tony had used the previous day.

Figure 18.2: My brother, Carl (left), with Tony (right)

"Carl! Wow! You made it. Where's Dad?" I asked him.

"He couldn't make it. We were sailing down from Mooloolaba to meet you here, but by the time we got to Eden, he wasn't well. He sailed into the harbour there, and I hitchhiked the rest of the way," he told me.

I was impressed that my father had managed to get that far down the east coast of Australia. He had done it in a nineteen-foot Hunter design sloop. It would have been a feat to take that small boat across Bass Strait.

"I'm just heading over to the yacht club to drop off mail. Why don't you come with me now?" I suggested.

"We have some mail for you. Rose has it now, she can give it to you when you get over to the yacht club," Tony told me.

"Oh... actually, I need to have someone certify that the mail has only written material and nothing like spare parts or something that would help me in a tangible way. You know, like radio transistors or something small," I told him.

"Alright. We can get one of the yacht club officials to do that, then," Tony replied. "I'll see if I can find the bosun."

I grabbed my mail package, climbed down into my dinghy, and we rowed together to reach the yacht club. Tony and Carl tied up their dinghy and climbed up onto the floating pontoon while I stayed in my

Figure 18.3: Receiving my first letters from Canada

dinghy, sculling occasionally to stay in the same position. Carl disappeared into the yacht club to look for the bosun to check on the rules about mail. No one seemed to know anything, so I decided that I would accept the mail, provided that it was opened and checked by a yacht club official. Carl went off again to fetch one of the club officials. Rose came and sat down on the pontoon, dangling her legs over the side.

Just then, Carl came back with the club commodore.

"Good morning! I'm Olaf Hedberg, the commodore of the yacht club," he introduced himself from high above on the jetty.

"I've been asked to examine this mail to ensure that it contains only written material. Is that right?" the commodore asked me.

"That's right. I'm not supposed to receive any aid, so if you can open it and make sure that there is nothing in the envelopes other than letters," I instructed him.

The commodore opened the envelopes and unfolded the many pages of letter paper inside. After a while, he looked at me with a sly look on his face.

"Hmmm...there seems to be a lot of letters from this Penny person. Perhaps I should read them out loud. I need to make sure she is not providing you with too much aid," he smirked.

"You'd probably find them a bit too...well..."

"Mushy?" he suggested. "You're good to go. They are just letters."

"Could you sign a statement to say that you have examined my mail and found it to contain only written material?" I asked him.

"Already done it. Your brother told me what you wanted," he replied. "Here it is."

He carefully handed Rose the mail and the statement he had just written. Stretching down, Rose passed the mail to me. It was my long-awaited connection with Canada.

I rowed back to *Laiviņa* while Carl and Tony accompanied me in the club dinghy. After a few photos, it was time to go. Going below, I changed out of my clean shore-going clothes and into my grubby sailing clothes.

I sailed out the anchor and manoeuvred among the moored boats under mainsail alone. After stowing the anchor chain, I set the genoa and spinnaker. A little way down the River Derwent, I came up to a large group of dinghies of various classes sailing around the buoys in a race. We managed to pick our way among them without getting too many curses from frustrated racers. Once clear, I settled down in a pair

Figure 18.4: Carl saying goodbye

of shorts under the warm sun to read my mail.

What fun it was to hear from everyone back in Victoria and Noosa. Every now and then I would laugh out loud at something funny. The crew of a nearby sailing boat must have thought me strange for they laughed back.

Towards sunset I was passed by a beautiful full-rigged ship going upriver under motor in the calm conditions now prevailing. It was a brig, and I wasn't able to see its name. Earlier they were under full canvas but had it furled by the time they were alongside. All I could see was her spars and furled sails as she progressed under motor. What a beautiful sight. How I would love to sail on such a ship.

The light breezes were now blowing upriver, and I was forced to tack in the gathering gloom of night. I worked over to the eastern shore, and for a while I thought that I might have to anchor for the night as the wind had died completely. Around 9 p.m. the wind came up again, and we were away on a tack heading for the western shore.

Figure 18.5: Unknown tall ship, brig rigged

CHAPTER 19

Tasman Sea

Sun, Mar 24, 1985: 43°26′S 148°59′E, Previous Day's Run: 79

I was tired and having difficulty keeping awake. We were abeam Tasman Island when I went below to check the chart. I sat down at the chart table and stared at the features on the chart. The next thing I knew, my head was resting on the chart, and it was wet with a pool of saliva. I had fallen asleep. As soon as I woke up, I rushed on deck to check the proximity of land. Everything was all right; we were sailing past the island nicely. Once I was safely clear, I crawled into my bunk and collapsed, falling asleep almost instantly.

The wind still blew strongly from the south, and we moved fast. I was pleased as I wanted to cross this dangerous sea quickly. At noon our position showed us to be over two-thirds of the way around the world, so I opened up a tin of Ovaltine, a tin of candy, and a tin of tomatoes to celebrate. I still felt tired and didn't get a break as I had to spend most of the day changing sails and navigating.

Mon, Mar 25, 1985: 43°32′S 151°12′E, Previous Day's Run: 97

I woke after seventeen hours of continuous sleep and had needed every minute of it. It was a beautiful, quiet morning, and the wind had gone down. I was able to bake a loaf of bread and write letters while becalmed in the leftover swell.

I put on the Vivaldi's *Four Seasons* tape and settled back to absorb some nice violins. Later in the evening I lay on deck under the stars and listened to the radio. What a wonderful way to relax!

Tue, Mar 26, 1985: 43°51′S 152°35′E, Previous Day's Run: 63

Today there was a steady, light westerly wind and little to do, so I worked out Mhora's next puzzle and successfully completed it. During the afternoon, I slept as I still felt a bit worn out.

Wed, Mar 27, 1985: 44°43′S 155°00′E, Previous Day's Run: 116

My noon position showed us to be nearly halfway across the Tasman Sea. We were heading for New Zealand now. I was reading and had almost finished *The Rise and Fall of the Third Reich.*

It was good sailing as we were under spinnaker for the last thirty hours and still surfing along, though the wind increased so I had to take it down. I had been getting plenty of sleep and was feeling stronger and stronger.

Thu, Mar 28, 1985: 45°18′S 157°55′E, Previous Day's Run: 129

Another pleasant sailing day. This was the easiest Tasman Sea crossing I had so far. I spent the day relaxing, reading, and eating popcorn.

Fri, Mar 29, 1985: 46°04′S 160°48′E, Previous Day's Run: 129

And yet another great sailing day. We were flying along under twin headsails, the number two genoa and the number one jib. However, the weather was unusual and the barometer was dropping, so I expected that we would get a blow.

I must have been among a lot of squid or other sea creatures, as *Laiviņa* was enveloped in a large flock of approximately five hundred grey-backed storm petrels circling around and around. They watched the boat's wake for squid and small sea life because the water in the wake upwelled and brought such sea creatures to the surface, where the birds swooped down and plucked them up into their beaks.

I would soon be approaching the New Zealand coast, so I got out the charts and started plotting my course through Foveaux Strait. I calculated safe transit bearings, compass bearings and vertical sextant angle limits of charted hill and lighthouse heights so I would safely pass various navigational hazards. I hoped to sight land in a couple of days.

The rest of the day was spent reading and eating pancakes. No wonder I was getting fat. It wasn't my bread!

Sat, Mar 30, 1985: 46°25′S 163°52′E, Previous Day's Run: 129

Well, I got the blow I expected. It was gale number nine. I wondered why every time I approached land the weather got difficult! I spent the day getting as many sun sights as possible to keep my position updated in case I was unable to get sights from an overcast sky. I figured that I would sight New Zealand the next day at dawn.

During the afternoon, we were lashed with a substantial hailstorm. The hail stones were a bit bigger than the size of peas. When it hit, I opened the hatch to see and was promptly struck on the lip and cut by one of the stones. Very soon, *Laiviņa* was white with the hail. I went out after it was over and enjoyed sucking on the cold, fresh ice.

Sun, Mar 31, 1985: 46°24′S 166°22′E, Previous Day's Run: 103

"Land ho! Land ho!" New Zealand! I sighted the Dark Cloud Range in southwestern Fiordland at 8:30 a.m., and a couple of hours later, the Solander Islands were in view. The wind was dying fast, leaving a heavy, lumpy swell that crashed the sails from side to side, shaking the mast violently with its heavy impact even though I had sheeted the sails in as hard as I could. One consolation was that the day was beautiful, warm and sunny.

During the afternoon, after being becalmed for an hour, I went on deck and noticed that the mainsail had torn halfway across. The heavy slatting from side to side was whiplashing the battens, and a tear had started at the batten end and spread to the leech and the middle of the sail. When a light north wind sprang up, I set the spinnaker and we started moving again for Foveaux Strait. By midnight, I had picked up the Centre Island light, and we headed for it in a nice steady breeze and smooth swell.

CHAPTER 20

Laiviņa's Homecoming

Mon, Apr 1, 1985: 46°48′S 168°54′E, Previous Day's Run: 106

April Fool's Day! I wondered what joke the weather was going to play on me, now that I was in Foveaux Strait with its reputation for violent storms and terrible seas heaped up by strong tidal currents. Although I was pretty groggy, I stayed awake all night to ensure that we did not run into the shore. When the first light of dawn illuminated the surrounding land, I was well into the strait. And what a dawn it was. "Red sky in the morning, sailors take warning." The sky, lit up with bold streaks of gold and red, was ominous and yet beautiful. So far, the weather was reasonably benign.

The barometer was falling quickly, and the wind freshened from the northwest. I photographed the changing sky and then quickly got ready for the blow. A fishing vessel, surging into a strong wind on its way to Puysger Point, passed me looking stark in the golden dawn light. The counter-current heaped up the seas and made the wind look worse than it really was. I hung on to full sail and surfed along on a broad reach towards the Dog Island lighthouse.

Just after we passed the lighthouse, the current started flowing with us and we scooted along. I had to change down to smaller sails, as the wind was now blowing quite hard. By the time I lowered the number one genoa and reefed the mainsail, I was forced to set the number two jib. The water was really churned up. Luckily, I had the wind coming straight off the land and the current with me. I stayed as close inshore as possible, so the seas were only a metre or so high by the time they reached me. I was sailing in brilliant sunshine, and the surface sparkled with light from the beautiful blue-green colour of shallow water.

By noon, we were out of Foveaux Strait and flying along the coast, close to the rocks and bold headlands. The wind blew harder, still coming from the land. I set the trysail instead of the fully reefed mainsail, and, in spite of the boisterousness of the weather, I was able to bake

Figure 20.1: Red sky in the morning, the storm develops

a loaf of bread. The off-shore gale kept the seas down and motion inside the cabin was smooth and predictable. I kneaded the dough while keeping a lookout through the portholes.

What a scene. The reefs close inshore were smoking from the heavy ocean swell breaking on them with spray being atomized by the gale. I watched a cormorant trying to fly against the wind and making slow progress. By sunset, we were off the Tautuku Peninsula when the wind died away to a moderate breeze. I debated putting on more sail, but the sky was covered over with threatening black clouds, so I decided to wait a bit. Close behind the headland, a couple of fishing boats were lying in the lee of the cliffs, sheltered in the calm seas.

Then it came. Almost instantly the wind blew storm force as I scrambled to lower the number two jib and set the storm jib. To balance the storm jib, I set the trysail. Even with only the storm jib and trysail, we were laid right over and flying along on a reach. A fisherman saw me and powered towards me from the shelter of the cliffs. I quickly hove to and waited. He came alongside me in my lee, and we screamed at each other in order to be heard above the shrieking wind.

"You better head for shelter!" he yelled "It is really going to blow!"

"Worse than this?" I shouted back

"Yes!" he screamed.

I told him who I was and asked him to contact Taiaroa Head lighthouse or the Otago Yacht Club and let them know where I was. I don't know how much he heard, but in parting I shouted that I would lay up behind Nugget Point lighthouse . He powered away towards the shelter of the cliffs while I swung *Laiviṇa* around and continued on my way towards the lighthouse, which winked at me through the gathering gloom. In such a strong wind, I could really only close reach. If I tried to point higher, I would stall the keel and lose laminar flow. After taking leeway into account, I wasn't making any distance to windward. By the time I was abeam of the lighthouse, I was still about three or four miles offshore. I would not be able to tack upwind to shelter behind the lighthouse.

Fishermen tend to think of running for shelter, as their crafts are likely to capsize in open water during a storm. Although the fisherman's advice was well meant, I had to assess the risks myself in view of my own experience and *Laiviṇa*'s capabilities. In the conditions in which we found ourselves, it would be too risky to try to work into the shelter behind Nugget Point lighthouse and drop the anchor by myself in such conditions. I would very likely lose my fingers. With the wind blowing off the land, I was quite safe, and we were making fast progress up the coast!

By midnight we were eight miles past the lighthouse, and I set a course to continue up the coast. For safety reasons I moved a bit further out to sea and then set the alarm to give me an hour's sleep.

Tue, Apr 2, 1985: 46°11′S 170°20′E, Previous Day's Run: 66

One hour's sleep? What alarm? A couple of minutes before dawn, I awoke much refreshed but with fear in my heart as I rushed up on deck to see where we were. The wind had died, and we were wallowing under storm sails well clear of the land. I set full sail, and we started to creep along. I managed to fix my position when the morning mist cleared and revealed the coastline to be ten miles away.

What a heartwarming sight! Mount Maungatua rose imposingly out of the Taieri Plains. I remembered the many times I drove freight trains along its flanks. I spotted Mount Cargill, overlooking Dunedin, Mount Charles, and Mihiwaka Hill. I remembered the winding road over Mount Cargill, which twisted its way upward through gorse, broom, and tough macrocarpa trees. Mount Cargill rose to 676 metres and overlooked

Otago Harbour and its channels, sandbanks, and bays.

I used to camp at Mihiwaka Hill among the trees at the base of the overhanging cliff. I would wait for the dawn sunlight to warm the face and then silently climb alone, save for the rock wrens and bell birds. As I surveyed the places I once called home, my chest felt tight and my eyes wet.

I switched on the radio and listened to the local stations. The advertisements mentioned stores I had forgotten and streets I used to cycle along, calling up more strong emotions.

All through the day we made slow progress, mostly because we were becalmed for much of the time. At least the current was carrying us up the coast. By 4 p.m. we were only seventeen miles from the Cape Saunders lighthouse. I spent the day sewing up the sails that had been damaged over the last couple of days.

While down below, I heard a motor. I came on deck and was greeted by a fisherman and his mate. They had taken a haul of grouper and were heading back to port. I told the fisherman about my trip, and he took down the names of the people I knew in Dunedin. He introduced himself as Alistair McMillan, and his mate as Quentin.

He was a friendly and easygoing fellow, and I took an instant liking to him. We spent quite some time chatting, and I regretfully declined his offer of fresh fish. After he left, he made very fast progress in his powerful semi-displacement boat. Soon after, the wind came up from the northeast and I tacked in towards the land. I cooked up some dinner, thinking of the grouper Alistair had offered me that I had to turn down. Many times in the past while sailing the New Zealand coastline, we had been given fish and crayfish by local fishermen.

By dark, I was getting close to St. Kilda Beach, and the lights of Dunedin were showing behind the sand dunes along the beach. I recognized the major roads by the yellow sodium vapour street lights and spotted steep Stewart Street going straight up from the centre of town to Roslyn on top of the surrounding ridge. As we sailed past White Island, I remembered the sailing race from Taiaroa Head to White Island and return in which I had participated during 1981.

Soon we were getting close to Tomahawk Bay, so I tacked when the sound of the breakers was becoming ominous and the depth sounder was showing only six metres of water. By midnight I was getting near the Cape Saunders lighthouse and moving slowly towards the Taiaroa Head lighthouse, still hidden around the corner of the Otago Peninsula.

Wed, Apr 3, 1985: 45°48′S 170°38′E, Previous Day's Run: 26

The wind, which had been blowing from the northeast, shifted to the northwest so that as I crept around the peninsula I always had it from dead ahead. Now it chose to weaken until I was only getting occasional light puffs. I reached Cape Saunders at 3 a.m. By first light I was in view of the Taiaroa Head lighthouse, which lies at the entrance to the Otago Harbour.

Although there was a little wind, the sea was chopped up by the ocean currents, and the last of the ebb tide was flowing out of the harbour. I could not make any way across the ground. Oh, the frustration I felt. There, a mile away, lay smooth water where I knew that I could work the back eddies to make my way up the harbour. I couldn't get anywhere. I tacked back and forth trying all sorts of tricks to make towards the harbour entrance but to no avail. Here was *Laiviṇa*'s home port where she was born, and we couldn't get in! I cursed and raged and tried whistling up a wind. Nothing. We could not make any progress.

Then an idea came to me. I went below and started cooking up breakfast. It never failed to bring a wind, because by the time I rushed up on deck and organized the sails, my breakfast was stone cold. This time it worked better than ever. Up sprang the wind from the southwest, dead ahead. I started tacking in towards the lighthouse, and before I reached it I had to reef the mainsail right down and set the number one jib.

It looked as though my familiar old harbour was going to put me to the test. It would be no easy trip up the harbour. I was going to have to fight for every metre, tack by tack. The ebb current was still rushing out of the harbour, so I worked in close under the lighthouse in the back eddy before coming out into the wind. We shot into the ebb current and I sailed close-hauled over to the mole. Near the mole and towards the beach was slack water in which I intended to work a couple of tacks before heading back into the current to get around the first bend in the channel.

Someone hailed me from the mole. It was my old friend Ian Gilmour with his wife Adrian and son Gweneth. I gave a wave, but I was too busy to talk. The wind was rising. A couple of tacks later, we were back into the channel and again fighting the ebb current.

I had sailed with Ian on *Icon*, a Hartley 32, the same design as *Laiviṇa*. We sailed together in the races, and we also did a couple of sailboat deliveries together, one from Christchurch and the other from Auckland. Ian and the rest of Icon's crew helped me do the final fit-out of *Laiviṇa*

Figure 20.2: Storm at the entrance to the Otago Harbour

in 1980 just prior to launching.

After a half an hour, we managed to make a mile up the channel, and was just about abeam of Otakau when the wind blew up a gale. I dropped the number one jib and tried to work across the narrow confines of the channel with its submerged rock walls, beacons and sandbanks to leeward. With difficulty, I was able to tack with only the mainsail, however we made little forward progress against the two-knot ebb current.

On the next tack, I was forced to turn around and gybe as the wind was really piping. It blew so hard that I could not control *Laiviņa* under a fully reefed mainsail alone. After a long time and an incredible fight, I managed to turn *Laiviņa* downwind before she crashed into the sunken rock wall off Otakau. I have never before had my skill, seamanship, and strength so tested by wind and tide. I felt that if I had been slightly less experienced or weaker I would have lost *Laiviņa* on the rocks.

We flew downwind, surfing along under the fully reefed mainsail until we were back out to sea again. I worked my way into the shelter of the cliffs at Taiaroa Head and hove to. It was the first time ever that I had been unable to tack up the harbour. I was literally blown out of it!

Figure 20.3: Alistair McMillan and Quentin

While I lay in the shelter of the cliff, Alistair McMillan had come back from fishing. He told me he had contacted Ian Gilmour. We chatted for a while as I rigged storm sails. I told him that I was going to wait until the wind eased and then have another go at getting up the channel.

After Alistair left, a speedboat approached me at a fast clip and I recognized Grant Fletcher, another yacht builder of Dunedin. He had with him two people who started filming *Laiviṇa* and me. They came alongside, and while the wind blew and the spray flew from the gale, I was interviewed for television. The cameraman had to keep wiping the spray off the lens, and I wondered how long it would last from the drenching it was getting. He was determined to film the interview in spite of the appalling conditions under which he was working.

After the interview, I set the trysail and storm jib and tacked towards the harbour entrance again. By this time the wind had eased enough so that I was able to quickly change the storm jib for the number two jib and set the fully reefed mainsail instead of the trysail. The current had also changed, and it was now flooding into the harbour, helping me along my way. Just as I reached the entrance, *Gremlin* came tearing downwind to meet us. On board were Stuart Ballantyne and Wilson Munroe with Roger and Grace Dudman.

"Ahoy, *Laiviṇa*!" hailed Stuart.

"Ahoy, *Gremlin*!" I returned.

We brought our vessels as close as we could to talk.

"We've come to escort you up the harbour," Stuart shouted over the wind.

"All right. I'll be with you, then," I called.

"The harbour master wants you to go to Carey's Bay!" Stuart called over the distance. "Let's meet in Deborah Bay, where we can talk better."

I used to race against *Gremlin* while Roger and Grace crewed with me in the races. When we left for Australia, Grace came with us as far as Nelson at the north of the South Island of New Zealand. It was great seeing familiar faces again.

Deborah Bay was about five nautical miles up the channel, and with the flood tide, it would take less than an hour. Away we went in company, tacking up the harbour with *Gremlin* leading. I was still under canvassed as the wind had eased some more. I managed to set the number two genoa, and now we started to move! *Laiviņa* picked up her skirts and flew along. After a while, I caught and passed *Gremlin*, and before long we were nearing Carey's Bay, the fishermen's port. We dropped anchor close to each other in the adjacent Deborah Bay.

"There's a new harbour regulation in force now. Every boat going up the channel must be in constant radio contact with the harbour master," Stuart told me.

"Oh...I don't have a VHF radio," I said.

"Yes, we figured that. Alistair had told us you had no radio when I contacted Ian Gilmour. That's why we came down to escort you up the channel," Stuart explained. "These new regulations say that boats without a radio must be escorted by a boat that has a radio. There's been too many incidents between boats and ships."

I remembered participating in one sailing race in the narrow channel where I had to conduct a series of very short tacks between the rock wall and the steep high sides of a ship making its way up the channel with barely sufficient steerage-way. It was heading towards the super phosphate wharf at Ravensbourne with *Laiviņa* barely gaining enough speed after each tack before we had to tack again.

"Even though I can escort you all the way, the harbour master wants you to only go as far as Carey's Bay," Stuart informed me.

"Oh...that's not going to work. I wanted to go up as far as the boat harbour at the Otago Yacht Club. It'll be easier for me to meet with my old friends there," I explained. "Perhaps if there is no shipping over the next couple of hours and the harbour master knew I was in the channel, would that work?"

"Let me give the harbour master a call," Stuart said, then disappeared inside his cabin.

I wanted to go right up to Dunedin at the head of the harbour, and I also wanted to sail old familiar waters. After a while, Stuart came back on deck.

"He's not happy with you going up into the head of the Inner Harbour. He says there's nowhere you can berth," Stuart said.

"Tell him I would anchor in my old spot just north of the boat harbour. It's off the channel and in shallow waters."

Stuart disappeared below again, giving me the opportunity to chat with Roger and Grace. In a short while, Stuart reappeared.

"He says there's not enough water there at low tide."

"Yeah, I know that. But there's a small area where the bottom is very soft mud. I've anchored there before. As the water level drops, the keel just spears down into the ooze. She stays upright. It's not a problem," I said.

Stuart went below again and this time he was there for a long time. Eventually, he reappeared.

"You're good to go. I told him that you had a fair wind and tide and you'd be there pretty fast. I also suggested that there probably wasn't any ship movements right now. He concurred. I also told him that you knew the harbour like the back of your hand."

"I do...well, I mean I did. I'm sure it'll come back to me. When we sailed from the entrance to here, all my memories of the sandbanks, back eddies, and shoals came flooding back. I'm sure that the same would happen when I get into the inner harbour," I said.

Stuart weighed anchor and set off. I hoisted the full mainsail and got the number two genoa ready to hoist. I sailed out my anchor using the mainsail, and once I had it on deck, I hoisted the genoa. As I came out of the shelter of Deborah Bay, the wind was even lighter. The tide was still flooding but would turn to the ebb around 2 p.m. It was now a bit after noon, so I didn't want to waste too much time.

Gremlin soon disappeared between the two islands marking the entrance to the inner harbour. Dunedin was a further eight miles up the channel. As each mile slipped under the keel, memories came flooding back. I was astounded that I remembered so much, or I should say, recognized so much. Before leaving Dunedin in 1981, I had sailed over two thousand nautical miles in this harbour alone, so I was familiar with every sandbank, shoal, back eddy, and wind shift that was caused by the hills flanking both sides of this long narrow harbour. The moderate southwesterly wind now blowing was a typical harbour wind. It was so typical that each tack I made was executed at the same place I used to tack years ago. It was such a joy to see the familiar landmarks.

I tacked through the islands and past Sawyers Bay, tacking right in behind the cliff at Roseneath Point, then across the channel to the edge of the Cross Ditch, then along the long edge of the submerged rock wall until we tacked just metres short of the railway line. Soon we were near St. Leonards, where my friend Andrew Jaket built *Teka Jay*, another Hartley 32. Andrew named his boat by reversing the letters of his last name.

Gremlin was now just ahead by a couple of boat lengths. I crossed tacks close astern of her on the port tack but on the next tack she was forced to tack astern of me. Now we were in the lead of this unofficial race. We made up ground quickly and managed to leave her some distance behind. The wind freshened again, and we were over-canvassed.

I hung on until I was nearing Ravensbourne. Here the channel narrowed down between the rock wall and a fertilizer ship unloading at the wharf. In this place, I could get into trouble and have nowhere to run. I could feel the fatigue of the last four days of sailing, all on only five hours of sleep, robbing me of my concentration. I found my mind wandering when I should have been concentrating on avoiding the many beacons marking the channel.

I quickly shackled the jib sheet to the second eye on the genoa clew and changed the tack snap shackle, turning the number two genoa into the smaller number one jib. That was a bit better; I could sail more safely now. On the next tack, the jib sheet snap shackle opened up. Damn! What a time for it to happen. I dropped the jib, and under the mainsail, I manoeuvred into the shallows at the edge of the channel. I let go the anchor, ran out about twenty metres of chain, and waited for the anchor to catch hold.

I waited and waited while we dragged slowly astern towards the railway line embankment. I veered more chain until I had forty-five metres out in only three metres of water. Still it didn't hold, and the embankment was getting very close. I manoeuvred away from the rocks until the anchor took hold.

It was now blowing a near gale. Lying to anchor, I set the storm jib and trysail. I was exhausted and a little concerned. Although I had only half a mile to go, I felt that I was reaching the end of my concentration and stamina. The dragging anchor had given me a fright and drained my nervous energy further. I managed to break the anchor out of the bottom, and we got under way.

I first worked up in the lee of the fertilizer ship's stern to keep out of the now ebbing current and heavy chop in the channel. When we came out into the full force of the wind, the ebb tide was accelerated between the side of the ship and the rock wall and I could not make any progress. The wind and current were just too strong.

After a while, I noticed that the wind had eased a bit, so I replaced the trysail with a fully reefed mainsail. This time, we managed to get past the ship. It was a good thing as my lungs had been filling with fertilizer that was blown downwind while I was at anchor. I found my old anchoring spot by lining up the two beacons that marked the channel and crossing that line with the line of the southern rock wall that sheltered the boat harbour. I dropped anchor, lowered the sails, and secured them.

So little had changed that I felt I had never really gone away. I was first visited by the Gilmours in their sailboat, then later by Michael Turnbull and Jenny Hyndman in their sailboat. The two boats tied up to my stern, and we talked and talked. It was just like old times. Later, Roger Dudman rowed out in a dinghy.

"I brought you some fresh food. I've got bananas, oranges, and some vegetables with me," Roger announced.

"Oh, no... I'm sorry Roger. I can't accept it. I'm not allowed to receive any help," I said.

"C'mon Peter, we won't tell," Ian said.

"No, really. I can't take it. Don't worry, I have plenty of good food, and I take a multivitamin pill and a vitamin C each day, so I won't get scurvy. But thank you for thinking of me."

The tide was now dropping, and they all had to get back into the boat harbour before the tide grounded them. Off they went, leaving me quietly at anchor in the fading evening light. The sun had set, and darkness closed upon the land.

It was a strange sensation, this feeling of belonging that I was now experiencing. I was very aware of every little detail, and rather than taking it for granted, I found myself wanting to absorb as much as I could. I wanted to take in all the nuances, the subtleties, every interaction I had with my friends, and hold it carefully in my mind like a precious gift. I felt supremely happy. My soul was so much at peace, and yet I was still elated in spite of my exhaustion. When I crawled into my bunk, I tried to replay in my mind the memories of the day's experiences but weariness overcame me. I soon fell asleep in spite of the new sounds of traffic, trains, and the crackle of bubbles that rose up and burst against the hull as the keel pressed slowly down into the muddy bottom.

Thu, Apr 4, 1985: 45°52′S 170°32′E, Previous Day's Run: 6

I slept well and woke at dawn. After breakfast, I busied myself with repairing sails and tidying up the cabin. By 9 a.m. I had just managed to get things shipshape, when I was hailed from ashore. I lowered the dinghy and rowed over. It was Frank McCarthy. He and I were in the same training classes with the New Zealand Government Railways and had become fast friends.

While Arvita and I were building *Laiviņa*, Frank bought a sixteen-foot trailer-sailor. It had a tiny open cabin and two berths. He had loaned it to Arvita and me one weekend, and we sailed it around the harbour, anchoring in Broad Bay on the Saturday night. At about 3 a.m. the wind came up very fast and was blowing a near gale just before first light. Our anchor dragged, and the little vessel was in danger of being driven onto the shore. The tide was high, and the wind-driven waves were breaking on the rocky embankment of Portobello Road, which ran right beside the water.

When the stern was a mere couple of metres from the rocks, I jumped overboard, and standing in a metre of water, I kept the little boat from being damaged. I stayed there for hours battling against the wind and waves until the tide dropped and the little sixteen-footer rested on the bottom. When the boat was high and dry, a woman who lived nearby saw our predicament and invited us into her home to have a cup of coffee and warm up. It was the first cup of coffee I had ever drunk. While I found the taste not to my liking, I enjoyed the wonderful warmth that it imparted.

Frank had been driving a train on the main railway line that ran along the water's edge and was surprised to see a sailboat anchored in my old spot. He knew it was *Laiviņa* as I was the only one who anchored there. We talked for quite a while, but eventually he had to leave to go to a second job. All through the day, I was tooted by the train drivers with whom I used to work as they drove their trains along the shoreline near where we were anchored. People rowed out to see me, and I rowed to near the shore to see those who didn't have dinghies. What a wonderful reception from my friends.

When Arvita and I were planning to build *Laiviṇa*, we built a boat shed on a vacant piece of railway land. Children from the nearby elementary school would visit us on their way home. Kerry, Michael, and Tony were three of the children who regularly visited us while we were building. Along with their friends, they would hoist themselves up to the ridgepole of the shed with the main sheet blocks and play around the boat, dressing in our coveralls and pretending to be boat builders. Kerry made a scale replica of *Laiviṇa* out of cardboard and cloth and presented it to us. On launching day, *Laiviṇa* was the topic of conversation in their classroom. Their teacher brought the whole class to watch the boat being sledded out of the shed, lifted by a crane, and put atop a flatbed trailer to be taken to the wharf.

I was visited by two of the kids, Tony and Michael, who had read in the newspaper of my arrival in Dunedin. They were about ten years old when I knew them; now they were around fifteen and very different. I didn't recognize them!

Figure 20.4: Anchored outside the Otago Yacht Club boat harbour

Later I was visited by an *Otago Daily Times* newspaper reporter who photographed and interviewed me. After the reporter left, I saw a man in a uniform rowing out to *Laiviņa.* He was rowing the dinghy like a pro, feathering the oars on the recovery and dipping the blades, clean and shallow at the catch.

"Here comes a seafaring man!" I hailed, as he came alongside and held onto the toe rail.

"Good morning! I'm from the New Zealand Agriculture Department. I have a couple of questions I need to ask you," he told me. "Do you have any fresh food aboard? Silly question really, but I've got to ask it."

"I can assure you that there is nothing fresh on board!" I laughed. "Haven't you smelt my clothes?"

"Yeah, I can imagine," he chuckled.

"Seriously. No, I haven't any fresh food left. I think I ate the last egg and cabbage at Easter Island months ago."

"That's okay, I've done my duty. Now tell me, how was it over the last few days? That was quite a blow, huh?"

We had a pleasant chat and then he had to leave, rowing as expertly back to the boat harbour as he had done coming out.

The tide was now starting to drop, the current was ebbing, and I wanted to get under way and head down to Carey's Bay for the night. I also needed to get back into the channel before my keel spent another night in the mud. Tomorrow was Good Friday, and I was told by my sailor friends that Easter Friday was the start of the Dunedin-to-Oamaru keeler race. I saw an opportunity to race with the fleet, just like old times. The last time I had raced in this particular event was in 1981, when I came in second place. The race was around forty miles in distance and headed north along the east coast.

I weighed anchor, and as there was only the lightest breath of wind, we gently headed downcurrent towards Port Chalmers. I was looking forward to chatting with Andrew Jaket at Carey's Bay that evening. Going past St. Leonards, a traffic officer switched on his flashing light for me and waved out his window. It was a wonderful gesture of support. I gave him a hearty wave in return.

After Sawyers Bay, I took the secondary channel through the islands instead of the main shipping channel and eventually reached Carey's Bay. I tied up to the pile moorings ahead of *Teka Jay.* Andrew arrived soon after with his crew for the race, and I chatted with him and his son Michael until 11 p.m., when we all went off to our respective bunks.

CHAPTER 21

Race

Fri, Apr 5, 1985: 45°24′S 170°53′E, Previous Day's Run: 32

At 4 a.m. the alarm woke me. I quickly dressed, came on deck, and looked around. The pre-dawn air was still, crisp, and quiet. Above me I could see a number of stars twinkling through patches of cloud. The only winds blowing were the soft night breezes drifting down the grassy hillsides and out across the harbour waters. The tide was ebbing, however I would have to get away quickly in order to sail the five miles to the mouth of the harbour and start line in the light airs. The race was to start at 7 a.m., and I wanted to be in position early. Taking care not to awaken the crews of other sailboats, I quietly slipped my moorings and eased *Laiviņa* out into the current. As we drifted slowly with the tide, I relaxed and allowed images of the past to flow into my brain.

It was nice to get away early, giving me a chance to get my mind attuned to the wind and current conditions. In the almost non-existent breeze, I drifted slowly in the channel with the tide. There was barely enough wind to give me sufficient steerage-way to keep *Laiviņa* pointed in the right direction.

Ahead of me, two tugs were bringing up a ship to Port Chalmers, and I had to get out of their way. I took *Laiviņa* out of the channel and into shallow waters. Once they were past and clear, I came back into the channel and continued to sail towards the harbour entrance in the light pre-dawn winds. By the time I reached Harrington Point at the harbour mouth, a large group of sailboats were close behind me, motoring to take up their positions. The sky was getting quite light with the coming sunrise, and with only twenty minutes remaining to the start of the race, a number of boats were milling around.

I met others who I hadn't seen for some years and had a brief opportunity to catch up while we manoeuvred into a good start position. So far, conditions didn't look promising as the wind was still faint. The minutes ticked by, and the manoeuvring became more intense and confusing until the moment of the start.

When the gun went off, boat after boat shot across the line and into the last of the ebb current. I managed to cross the line in the middle of the fleet, and I worked *Laiviņa* over to the port side to get plenty of room to set the spinnaker and not worry about bumping into anyone else. Perhaps they all manoeuvred over to the starboard side to give me a wide berth.

Unfortunately, I sailed into a hole in the wind and was left becalmed while everyone sailed past. Now I was in the last position. Eventually, the wind came up for me, and I caught up to and passed *Laiviņa*'s sister ship, *Teka Jay*. Andrew was having trouble setting his new spinnaker, and as he had not yet purchased a spinnaker pole, the sail wasn't pulling well. At this stage in the voyage, *Laiviņa*'s hull was becoming encrusted with tiny gooseneck barnacles on her hull, yet it wasn't having too much of an impact on our speed.

My spirits were high as *Laiviņa* surged along the New Zealand coast, her old spinnaker pulling well. The sun had risen high in the sky, warming my body and colouring the clear coastal water a translucent light blue. We picked up speed as the wind increased, and I started overtaking the slower boats until I was about the middle of the fleet again. A half-hour later, *Teka Jay* was just a sail in the distance behind. Next, I overtook *Bonita*, a twenty-five-foot Nordic Folkboat that Ian and I had delivered for Michael and Jenny. They were sailing very well to be where they were.

Up ahead was a large ketch with its red and white striped spinnaker. Her crew was having trouble keeping the spinnaker drawing properly, and eventually it twisted. They lowered the spinnaker on deck, and the distance between us shortened. *Laiviņa* saw her chance. In a panic, the crew of the ketch, *Caspan*, saw me coming and hoisted the spinnaker hastily. Unfortunately it filled prematurely, twisted and formed a wine-glass shape. By the time they had pulled it down and re-hoisted it, I was ahead. Once they had it set, they tried to catch me, and for quite a while, I was able to stay in front and even increase the distance between us.

What a glorious day for a sail! The miles just slipped by. I was visited by the Sea Scout training vessel the *MV Clematis*, still chugging along at a respectable rate of knots. I called to the skipper, who answered back through a megaphone. I used to see the *MV Clematis* often when I sailed in the Otago Harbour; it was a beautiful little ship.

Around noon I went below, cooked up a meal, and ate it on deck while keeping an eye on the rest of the fleet. *Caspan*, the large ketch I had previously overtaken, had made up the distance between us and was slowly overhauling *Laiviņa*. As they passed me, I engaged in a conversation with the crew.

"We've decided to throw our skipper overboard. If we do, will you pick him up?" one of the crew joked.

"How come?" I asked.

"The stupid fool didn't concentrate on steering properly back there, and the spinnaker hoist fouled up."

"I'd only do that if your skipper was a woman," I joked back.

"Is it really that bad?" he answered back

"The longest period of celibacy since I was a virgin."

"I don't envy you, mate!" he laughed.

Mid-afternoon, *Laiviņa* passed Cape Wanbrow, and we headed for the finish line. I have never liked the finish line at Oamaru, and this time I was very nervous. With this strong southerly wind, the wave-washed, stone-covered lee shore lay a half mile away. Swells from the storm a few days before were crashing noisily on the rock and shingle beach. To cross the finish line, I would be heading for that terrible lee shore. To get the spinnaker down, I had to work out a plan of action that wouldn't get me into trouble, and it had to work flawlessly.

As I came up to the finish line, heading for the shore, I saw a small motorboat about five metres in length, and low in the water. Aboard were two race officials dressed in yellow wet-weather gear and wearing sou'wester hats. Just as I crossed the line at 3:17 p.m., they powered after me, waving and shouting.

I went into action. I raced aft and set the self-steering for a reaching course to run parallel to the beach. The wind was fresh, and the spinnaker protested as *Laiviņa*'s bow swung closer into the wind. The men in the tiny motor launch raced after me, still waving and shouting as they plowed through the choppy seas in pursuit. I didn't have time to talk to them. The spinnaker had to come down.

I unclipped the snap shackle from the end of the boom I used for leading the spinnaker sheet when I wanted a stable rig. I attached the snap shackle to the sheet and pulled the sheet in against the strain until I could clip it to the cap shroud. Now when I released the tack, the spinnaker would be close to the dead air behind the mainsail. I ran up to the bow and released the tack. In a smooth arc, the spinnaker swung around until it rested limply behind the mainsail. *Laiviņa*'s speed slowed now that only the mainsail was driving her.

Behind me, the crew of the small motor launch persisted in dogging me. They had stopped waving, but were determined to keep with me. By now they were well away from the marginal shelter of South Head, and the seas in which they were navigating were large enough to send spray flying back from the bow as the plucky little craft leaped off the top of the swells from the storm a few days before. When I glimpsed back, the image I saw was of two men in yellow, water running off their faces as they ducked to avoid the spray from wavelets slapping the starboard side of their little vessel.

Now it was an easy matter to lower the sail down the main hatch. After tidying up the running rigging, I gybed around and pointed *Laiviņa* towards the entrance of Oamaru Harbour. The race officials motored up beside me in my lee.

"We've got something for you!" one of them shouted. "We'll try to get close to you to pass it over."

"I'm heading back to the harbour as soon as I get everything squared away here!" I shouted back.

"We thought you were going to head out to sea," he called.

"Not yet, I want to get a chance to say a proper goodbye to my fellow sailors first."

"All right, then. We'll see you in the harbour."

They turned their craft around and began the long trip back to the harbour against the wind and waves. After they left, I finished tidying the gear, and faked about twenty metres of anchor chain on the foredeck, taking some turns around the brass bollard, cross-cleating it, and finishing with a final turn. I untied the anchor lashings and secured the anchor crown with an easy-to-release slip knot. In my mind I was planning the tacks I would need to make to get past the tricky harbour entrance. I uncoiled the main and jib halyards, back laid them both, and stowed the lines along the handrails on the cabin top so they were ready to run when I dropped the sails. I uncleated the halyards; now only the turns on the winch and winch drum cleats were holding the halyards. I was ready for fast action when I needed it.

Oamaru Harbour was a small harbour sheltered by a breakwater on the eastern side with Holmes Wharf coming out from the beach to almost meet the end of the breakwater. In the past, the entrance was kept dredged as large vessels used to call into Oamaru. Only fishing and sailing boats used the harbour now, and the entrance had a sandbank extending from the end of the breakwater to near the jetty. The distance between the sandbank and Holmes Wharf was only about forty metres.

I was approaching the harbour from the north into a southerly wind. After tacking near the middle of Holmes Wharf, I headed for the tip of the sandbank on the starboard tack. People were shouting and warning me to keep clear. I needed to get as close as possible to the sandbank because my next tack would have to take me the short distance to the end of Holmes Wharf, very little room to get enough speed to tack again before I reached the wharf. I wasn't unduly worried as the sandbank was to weather of us and I could get off it and back into deep water if we ran aground. I watched the depth sounder and tacked just before we grounded.

I stood astride the tiller, steering with my knees, my left hand holding the port jib sheet ready to let fly and my right hand holding the starboard jib sheet ready to sheet in. I turned *Laiviņa* smooth and fast, keeping laminar flow along the rudder and not stalling the keel. As soon as the headsail backed, I let fly the port sheet and snapped in the starboard sheet before it became loaded with the force of the wind.

Out of the corner of my eye, I watched *Laiviņa* accelerate towards the end of Holmes Wharf, a concrete walkway built on a breakwater of rocks. I barely had time to get the gear ready before I had to tack again or we would hit the rocks. My eye flitted from the depth sounder, to the flutter in the luff of the mainsail and to the rapidly decreasing distance between *Laiviņa* and the rocks. I back laid the starboard jib sheet by feel so it would run freely when I let it fly. In my mind I heard the calls.

"Ready to go about?"

"Ready."

"Lee ho!"

"Let fly!"

We came around fast and smooth. The port winch spun furiously, taking up the slack, and then stopped dead when the wind loaded up the sail.

From the end of the wharf, the large crowd of people cheered and clapped. Word had spread about this crazy person sailing alone around the world. Although I was now in the harbour, I needed to tack once again as I was running parallel to the edge of the sandbank under my lee and heading for the eastern breakwater. There was plenty of time now, as the distance to the breakwater was almost two hundred metres. I tidied the jib sheets and prepared for my last tack.

Around *Laiviņa* came, clean and smooth but much more gently. As soon as the genoa backed, I lashed the tiller quickly and raced forward. I whipped the jib halyard off the winch and dropped the number two genoa onto the deck. Under the mainsail alone, *Laiviņa* nosed up into the wind and stalled. This gave me time to lash the genoa to the lifelines and out of the way of the anchor chain.

I saw a good spot to anchor in among the boats and sailed towards it. We were approaching it on a reach with the mainsail fully out to keep our speed slow. At the right moment, I tugged on the slip knot holding the anchor crown and gave it a push over the rollers. The anchor chain paid out evenly. When it reached its limit, the CQR anchor caught, and *Laiviņa* swung gently around and feathered into the wind. Down came the mainsail; I lashed it to the boom, and after a bit of tidy-up, I could relax.

It turned out that I had arrived before *Teka Jay* by three-quarters of an hour. A number of larger boats had crossed the finish line after *Laiviņa*. They were a bit embarrassed at being beaten by a solo sailor in a barnacle-encrusted boat. I assured them that it was only because I had plenty of practice. I felt I had done well. While I was at anchor, I had an opportunity to talk with friends whom I had missed when I was at anchor in Dunedin.

I was visited by an official of the Oamaru Yacht Club, which hosts the race. The club gave me a certificate stating that I had taken "LINE HONOURS Overseas Entry." I had a chuckle at that since I was the only "overseas" entrant in the race. One could argue that as *Laiviņa*'s home port was Dunedin, I wasn't an "overseas" entrant. I just had to sail over two thirds of the way around the world to get to the starting line.

This year it was the centennial occasion of the Dunedin-to-Oamaru keeler race, and I thought people would remember this race for many years to come. Eventually it was time to leave. I thanked the sailors for accompanying me on this leg of the voyage, consigned my mail to Andrew and prepared *Laiviņa*'s sails.

I hoisted the mainsail, backed it to force *Laiviņa* onto a tack, and started to sail out the anchor. I held *Laiviņa* to a close reach until the anchor pulled the bow around onto the other tack. I easily took in most of the slack chain. Eventually one of the tacks ran over the anchor, and I snubbed the chain on the bollard. The anchor broke out of the bottom, and I hastily hauled it up and onto the rollers, quickly securing it. I would stow the anchor chain as soon as I was outside the harbour and I had some more sea room. Before I hoisted the genoa, I sailed close to my friend's boats for a last farewell. I passed close to *Teka Jay*.

"I better not screw up this departure—I'd never live it down," I confided in Andrew.

"You'll be fine!" he assured me.

From the anchored boats came a cheer.

"Hip, hip, hooray! Hip, hip, hooray! HIP, HIP, HOORAY!"

I felt the blood rush to my face.

As I approached Holmes Wharf, one of the onlookers called out, "Good luck, mate!"

I raced below, grabbed my globe, and bounded up the companionway back on deck.

"Which way is America?" I asked.

"Go straight out and turn right a bit. You can't miss it," someone replied.

"Blue is water, isn't it?" I said, pointing to the globe.

"You're holding it upside down, mate," another replied.

Soon the jetty was receding astern.

"Goodbye, New Zealand!" I called out, my final farewell to them all.

Laiviņa was now pushing out into the world's greatest body of water, the Pacific Ocean. I set the course and trimmed the sails. After I stowed the chain, secured the anchor, and stored everything for the open sea, I rested up against the backstay. Without thinking about it, I started singing some verses from the sea shanty, "Rio Grande."

Rio Grande

Our ship is a-sailing out over the bar,
Away for Rio!
We're pointing her bow to the southern star.
And we're bound for the Rio Grande!

Then away, boys, away,
Away for Rio,
So fare thee well, my bonny young girl,
We're bound for the Rio Grande.

She's a deep-water ship and a deep-water crew.
Away for Rio!
You can keep to the coast but we're dammed if we do,
And we're bound for the Rio Grande!

Anon

Very soon, tears were running down my face, mixing with the cold, sharp sting of ocean spray. Parting is such sweet sorrow, and I had really wanted to stay. Alone again after a close emotional connection with my friends, I felt the loss of human contact acutely.

I planned to sail straight out to sea to get some sea room so I could sleep, as the accumulated weariness was preying on me. As the daylight failed and darkness approached, I saw on the horizon the lights of many squid fishing ships and realized that before I could sleep I would first have to run that gauntlet.

Around 10 p.m. I was among them. I had managed to skirt around most of the ships but still had to pass between a few. These ships were lit up with something in the vicinity of 100,000 kilowatts of power, and one ship alone could be spotted by the glow of light in the sky from many miles away and over the horizon. I counted forty-five of these ships. The light was so bright as I sailed past them that from many miles away, I could read a book below in the cabin. Close to one, I was blinded.

The bright lights were used to attract squid, which were caught automatically by a multitude of lines and hooks extending over both sides. Each ship was a squid-catching factory and would sit in one spot until most of the squid in that spot were caught. I had one tense moment when one of the ships moved to a new spot, and for a while I thought that it was going to sit right where I was. By midnight I was past them, but sailed on a bit further before I dared go below to sleep. Eventually I crawled into my bunk and blissfully fell asleep.

CHAPTER 22

Chase the Trades

SAT, APR 6, 1985: 44°39′S 172°48′E, PREVIOUS DAY'S RUN: 93

I awoke at 9 a.m. groggy from the last week of excitement and strong winds. The wind had died down and we were moving along very gently. I changed the number two genoa for the number one genoa and that was the only work I did as I spent the day staggering around the cabin, preparing my meals and sleeping between meals and navigation. I was recovering from the last five days of excitement.

My noon position showed that I had crossed to the north of forty-five degrees south latitude. It was time to celebrate another milestone on the way home. Rummaging in one of the lockers, I found Patrick's present and opened it. What a fantastic surprise! It was *The Brendan Voyage* by Tim Severin.

SUN, APR 7, 1985: 44°48′S 174°05′E, PREVIOUS DAY'S RUN: 55

I had another excellent night's sleep, but I still felt worn out and groggy when I awoke. Today I managed to bake a loaf of bread. The wind was still very light, but luckily it was blowing from the northwest. I set the spinnaker out on the jury bowsprit to give us a little more speed. It worked; I noticed that the needle on the log showed a slight increase in knots.

MON, APR 8, 1985: 44°36′S 175°10′E, PREVIOUS DAY'S RUN: 48

Another great night's sleep, but still I felt exhausted, although I did notice a little improvement. The wind was very light and still blowing from dead ahead. I was close-hauled and moving north. During the afternoon I felt alert enough to check the route across the Pacific, plan my strategy, and work out the best route for the leg from Santa Barbara to the Juan de Fuca Strait. The weather was warm enough for me to go barefooted.

Figure 22.1: Spinnaker pole on jury bowsprit

Tue, Apr 9, 1985: 43°17′S 175°12′E, Previous Day's Run: 79

I had another excellent night's sleep, but I still felt a bit groggy. I figured that one more night would see me back in top form. I spent the day taking it easy and reading *Blue Highways* by William Least Heat-Moon.

Wed, Apr 10, 1985: 43°30′S 177°30′E, Previous Day's Run: 101

I awoke feeling great for the first time in days, however there wasn't a lot to do so I had a lazy day reading and finishing *Blue Highways.* I really enjoyed the book.

Ever since the Dunedin-to-Oamaru keeler race, we had been sailing in a large high-pressure system and its associated light winds. This was the fifth day of high pressure. I hoped the barometer would drop soon and give me some wind as my noon-to-noon runs were very poor. I couldn't really complain as the sky was blue and cloudless and the temperature was mild with warm sunshine.

Thu, Apr 11, 1985: 43°49′S 179°50′E, Previous Day's Run: 103

The barometer still refused to drop, and we continued to get light northeasterly headwinds. We were being forced slowly southward now, and it looked as though I would pass south of Chatham Island. My noon position showed me to be approximately seven miles from the 180-degree meridian, where the longitude would change from east to west, another milestone. I spent the day reading *The Brendan Voyage* and found it fascinating.

Fri, Apr 12, 1985: 44°05′S 179°30′W, Previous Day's Run: 33

The barometer continued to stay high and refused to drop. We had light winds through the night and a pathetic thirty-three miles for our noon-to-noon run.

I finally kicked myself out of my lazy mood and did some work around the boat. I put some fresh leather chafing patches on the pulpit, tidied up the lines, and checked the shackles, finding one almost undone. I put new grease nipples in the self-steering bearings as some of them had almost rusted away. Once that was completed, I gave everything on the self-steering a good greasing.

Later, I climbed the mast and repaired the wind indicator, which was about to fall off. It had been damaged when the mast speared into the water during the near roll-over southwest of Île Kerguélen. Finally, I fixed the clew outhaul on the mainsail where a shackle pin had popped out and gone overboard.

During this period of light winds, I saw large groups of seabirds sitting on the water waiting for a stronger wind to enable them to soar effortlessly in their hunt for food. After we passed a group of resting birds, they took to the air, flew ahead of *Laiviņa*, and then landed back down on the ocean surface. They must have thought *Laiviņa* was a big bird with her white sails and wanted to stay in her company. As we encountered group after group, they joined us.

Eventually there was quite a congregation of great wandering albatrosses, black-browed albatrosses, and petrels keeping our company. At the end of these days of light winds, I was surrounded by over 200 birds. They became rather indignant whenever *Laiviņa* sailed up behind them, threatening to run them down, and forcing them to take to the air. They left at the last possible moment with a squawk and heavy paddling of their feet. The great wandering albatross, with its three-and-a-half-metre wingspan, required a lot of effort to get airborne when there was no wind. It beat its wings, thrashed its tail and ran along the water for a hundred metres before it finally broke free of the surface.

During the afternoon, a pod of dolphins came fast through the resting birds, and I wondered if any would be eaten. But the dolphins and the birds didn't seem to notice one another.

Sat, Apr 13, 1985: 43°25′S 178°09′W, Previous Day's Run: 71

At last the barometer started to drop, and the wind sprang up from the northwest. Now we would be able to pass to the north of Chatham Island. I was looking forward to crossing the International Date Line, where I would gain another day. I had another busy day replacing one of the boom foreguys and splicing up two self-steering lashings.

Sun, Apr 14, 1985: 42°20′S 176°00′W, Previous Day's Run: 115

We had a good wind all night, which veered from the northwest around to the southeast, and we passed to the north of Chatham Island safely. The next danger was the islands around Tahiti. I spent the day baking a loaf of bread, writing, and reading *The Stand* by Stephen King.

MON, APR 15, 1985: 41°26′S 175°00′W, PREVIOUS DAY'S RUN: 70

The barometer had risen again, removing any possibility of an increase in the wind. This was day ten of light breezes and I was beginning to wonder when I was going to get some decent conditions. The wind was blowing from dead ahead again. It was very frustrating to not be able to move at a reasonable speed.

Just after noon, I was writing up the log down below when I came up on deck to see the stern of a large oil tanker. It must have passed quite close astern of me, and as it was downwind, I didn't hear its engines. I received quite a fright from seeing it so close. It appeared to be coming from New Zealand and heading for Panama.

The wind today was a strange and frustrating one as it varied in strength from dead calm to force 4 at random intervals between a quarter of an hour to an hour. It was quite unusual. It meant that I was constantly adjusting the main rudder weather helm to keep us on course.

I started working on a "two-in-one" jigsaw puzzle with a different puzzle on either side of the pieces. It made it challenging to determine which side of the piece belonged to which picture. I used the rubber collision mat as a tablecloth to assemble the jigsaw puzzle so the pieces gripped the rubber and didn't slide off when we heeled.

TUE, APR 16, 1985: 41°49′S 173°40′W, PREVIOUS DAY'S RUN: 64

What a terrible night! I hardly slept at all as I was up and down all night adjusting the weather helm on the main rudder. The wind went from dead calm to whitecapping the surface of the water, and all day, the same conditions prevailed. What crazy weather.

I finished the jigsaw puzzle and finished reading *The Stand*, which I found okay but a bit too metaphysical for my liking.

TUE, APR 16, 1985: 42°00′S 172°10′W, PREVIOUS DAY'S RUN: 68

No, the date above is not a mistake. I crossed the International Date Line and gained an extra Tuesday, another milestone. Here, the line is seven and a half degrees east of the Greenwich antipodes. I celebrated by eating a bar of halva and some bacon bits. During the night, the jib clew snap shackle broke, so now I was using an ordinary shackle, and it took a little longer to change sails. It had been another night of up-and-down wind and I hardly slept a wink as I was constantly changing sails and course all through the night. All that lovely rest I had was being used up, and I felt worn out again.

The Roaring Forties, where the westerlies blow! Ha! More like the Whimpering Forties. Except for a couple of hours, I hadn't seen any westerlies for twelve days. During the day I read *The Dead Zone*, another story by Stephen King. I found it excellent, except for the very last paragraph, which I thought spoiled the story.

Wed, Apr 17, 1985: 42°20′S 170°00′W, Previous Day's Run: 98

The barometer was still high, and we were continuing to get northeasterly winds, which were now fluctuating from force 2 to 5. I was beginning to wonder when I would ever break out of these frustrating easterly winds.

When I awoke this morning, I found a small squid washed up onto the deck. Although it was dead, as soon as I began to handle it, ink started coming out of its clear body.

Thu, Apr 18, 1985: 42°23′S 168°52′W, Previous Day's Run: 50

Today we had light northeasterly winds again, so I spent the day reading *A Man Called Intrepid* by William Stevenson. It's a true story about wartime intelligence operations.

Fri, Apr 19, 1985: 42°27′S 167°43′W, Previous Day's Run: 51

We had the same winds again, today and still the barometer was very high. It hadn't moved at all and the wind was still blowing from the northeast and very light.

I had been eating popcorn and unfortunately crunched down on some un-popped kernels which broke two of my dental fillings. This was a bit of a nuisance and it was one of those events on which I had not planned. I removed the broken pieces from my teeth and determined that I would have to clean the cavities very carefully to prevent any decay.

Sat, Apr 20, 1985: 42°20′S 166°00′W, Previous Day's Run: 76

Finally the barometer started to drop a bit and the wind was beginning to rise and become more steady. This was the first time I had been overjoyed to see a dropping barometer. It had been a record sixteen days with the barometric pressure above 1,030 millibars. I had never experienced anything like this before in the Roaring Forties. In the past, I usually found that I might get up to a maximum of five days of such high pressure. It was even more unusual in that we were nowhere near the South Pacific high pressure system.

I spent the day reading *And Vets Might Fly* by James Herriot. I had a good time laughing out loud as I read the book. I opened another of Mhora's cards, and I was quickly able to work out the cryptogram. I really enjoyed these puzzles as they brought a new kind of thinking to my day.

Sun, Apr 21, 1985: 41°57′S 163°30′W, Previous Day's Run: 114

During the early hours of the morning, I was jarred awake by a loud bang. I went on deck and discovered that the jib fairlead on the starboard side had separated from the slide attached to the track. The five-sixteenth-inch retaining pin had sheared from metal fatigue. To apply a workaround, I exchanged the broken one for the portside fairlead, and we were soon sailing again.

The wind continued to rise slowly all day, and the barometer dropped until we were making good progress again. For the wind we were getting, the noon-to-noon run wasn't that exceptional, so I suspected that the gooseneck barnacles were slowing us down. I had noticed that the antifouling was losing its potency. Soon we would be in warmer waters where I would be able to go over the side and clean the hull.

Mon, Apr 22, 1985: 41°00′S 161°00′W, Previous Day's Run: 126

The wind continued to strengthen, and the barometer dropped. In the afternoon it blew a near gale for a while before easing. By sunset, the barometer had stopped falling and the seas were quite sloppy. There was only a light westerly wind which was not strong enough to drive us through the choppy wavelets. I saw an albatross and wondered if that would be the last one I would see until the next time I was in the Southern Ocean.

I spent the day reading a Zane Grey western. I found it to be very predictable! Cowboy meets cowgirl, and they fall in love. Another cowboy lusts after the cowgirl. The two cowboys fight. The good cowboy wins. Some other stuff about robbing a stagecoach and tracking the culprits down.

Tue, Apr 23, 1985: 40°26′S 159°30′W, Previous Day's Run: 76

In the morning, I repaired the broken jib fairlead by making a bolt using a piece of stainless steel threaded rod, pin-punching the thread and peening a nut on the end. I filed the nut down so it was shallow enough to clear the track, and once done, it was definitely as strong as the original.

Figure 22.2: Great wandering albatross

It was a nice sunny day with a brisk westerly wind coming up during the afternoon. I baked a loaf of bread and set the spinnaker, but unfortunately it wasn't up for long before the clew tore off. Damn! It was another big sewing job. The material had been in the sun too long, and was getting weak.

I saw two albatrosses today. By its markings, I recognized that one of the birds was the same bird I had seen yesterday accompanied by a new bird.

Wed, Apr 24, 1985: 39°26′S 158°20′W, Previous Day's Run: 81

At last we were officially out of the Roaring Forties and into the Variable Thirties, and again I was accompanied by the same two albatrosses as the previous day, circling around on steady outstretched wings. The wind was coming from the west but it was still only very light. A heavy southwest swell was rolling through from a storm in the Southern Ocean, making me feel pleased to be away from that place.

I started repairing the spinnaker and managed to get half of the sewing done, though I was worried that I was getting low on patching material. While I repaired the spinnaker, I flew the old number one genoa unhanked and off the pole as a spinnaker.

Thu, Apr 25, 1985: 38°41′S 156°54′W, Previous Day's Run: 81

The heavy six-metre swell was continuing to come from the southwest, and I was still only getting light westerly winds. As some compensation, I was being accompanied by three wandering albatrosses as another one had joined my group. I spent the day relaxing and reading *Under Western Eyes* by Joseph Conrad. I worked a little on the spinnaker, but it still needed another day's work. I was starting to get the moon now in the evenings, which gave me light when changing sails.

As I was going down into the cabin carrying the sextant, I slipped on the companionway tread and landed on my elbow on the sharp edge of the brass strip on which the hatch slides. I didn't realize that I had cut my elbow until I noticed the blood dripping through my sweaters and onto the chart.

Fri, Apr 26, 1985: 37°24′S 155°35′W, Previous Day's Run: 99

I had a busy day sewing up the rest of the spinnaker and wondered how long it would last before I blew it out again. I probably wouldn't need it until we reached the doldrums. My three albatrosses were still with me, but they would soon leave as I moved north into warmer waters.

During the afternoon, I decided to repair the worn jib sheet. I found it to be badly frayed in three places so I decided to replace it with a brand new line. I cut out the bad sections of the old sheet and spliced the good pieces together. I used this recovered line to replace one of the very old and worn out boom foreguys.

Sat, Apr 27, 1985: 35°56′S 154°28′W, Previous Day's Run: 103

The albatrosses were no longer with me; I was on my own again. The wind was now southeast, and I wondered if it would carry us into the trades.

Now that I was using a regular shackle instead of a snap shackle to attach the sheets to the headsail, it was taking much longer to change sails. I also had to keep a wrench in the pocket of my wet weather jacket to undo the shackle pin. Additionally, there was the risk of losing the shackle overboard. I decided to try out a new idea to attach the sheets to the headsail clew that would be quick and not require any tools.

I seized a heavy piece of line onto a bight in the middle of the jib sheet. The idea was to poke the bight through the clew grommet and thread the heavy piece of line through the bight, locking the sheet onto the sail. It functioned in a similar way to the wooden toggle fasteners on pea jackets. My jury-rigged system seemed to work okay, although time would tell if it was rugged enough to last the voyage.

Today I also reached the three-quarters point of my voyage around the world, so I celebrated with Ovaltine, halva, apricots, and butterscotch candies. I made sure to brush out the missing filling holes in my teeth afterwards.

Sun, Apr 28, 1985: 34°32′S 153°15′W, Previous Day's Run: 103

The barnacles were now ten centimetres long and covering most of the hull and I estimated that I was losing about one knot of speed. I needed to go over the side as soon as I could to clean the bottom.

The rope system that I rigged up yesterday for the clew attachment on the jib sheet failed as soon as a lot of force came on the sheet. I determined that the locking line was too small a diameter. To make it larger, I thickened it up by back-spliced it and it seemed to work okay. I would have to wait until a strong wind to see if the changes were successful.

Mon, Apr 29, 1985: 33°17′S 152°36′W, Previous Day's Run: 82

The wind was now blowing from the east and getting up to a near gale. I noticed that although the thickened locking line was holding, the seizing on the jib sheet that was keeping the locking line in place was slipping. I tied a knot in the sheet to keep the locking line from sliding along the sheet. I spent the day reading while cursing the rough weather.

Tue, Apr 30, 1985: 31°46′S 151°20′W, Previous Day's Run: 111

The winds died down a bit, so during the afternoon, I went over the side with a steel plasterer's float to scrape off some of the barnacles. I managed to clean off half of the port side, but the leftover swell from the near gale was causing *Laiviņa* to leap around violently. After I got hit by the hull while I was holding my breath underwater, I realized that the conditions were too dangerous for such work. If I were struck on my head by the hull coming down, I might be knocked unconscious while I was underwater.

There were still a lot of gooseneck barnacles to take off, however even if I had calm weather, the water was still too cold. I hadn't had enough cardiovascular exercise on the voyage and could only stay underwater for very brief intervals of time and the cold reduced the time I could hold my breath underwater. I came back on board, dried off, and warmed up in the cabin.

This was a good time to get out the next two weeks' supply of food. After I had the food squared away in the food locker above the sink, I celebrated *Laiviņa*'s birthday. Five years old today!

Wed, May 1, 1985: 30°11′S 150°50′W, Previous Day's Run: 98

The wind was back to blowing from the northeast again. I was getting a lot of headwinds on this section! During the afternoon I saw flying fish for the first time since I entered the Pacific Ocean, a good sign that the waters were getting warmer again. I went over the side again to clean the bottom, and the water temperature was noticeably warmer than the previous day. We must have sailed into a current coming down from the north. With the warmer temperature, I was able to stay in the water for much longer.

Unfortunately I had only managed to clean half of the starboard side when I cut my arm and leg on the steel float. I felt the sting before I saw the tendrils of blood drifting around me. The sky was overcast, making visibility less than ideal, and coupled with the blood in the water, I felt it prudent to get back on board and not tempt any roving sharks. I usually preferred to go over the side during the middle of the day when the sun was the highest in the sky and visibility was the best underwater.

To clean the bottom of the boat, I would take a deep breath, dive down and clean as much as I could before I ran out of air, come back to the surface carefully watching the movement of the hull so that it didn't hit me, blow the snorkel, and look around for sharks while catching my breath for another dive.

Later in the afternoon, we crossed the thirty-degree parallel. To celebrate, I baked a tasty loaf of bread and opened the first of Dug's presents, a pavlova mix. I would have to figure out how I was going to cook it as it required an oven.

This was the spot where I hoped to meet the trades, but as I had been held up, the trades had moved north for the winter. I now expected to meet them around twenty-five degrees south.

I also turned over a new leaf of the calendar and opened another can of Ovaltine, a tin of sweet corn, a jar of Vegemite, and a packet of dried apricots. Now we only had May and June to go.

Thu, May 2, 1985: 29°23′S 150°00′W, Previous Day's Run: 65

The wind came up a bit today, and it was too strong to go over the side. The water was getting warmer, though, and there were more flying fish around, with some landing on the deck. In spite of the warm water, it was a cold day with a grey sea and a grey sky. I spent the day reading and relaxing.

Fri, May 3, 1985: 28°25′S 148°03′W, Previous Day's Run: 118

It was another day of heavy overcast and the north wind increased in strength. By the afternoon, I was down to just a storm jib when it blew a gale. Just when I went on deck to lower the mainsail, a strong gust split the mainsail from luff to leech about two metres below the head a few seconds before I had it lowered. I had another big sewing job ahead of me.

This wind was worrying me as it could be a late cyclone, and with an overcast sky, I was unable to get a position fix. At least the nearest land, Rapa Island, was still 150 miles away.

Sat, May 4, 1985: 28°25′S 146°47′W, Previous Day's Run: 67

It was yet another day of heavy and total overcast. I was becoming worried about Rapa Island as it was getting close and to eastward of me. Luckily, the wind was now blowing from the northwest and I was moving more towards the northeast. I found a couple of large flying fish washed up on deck.

During the afternoon there was a furious rainstorm which blew at storm force and stung my legs. The weather was now warm enough that I could be naked below decks and I only needed to wear a sweater while on deck. I was reading *King Rat* by James Clavell and enjoying it very much.

Sun, May 5, 1985: 27°12′S 146°07′W, Previous Day's Run: 81

Although it was cloudy, I managed to get a couple of sights to fix our position. My morale was way down today, and I was suffering from the blues. To escape, I read *Shōgun*, also by James Clavell.

To assist in chasing away the blues, I decided to make yellow pancakes. I had discovered that the only way to cook Dug's pavlova was to beat it by shaking it in an old Ovaltine tin and then fry the thickened mixture like a pancake. It worked out well, and they were quite tasty. Pete's pavlova pancakes!

Mon, May 6, 1985: 26°35′S 144°35′W, Previous Day's Run: 90

Just after noon, I finished reading *Shōgun* and had kicked the blues. I went over the side in bright sunshine and calm seas and cleaned the whole hull. It took a couple of hours but was relatively easy as the water was now comfortably warm. I also scrubbed off some of the slime that was starting to grow on the rudders. While in the water, I cut myself again, but this time I stopped the bleeding with a tight bandage. After that bout of hard work, I was pretty tired, so I slept for a straight fifteen hours.

Tue, May 7, 1985: 25°56′S 143°14′W, Previous Day's Run: 82

I was looking forward to crossing the Tropic of Capricorn, my next milestone. It seemed as though I would be celebrating soon as I might reach it in a couple of days.

I finished sewing up the mainsail and replaced the number one jib, which I had been using in its place. I also baked the best loaf of bread so far. Now that I was once again into warm waters, I could let the bread rise four times, which improved the texture quite a bit. It helped that the cabin temperature was up to thirty degrees today. During the afternoon, I sunbathed. At this time of my life, I believed that I needed a tan to protect my skin from the hot sun of the tropics. At the time of writing this book, I know better and use sunblock.

Later I started repairing the luff cringles of the trysail and managed to repair two out of the seven that had torn out during the gales along the New Zealand coast. I made my own cringles using a piece of thin-walled stainless steel tube and washers that the tube would just fit through.

I cut the tube into pieces about fifteen to twenty millimetres long. I heated up the end of my tube stock over the stove and used the red-hot end to burn through the patched sailcloth. It left a sealed hole the size of the tube. I slid one of the tube pieces through the hole in the sailcloth and put a washer on either side. With a ball-peen hammer clamped in the vice that was attached to the companionway, I rested the tube piece on top of the ball of the ball-peen hammer, put the ball of another ball-peen hammer on top of the other end of the tube piece, and then hit the flat part of the top ball peen hammer with a blacksmith's hammer. It peened the tube over and on top of the two washers. When I was finished, it looked like a regular cringle or grommet.

Wed, May 8, 1985: 25°18′S 142°00′W, Previous Day's Run: 77

There was still no sign of the trade winds however I thought we might reach them in a day or so. The wind started in the north, then moved to the northwest, and then finally settled in from the southwest before dying away altogether. It was a really beautiful day with light winds and nice sunshine, so I took advantage of the conditions to get some work done. After breakfast, I finished putting new cringles in the trysail and then mended a tear in the foot of the North number one genoa. After I had folded and stowed the sails, I went for a swim to cool off.

Laiviņa was only moving very slowly in the light winds, so after dropping the genoa on the deck and trailing a thirty-metre line with a monkey's fist on the end, I felt safe going over the side. When I went swimming, I always wore flippers, mask, and snorkel for safety reasons. The flippers let me catch up to *Laiviņa* in a hurry, and the mask and snorkel helped me keep an eye out for sharks.

My favourite trick was to quickly swim ahead of *Laiviņa* then dive deep and watch the hull and keel pass over me in the crystal clear water. After surfacing just behind the rudder, I swam ahead for another try. I felt like a dolphin at home in the water, frolicking around, diving and twisting down and around the keel. Today there were lots of plankton of different types floating around in the water, some like floating spider-webs, some like cocoons and doughnuts and other weird but beautiful shapes.

After my swim, I went around adjusting the rigging and tightening the stays and shrouds in preparation for the trade winds.

I decided to sit on deck just before sunset and watch the sun going down into the water. I was lucky to witness a phenomenon called "the green flash." I had been watching for it ever since I heard about it from Captain Church, my navigation instructor in Dunedin. Just as the last bit of sun disappeared below the horizon, the deep red light changed rapidly from red to yellow to white and then to green. It all happened so quickly that it appeared as a flash, with green being the last colour seen and remembered by the eye. Because I had never seen the phenomenon over years of sailing and watching for it, I was beginning to wonder if it was only seen in still waters and high up from the bridge of ships.

After such a beautiful day I was feeling very mellow, so I brought my guitar on deck and, in the fading twilight, serenaded the sea, sky, and stars for a couple of hours.

Thu, May 9, 1985: 24°51′S 141°42′W, Previous Day's Run: 32

After a quiet night of very light winds and periods of dead calm, my noon position showed a run of only thirty-two miles. For a while I thought we might get to the trades, but the wind was just boxing the compass and was now blowing northeast and from dead ahead again. Damn! Because of the light winds, it was quite hot, so I went swimming again through the day and relaxed after sunset by playing my guitar in the cool air on deck.

Fri, May 10, 1985: 24°20′S 141°27′W, Previous Day's Run: 34

It was another quiet and hot day, so I went for swim to cool off. I was feeling lazy, so I spent the rest of the day reading and baking bread and even baking buns in the frying pan, which worked out well. During the cool of the evening, I played guitar again. The wind moved around to the south-southwest, so I wondered if we would get the trade winds the next day.

Sat, May 11, 1985: 22°55′S 140°45′W, Previous Day's Run: 93

The wind went back to the north again, and there was still no sign of the trade winds. I was now well into the southeast trade wind zone, as my noon position showed us to be north of the Tropic of Capricorn. I celebrated our entry into the tropics in the usual fashion by eating some treat foods. Thankfully, the wind was fresher and steadier today, so we managed to make a reasonable day's run.

Sun, May 12, 1985: 22°15′S 139°37′W, Previous Day's Run: 74

The day started with an increasing north wind and an overcast sky. It looked as though we were in for another blow. By noon, the wind had increased to a near gale, and I was down to a storm jib and fully reefed mainsail. For the rest of the day, the wind raged until sunset, when it eased for a bit. It blew up again, this time accompanied by flashes of lightning. I was concerned as we were getting close to the Tuamotu Archipelago, through which I had to navigate. Luckily the winds allowed me to approach an area that was not so saturated with atolls and reefs.

From my noon position, it appeared that we would pass close to Moruroa Atoll, the site of the controversial French atomic tests. I wondered how much radioactivity was still present. After sunset, when it was dark enough, I saw the glow of the lights of the atoll ahead on the horizon. It was hard to estimate the distance to the atoll because of the overcast conditions and the resulting inaccuracies in my noon position.

I decided to heave to for the night so that I would not crash into any of the reefs surrounding the atoll in the heavy seas now running. By heaving to with just the storm jib alone and on the port tack, I figured that the boat's drift would counter the prevailing westerly current and we would stay put in the one place. With nothing more to do, I climbed into my bunk for some sleep.

During the night, I awoke feeling ill. It wasn't seasickness but something I had eaten. It may have been the coconut I had eaten that day, which could have gone rancid. I had stomach cramps and almost vomited. In spite of it all, I managed to get some sleep.

Mon, May 13, 1985: 21°35′S 138°30′W, Previous Day's Run: 74

When I awoke in the morning, the wind had abated a bit, and my stomach was back on an even keel. A few miles to the north, I could see the palm trees on Moruroa Atoll, so it seemed we had stayed in the same spot all night. The wind had shifted to the west, so I got under way again, heading in closer to the atoll so I would be able to see the reefs.

Figure 22.3: Moruroa Atoll

As we got closer, I saw the heavy southwest swell breaking on the reef just off the beach on the southern side. With a roar, these huge swells coming straight out of very deep water reared up and curled over, forming a beautiful hollow tube before collapsing on the exposed coral. I wished that I had my surfboard with me as the wave was perfect, with really fast sections.

Moruroa Atoll was basically oval shaped, with the long axis running east to west and about fifteen miles long. As I got closer, I could see a heavy power cable, held aloft by poles and running the full length of the southern shore. This southern shore was a series of palm-tree-covered islets separated by reefs. The cable crossed the gap between the reefs in one place supported by a suspension system. It seemed incomplete, and one section of the cable was not yet attached to the poles. It looked as though they were still stringing it up.

From the masthead, I could see the beautiful blue waters of the lagoon beyond. I thought it would be nice to sail in and stop for a swim however the thought of radioactivity disabused me of that notion. On some of the islets, I noticed some rude shacks. On the main islet was a large concrete bunker dominating the scene like a windowless hotel. What a pity that a beautiful place had such dirty overtones. I figured that the power cable was used to directly connect the bomb with the bunker at the east end. When I passed the main islet, I set my course and headed away from this sad place.

Later I researched and discovered that the French government had conducted nearly 200 nuclear tests at Moruroa over three decades from 1966 to 1996. Initially, the bombs were detonated in boats floating on the lagoon which caused high radioactive fallout. Later the bombs were suspended from balloons. This practice continued to 1975 after which shafts were drilled into the basalt base of the atoll and the bombs were detonated deep underground. On July 25, 1979, an underground test was conducted at a shallow depth of 400 metres after the bomb became stuck halfway down to the planned 700 metre depth. It caused the atoll rim to crack and produced a tsunami that injured six people in the Tuamotu Archipelago.

The French government had detonated an eighty kilotonne atomic bomb in a test named called "Nisos" on May 8, a week before I sailed past the island.

I took my noon sight and went below to process it. As I was plotting the fix on the chart, the wind suddenly increased from a small squall to gale force, and I dashed on deck to lower sails. I was just about to lower the genoa when the luff tore to shreds. I was shocked, as it was the North number one genoa, the new one, although not so new now.

I blamed the failure on the fact that there were insufficient hanks to support the luff, as they were only placed every three feet, whereas my Hood genoa had the hanks placed every two feet. Also, the luff reinforcing was badly designed. The luff tape stood out from the sail edge instead of being wrapped around the sail edge and reinforcing it. The hank cringles were half through the sail edge, so there were only two layers of cloth holding the cringles in place on one half and four layers on the other half. This unevenness, combined with cringles being placed in the middle of the edge of the sail instead of through a spot back from the edge, made them vulnerable to failure.

I was not impressed with North Sails. I just didn't get their lack of understanding about the basic effect of forces on a structure. Didn't they have any engineers working for them? Sometimes it seemed that these days, boats and sails were being designed for occasional day sail usage, not for ocean sailing.

For the rest of the day there were other squalls, and although they looked worse, they were not as vicious.

Tue, May 14, 1985: 19°59′S 137°00′W, Previous Day's Run: 128

The wind stayed fresh all night, and as we were on a reach, we made good progress, the best for the last five weeks. By noon, we were mostly through the Tuamotu Archipelago, with only two more atolls to get past. We were now north of twenty degrees south latitude with still no sign of the southeast trade winds. It was highly unusual not to have reached them this far north. The wind was still blowing west-southwest but slowly losing its kick. With the sail damage and no southeast winds, my morale was low. I was escaping into *Exodus* by Leon Uris.

Wed, May 15, 1985: 18°58′S 135°23′W, Previous Day's Run: 110

Another good day's run and still no trade winds. During the morning, the wind had shifted around until it was blowing from the south. I started thinking that at last I had reached the southeast trades, but later the wind moved back to the west. I glumly went below and spent the rest of the day reading.

Thu, May 16, 1985: 18°08′S 135°00′W, Previous Day's Run: 55

During the night, the wind still blew from the west, but it was getting lighter and lighter. At times we were totally becalmed, and I didn't sleep very well for most of the night. I cursed the crashing and banging of the sails, blocks, and other gear as *Laiviņa* rolled and pitched in the heavy southwest swell. At dawn I awoke with my nerves rubbed raw by the situation that fate had dealt me. Where in the hell were the damned southeast trade winds?

During the night, the mainsail had split halfway across at a seam, which didn't help my mood any. Luckily it was only a stitching failure, which I was able to resew quickly. The stitching on the mainsail was very weak now after five years of usage. I could tear a seam quite easily with my fingers, but luckily the sail had only to last another 5,000 miles or so. For the rest of the day and night, we lay becalmed, and I hoped that we would get the trades the next day.

CHAPTER 23

Towards Northern Waters

Fri, May 17, 1985: 17°50′S 135°05′W, Previous Day's Run: 19

All through the night, we rolled and pitched in the still air. The water was greasy with the calm, and I slept poorly, getting up many times to see if there was some wind. In windless conditions with a heavy swell running I have to sheet the genoa and the mainsail in as tight as I can to ease the rolling and the damage to the gear. The self-steering auxiliary rudder was lashed amidships with two eye-spliced lines fitted over the end of the trim tab shaft to prevent damage. Sometimes a swell threw *Laiviņa* astern, and if the auxiliary rudder was not lashed, it would slam it sideways and put a heavy load on it.

When the sun rose, I saw the first fingers of wind rippling patches of water. Then I felt it. The wind was first from the northeast and then as it strengthened it slowly veered. At long last the trades were starting. By noon, the wind was blowing east-southeast. The previous day's run was only a pitiful nineteen miles as we were becalmed most of the time.

The starting of the trades at eighteen degrees south ended what I would say was the worst piece of ocean weather I had sailed in. It was so unusual and not at all what it should have been. I was unlucky to be in the wrong place at the wrong time. I now felt that the Southern Ocean was much better than this, as I had never had a more frustrating time sailing.

The main problem with my morale was that if I expected rough weather and I got it, that was okay. If I got good weather, I was elated. But if I expected mild conditions and I got atrocious weather, I was furious. With the coming of the trade winds, my morale went up, and I went to work repairing the luff of the North number one genoa.

When North Sails had that sail made, I asked them to allow for stretch in the luff. Now it was chock-a-block, and there was still not enough tension in the luff, so I had to first shorten the luff. At the topmost panel seam, I unpicked the stitching, cut off twenty centimetres, and resewed it with the leech flush. This made the luff uneven, but recutting the luff later would fix this problem.

I needed a way to stretch the thirty-seven-foot luff, but *Laiviņa* was only thirty-two feet long. To get the extra five feet, I lashed the spinnaker pole to the pushpit rails so that it extended about six feet beyond the stern and upwards to get the height needed to clear the pushpit rails. I laid the sail out on deck and stretched the luff between the pulpit rails at the bow of *Laiviņa* and the end of the spinnaker pole at the stern. By adjusting the tension holding the sail and lifting the belly off the deck, I was able to see the natural camber in the sail and see where the edge of the luff should be cut.

I unpicked the old luff tape and removed it from the sail. Next, I marked the new shape of the luff with a marker pen and recut the whole of the luff with a pair of scissors to get rid of some of the excess camber (belly), which had been stretched into the sail through its heavy use over the last seven months. I marked and cut it to produce a slightly flatter, more efficient sail.

I was unhappy with North's weak design for the luff, and I wanted a stronger luff. My plan was to take the old luff tape, which was torn where every hank had ripped out, cut out the bad sections, and rejoin it. I would add extra material at the foot or head to make up for the missing amount. Finally, I would sew the tape back on the luff and make new grommets. It would be a big job.

North Sails placed the grommets for the hanks every three feet because that was the width of the sail panels. They were able to place the grommets on the seam between the panels where the sailcloth was thicker. This makes sense. The problem was that the hanks should have been placed every two feet as Hood had done with my original number one genoa. Some of the grommets for the hanks would have ended up in between panel seams and would have needed to be reinforced. But that was exactly how a sail should be built.

As I did not have enough hanks to rebuild the luff with hanks every two feet, I decided to stay with the three-foot distance between hanks and rely on a more properly sewn luff tape that was flush with the edge of the sail. By having the luff tape flush with the edge of the sail, I could place the grommets back from the edge so that there was an adequate and even thickness of sailcloth. This would act to spread the load more evenly over the sail in the area of a hank. Wind forces were trying to pull the hank towards the luff edge of the sail, and the reinforcement needed to be strong enough to prevent the hank from pulling the grommet towards the edge of the sail and ripping it out.

North Sails wisely used the stronger double portion of the seam in order to get the reinforcing effect of two layers of sailcloth plus two layers of luff tape—four layers of cloth. Unfortunately, the edge of the grommet hole that was cut into the sail went within a millimetre or two of the luff edge of the sail. This weakness was concealed by the luff tape, which was not flush but stood out a centimetre from the edge of the sail.

When force was applied by a strong wind, there was only a couple of millimetres of seam cloth to tear before the grommet was only held by the two layers of luff tape. These two layers tore easily and after all of the hank grommets tore out of the sail, only the bolt rope was holding the hanks in place. The bolt rope should have added strength to the sail but it was only stitched at the tack and head of the sail.

As soon as one of the hanks chafed through the bolt rope and severed it in two, the rest of the bolt rope just threaded through the luff tape and pulled out of the luff. The bolt rope should have been stitched to the luff tape all the way along the luff. It was another weakness in North's design. North probably manufactures sails that way as it requires less cloth and stitching, is quicker to manufacture, and cuts down on the number of hanks needed. Overall, they reduce their costs. I was not impressed with the way this sail was built.

Sat, May 18, 1985: 16°06′S 135°00′W, Previous Day's Run: 104

The trade winds were a nice steady force 3, and we were making good mileage. It was a beautiful sunny day, and I quickly got to work sewing up the luff of the North number one genoa. I also repaired a tear in the seam of the Hood genoa, which had opened up in the violent crashing while we were becalmed the day before.

I baked a loaf of whole wheat currant bread. I normally use half white and half whole wheat flour, but this time, I was able to bake a pure whole wheat loaf that rose properly. In the mix, I had added a cup of currants that were starting to ferment a bit. When the bread started to cook, I took the lid off the pressure cooker to check it, and the aroma of alcohol fumes nearly knocked me over.

I had to stop sewing the genoa because I ran out of ready thread. I spent the rest of the afternoon unravelling the strands from the reel of whipping twine. I hoped I wouldn't run out; this ball of whipping twine was getting down, and it was the last source of thread. So far I had used a mile of thread in sewing up the sails!

At sunset I was lucky to see the green flash again.

Sun, May 19, 1985: 14°16′S 134°15′W, Previous Day's Run: 118

The trade winds were getting fresh; the wind was now blowing at force 5. It was quite rough inside and outside the boat. Because I had crossed to the north of the fifteen-degree parallel of latitude, I opened another of Dug's presents and discovered a tin of butterscotch candies! Quite a treat since my main diet of oatmeal, canned tuna, and rice was now quite monotonous.

It was another busy working day. I had to repair an old patch in the number two genoa. I noticed one of the mainsail seams was starting to let go. I took it down, stitched it up quickly and rehoisted it. I had to adjust the timing of the bobbin in the sewing machine because it was missing stitches and balling up the thread. I was also able to make up a better locking rope for the clew attachment of the jib sheets. It was just two back splices in a short piece of sixteen-millimetre-diameter laid rope, simple and effective.

Mon, May 20, 1985: 12°42′S 133°00′W, Previous Day's Run: 119

I was still wondering if we were really in the trades as it was now blowing a near gale. These were the strongest trade winds that I had ever experienced. The barometer fluctuated as the wind shifted in strength and direction. This wind strength was too much variation for normal trade winds. I guessed it was just my luck! The weather was too rough for anything except reading.

Tue, May 21, 1985: 10°55′S 132°00′W, Previous Day's Run: 122

The wind eased a bit, and it was no longer blowing a near gale. It fluctuated so greatly that I had to reef and unreef the mainsail as the wind went up and down. It was still too rough to do anything else except read.

Wed, May 22, 1985: 9°00′S 131°00′W, Previous Day's Run: 129

The weather was a bit better today as the wind had dropped back to force 5. It was still fluctuating in strength, and I was spending a bit of time changing sails to meet these variations. These were unusual trade winds.

I baked a white sultana loaf that turned out quite nice, though I preferred whole wheat as it had more flavour. I had a lazy day reading a Steinbeck novel and eating the fresh bread.

Thu, May 23, 1985: 7°11′S 129°52′W, Previous Day's Run: 128

Up went the wind again until it was blowing a near gale. These were certainly unusual trade winds. I spent another day reading while cooped up in the damp cabin.

Fri, May 24, 1985: 5°23′S 128°49′W, Previous Day's Run: 125

This was an exciting day. Although the wind was still blowing hard, it was not blowing a near gale as it had the day before. I busied myself getting out the next chart, which had Victoria (and home) on it, and noticed at noon that we were just south of the five-degree parallel of latitude and just off the edge of the new chart. We had only about three days of sailing before reaching the equator, where I would really celebrate! I spent the rest of the day reading and relaxing.

Sat, May 25, 1985: 3°34′S 128°05′W, Previous Day's Run: 118

The wind was easing slowly now and down to force five. I could sunbathe on deck without getting washed overboard. It was not so rough down below, so I baked another loaf of bread. I was also able to plot my noon position on the new chart. This was always an exciting proposition and I was treated to the sight of my outbound track from six months before.

Sun, May 26, 1985: 1°49′S 126°54′W, Previous Day's Run: 127

Now the wind was as it should be, a gentle force 3. I was getting excited, as I should cross the equator the next day. I had only about 3,000 great-circle miles to go until Victoria. For the last week, I had been noticing the Big Dipper in the northern sky at night, and my favourite, the Southern Cross, was still with me. During the day, I had been reading a James Michener novel. It was a big thick book with lots of words, and the plot covered a long time period... a few billion years. I found it to be quite typical of Michener's books.

Mon, May 27, 1985: 0°00′125°40′W, Previous Day's Run: 132

Exactly at noon, I crossed the equator! When I took my morning sights, I knew that my noon position would be very close to the equator, and after processing the noon sight, there it was—zero degrees and zero minutes. To celebrate, out came the Montecello, sweet corn, fruit leather, and a packet of granola. I opened one of Dug's presents, and I was quite surprised. It was a plum pudding. By the end of the day, I was stuffed full. I could see that it was not my bread that was making me fat—it was Dug's plum pudding.

Today the weather was typical trade winds at last, and later that evening I listened to Rimsky-Korsakov's *Scheherazade* while on deck. Hearing the music "The Sea" with the real sound of the sea in the background brought tears into my eyes. I remembered the many months and miles I travelled on the sea. I was listening to the sea in realistic quadraphonic!

Tue, May 28, 1985: 2°02′N 124°26′W, Previous Day's Run: 143

Another beautiful day with perfect sailing conditions. We must have picked up a north-going current as we clocked up an impressive 143 miles over the last twenty-four hours. I spent a lazy day reading and looking for signs of the doldrums.

Wed, May 29, 1985: 3°38′N 123°00′W, Previous Day's Run: 129

As we zipped along towards the doldrums, I spent the day relaxing and reading *The Final Days* by Bob Woodward. It was about Richard Nixon's downfall. I found it fascinating because that period had been my most politically formative years.

The wind was light during the evening, so I brought a squab up on deck and lay under the stars listening to the radio. I was able to pick up AM stations in Mississippi and Texas over 2,000 miles away with the best reception I have ever received. On shortwave, I listened to Radio Canada and heard about Steve Fonyo's arrival in Beacon Hill Park in Victoria. Steve was running with his one artificial leg to raise money for cancer research. Boy, was I excited to hear about Victoria on the news.

It was a beautiful evening with a three-quarter moon overhead and the stars out in full force. Later I saw the first ship I had seen since Chatham Islands, heading down to the South Pacific.

Thu, May 30, 1985: 5°00′N 121°55′W, Previous Day's Run: 105

Figure 23.1: Approaching the doldrums

At noon, we officially entered the doldrums as I was at five degrees north latitude. With a lot of high-altitude cloud around, coupled with the wind now blowing from the south, I figured that soon we would be feeling the doldrum weather. The wind had veered to the south-southeast so I hoisted the spinnaker and away we went on a fast reach. I wondered how long it would take to get through the doldrums and reach the northeast trades.

During the day, I was busy getting out the next few weeks' supply of food and celebrating the start of the doldrums with a packet of crystallized ginger and a packet of dried apricots for later. Afterwards, I folded up the sails I had used in the heavy trade wind conditions. When that was done, I continued work on the luff of the North number one genoa. I was nearly finished sewing up the luff and when that was done, I just had to make the grommets.

I baked another loaf of bread, an easy chore as the warm temperature caused it to rise quickly. I definitely had my baking technique down pat after many months. I had been baking bread on the boat since I last crossed the doldrums. I didn't have a lot of flour left so I was into rationing my bread.

Fri, May 31, 1985: 6°54′N 120°46′W, Previous Day's Run: 133

At dawn, I was awoken by a light sprinkling of rain falling through the open hatch on my face. I got all the rain-collecting gear out, but the shower passed before I could collect any water. Later we just missed a heavy downpour to the east and another to the west. My noon position showed us to be almost in the centre of the doldrums and the large mass of cumulonimbus clouds verified it. This homeward crossing had been very sunny, unlike the outward crossing, which was in heavy overcast and constant drizzle.

At noon, the wind suddenly shifted from south to east and then to west, so I moved the spinnaker over to the starboard side. If the wind got light and we were becalmed, I planned to go over the side and check the growth of barnacles on the hull. During the afternoon, I got busy and finished sewing up the luff of the North number one genoa and put on some of the grommets.

Later that night, it rained and I managed to collect twenty-five litres of fresh water off the mainsail. It sure was nice to be drinking fresh water again instead of the algae-infected sludge I had been drinking the last few months. The starboard water tank was empty, and there was only a little water left in the port tank. The remaining water in the port tank was full of algae. After I pumped it out into a container, I strained it through a handkerchief. It tasted terrible, so I mixed it with a bit of concentrated lemon juice.

Sat, Jun 1, 1985: 7°32′N 120°20′W, Previous Day's Run: 46

During the night, I saw the North Star, Polaris, for the first time since leaving the northern hemisphere. These little milestones thrilled me!

I was awoken again at 2 a.m. by another shower of rain and managed to collect another twenty litres of water, a sure sign that we were in the doldrums. Another sure sign was that the wind died and we were moving very slowly. It figures!

During the morning, a small sparrow came and settled on a line on deck for a few hours. It must have been exhausted as it was a very long way from land. I tried feeding it oats and rice by scattering the grain near it, but it wasn't interested and later flew away.

I finished putting the grommets on the luff of the North number one genoa and fitted what unbroken piston hanks I had left. I had no more spare piston hanks so used regular shackles. It would take more time changing sails as I would have to unscrew the shackles to take the sail off the forestay. I decided I would scavenge some hanks from the worn out Hood genoa and fit them on the stronger North number one genoa.

I hoisted the repaired North number one genoa and checked out its shape. In the light wind, the sail seemed to set okay, but it would need a stronger wind before I could tell if the shape was right after recutting the luff.

I overhauled the Tilley storm lantern by putting in a new mantle and generally cleaning it up, but unfortunately, the salt air had corroded the aluminum fittings in the pump, making it difficult to pump up.

I went over the side into the hot tropical water and noticed that the gooseneck barnacles were starting to grow again. They were only a few millimetres long, so I decided to leave them for now. I would go over the side and scrape them off if we were truly becalmed and not moving at all through the water. I expected to get to Santa Barbara before they got too big and started slowing *Laiviņa* down again.

At sunset I was treated to the most spectacular sky I had seen in a long time. A nearly full moon had risen and added a silvery tinge to the colours. There were reds, golds, yellows, brilliant blues, and steel-grey clouds mixed with brown clouds and the silver moonlight. What a sight all around me, with the clouds' powerful shapes heaping up into the sky.

Sun, Jun 2, 1985: 8°40′N 120°15′W, Previous Day's Run: 68

Well, the spectacular sunset was certainly a clue to what we were in for because all through the night, I worked. It rained and rained and rained as the wind shifted in direction and strength. I was changing sail and setting the spinnaker only to haul it down a few minutes later. It would be nice not to bother and wait for a steady wind, but such a wind doesn't exist in the heart of the doldrums. The old sailors on the fully rigged ships cursed the exhausting work they had to do. They would be constantly changing the angle of the yards to catch every wind change, while they slowly worked through to meet the trades again.

From all the rain, I collected an amazing 122 litres of fresh water. I filled the starboard tank, which holds 100 litres, and started filling the nearly empty port tank. I had not slept for twenty-four hours and felt tired, but the wind shifts required my constant attention to the sails. Around noon, another bird, an Arctic tern, settled on the aft hatch for a

Figure 23.2: Arctic tern

rest. It only stayed a short while as I was constantly moving about the deck and scared it off.

During the morning, we passed a turtle resting on the surface of the water sound asleep, something I have often seen at Noosa, the coastal village in Queensland, Australia in which I grew up. We passed quite close to it, but it didn't wake up. It would have gotten a shock if we had run into it.

I noticed that my morale was getting stronger now that I was nearer my home; trying events did not seem to faze me as much.

Mon, Jun 3, 1985: 10°00′N 120°55′W, Previous Day's Run: 89

After a second sleepless night, I was beginning to feel like I was in a bit of a stupor, yet I was still excited to be getting close to the end of the doldrums. As the morning progressed, it really started to pour, and I collected all the water I needed. After filling the port tank and every available container, I started washing myself and my clothes and was amazed at their condition. My woollen undershirt was saturated with body oils and had turned waxy. A lot of dishwashing detergent and soaking in a bucket got it clean. That came from living in my clothes continuously, night and day, for many months in the high latitudes.

The wind was fitful, rapidly changing direction, blowing for a minute or so and then dead calm. It blew from all directions with the result that the sea became tortured. What a sea! It was the worst clapotic sea that

I have ever experienced. Even though the wind was strong enough to have us sailing at five knots in normal conditions, we could not move. Swells were coming from all directions. *Laiviņa* was stopped dead in her tracks.

We pitched and rolled and kicked and bucked. I sheeted the sails in as hard as possible, but during the calms when conditions were at their worst, *Laiviņa* still rolled her rails underwater, and the foredeck and aft deck were awash. Such violent motion put a huge strain on the mast, rigging, and sails, and I dared not take the sails down for fear that *Laiviņa* would be thrown on its beam ends and the mast torn out from the terrible whiplash. At noon, after an hour of such motion, the mainsail finally couldn't take any more and split from luff to leech even though there wasn't a breath of wind.

Ten minutes later, a steady northeast wind blew, and with the trysail set instead of the mainsail, we crept forward. We were in the northeast trades. What a welcome! If only the mainsail had lasted a few minutes longer. I took the torn mainsail down below and dumped it on the cabin sole. I was thoroughly dejected. More work. I cursed and cursed, but that didn't fix the sail or make me feel any better. I was mentally and physically exhausted after not getting any sleep for the past seventy-two hours. The good thing was that at last we were in the trades and *Laiviņa* could look after herself.

The wind freshened, and I changed the number one genoa for the number two genoa and then celebrated entering the trades by getting out a can of sweet corn and opening a jar of Horlicks along with some granola and a halva bar. With nothing more to do that required immediate attention, I fell on my bunk and slept.

CHAPTER 24

California Dreaming

TUE, JUN 4, 1985: 11°44′N 122°03′W, PREVIOUS DAY'S RUN: 124

I awoke in the dawn light after having slept a good fifteen hours straight. I changed the trysail for the number one jib in place of the torn mainsail. With the newly cut number one genoa and the number one jib, which set better than the stretched mainsail, *Laiviņa* pointed well. The North number one genoa did not have the stretched bagginess in the luff anymore, and the number one jib was flatter than the worn-out mainsail. We could sail in quite strong winds before needing to reef, so I decided to leave the jury-rig for a while to see what sort of day's run we would get. Still quite groggy, I spent the rest of the day just reading and sleeping.

WED, JUN 5, 1985: 13°05′N 123°33′W, PREVIOUS DAY'S RUN: 120

During the morning, I felt stronger, so I scavenged the hanks from the Hood genoa for the North genoa and replaced a couple of the grommets that had worked loose from the violent motion in the doldrums. I managed to learn more of *The Rime of the Ancient Mariner* but still had the last two parts to memorize. Later the wind died down a bit as a front came over.

THU, JUN 6, 1985: 14°30′N 124°40′W, PREVIOUS DAY'S RUN: 107

It was another lazy day, which I spent baking, eating bread, and reading.

FRI, JUN 7, 1985: 16°16′N 125°25′W, PREVIOUS DAY'S RUN: 115

It was yet another lazy day. We crossed the fifteen-degree parallel, and I opened the last of Penny's presents, a glass pyramid that changed colour when viewed from different angles. Around noon I was visited by three white seabirds with long whips for tails, which I first thought were gannets. I recognized that I needed to learn more about the different kinds of seabirds. Later I identified them as red-billed tropicbirds.

In the evening the wind was softer, so I dragged a squab up on deck and lay on it looking up at the stars. Many years later, I wrote a poem to express what I experienced that evening.

Passage

I lay on my back on a cool hard deck
With the star-pierced night poised above.
The Southern Cross stood on the horizon
While the Hunter attacked from high.

A cool air brushed my bare chest
Hardening me with its fingers
Mixing with warm exhalations
As it slid into tossed foam.

White ghost sails purred and surged
Thrusting with purpose
Sliding my sleek shining ship
Into parted and waiting waves of joy

Of exaltation
Of experience

Wetness touched me
Clinging with comfort
Drying coolly in the aging night.

Peter Freeman (November 1994)

Sat, Jun 8, 1985: 17°35′N 126°20′W, Previous Day's Run: 95

We were getting into colder water now. The air was cooler, and for the first time since being in the South Pacific, I covered my body with my wool undershirt, clean and smelling of the lemon dishwashing liquid I used to wash it in the doldrums. Surprisingly, I was getting tired of reading novels and wanted to sink my teeth into something that would work my brain a bit, so I dug out some technical notes and software descriptions and buried myself in computer literature.

Sun, Jun 9, 1985: 18°31′N 127°23′W, Previous Day's Run: 82

The previous day's reading inspired me to spend the day writing a computer program that made a computer simulate an HP-11C calculator. Once I was home, it would help me to write programs for the calculator a lot faster as I would be able to see what was happening in the various registers.

The air was pleasantly cool, and the sun was now getting higher and higher in the sky. It was almost the summer solstice, and we would soon pass under the sun somewhere near the Tropic of Cancer. So far the northeast trades were quite light, so our days' runs were not as much as expected. It looked as though I would be two to three weeks overdue at Santa Barbara, causing Penny and my friends to fret.

Mon, Jun 10, 1985: 19°39′N 128°18′W, Previous Day's Run: 86

This computer program was fascinating me. I spent another day totally engrossed in its mathematics and logic. In the evening, I brought the radio on deck and listened to the AM stations, 1,000 miles away. I was treated to a short story by Pushkin and *The Adventures of Red Ryder*, a western radio drama.

Because the radio's internal aerial system didn't work down below, I listened to the radio on deck. A ferro-cement boat with its armature of wire mesh was just a floating Faraday cage blocking radio signals—especially *Laiviņa* as the cabin was also ferro-cement. The only wood was in the hatches and rudders. I also had to put the radio up against the backstay before I got a signal, because it acted as a high aerial.

I was now wearing my trousers and a sweater as I lay on my back in the chilly night air looking at the stars and jets flying overhead bound for Tahiti.

Tue, Jun 11, 1985: 21°19′N 128°55′W, Previous Day's Run: 106

After having recovered sufficiently from the doldrums, I struck into my belated chores. I baked a loaf of bread and tidied up the forward area of *Laiviņa*. Later I repaired the mainsail and took the opportunity to remove some of the belly in the luff by recutting the panel to improve the shape. I also stitched an extra row of stitches onto each seam so everything was now triple-stitched. With the mainsail repaired, I took down the number one jib, which I had been using in the mainsail's place, and hoisted the newly cut mainsail. It looked good. The recutting had improved the shape in the lower third of the sail, but the upper two-thirds of the sail was still quite baggy. I wished that I had recut those panels when they opened up. Ah, well...

Wed, Jun 12, 1985: 23°11′N 129°31′W, Previous Day's Run: 117

I had calculated that we might pass under the sun today, and after taking my morning sights it appeared that this event might occur close to noon. I had sailed under the sun twice before and always hoped I could experience the rare circumstance of being exactly under the sun at noon.

I remembered Captain Church telling me how he experienced it as an officer in the merchant navy. The two mates stood back to back with their sextants right on noon and the sun directly overhead. Instead of the sun kissing the horizon to the north or south, it touched the horizon all around the full 360 degrees.

I stood there with my sextant waiting as it got closer and closer to noon. The sun was still towards the exact east twenty seconds before noon and ten seconds before noon. A few seconds before noon it was difficult to find the "kissing" point as I spun around the horizon with the mirrored image of the sun constantly touching the horizon. A few seconds later, the sun was kissing the exact western horizon. I was elated at experiencing such a rare event. The sextant read 89°46.2′, which after correcting for the semi-diameter of the sun, dip, and index errors, came out to 90°00′.

Later that afternoon I worked some more on my computer program.

Thu, Jun 13, 1985: 24°00′N 130°00′W, Previous Day's Run: 56

The northeast trade winds were gone. Dang! The wind was quite light now, and we were moving very slowly. My noon position showed us to have passed the Tropic of Cancer, so I celebrated with a tin of candy, granola, and a fruit leather.

I noticed a school of fish, which I first took to be shark but later thought were tuna. There were a dozen or so in the school. To see them better as they followed the keel, I leaned over the side wearing my mask and snorkel. They were mostly green with tinges of orange, but it was difficult to see. Wavelets dunked my head under, and I ended up with an ear full of water for my trouble. Ultimately, I determined that they were dorado.

That afternoon, I brought out the next couple of charts for the approach to Santa Barbara. I spent some time using the pilot charts to refine the point where I would go from being on the starboard tack to the port tack. If I calculated correctly, my port tack would lead me right to Santa Barbara.

Fri, Jun 14, 1985: 25°08′N 130°20′W, Previous Day's Run: 70

After processing my noon sight and plotting our position on the chart, I decided to go about and head on the port tack as it was more favourable and we were close to the spot where I planned to tack.

The school of fish was still behind the keel following *Laiviņa.* I wondered why they were continuing to stay and thought that they may have been using *Laiviņa* as a form of protection. I tried catching one of them, but they weren't interested in my lure even though I put a piece of bread soaked in vegetable oil on the hook.

During the afternoon I finished working on my program and rewrote it. With the used sheets of paper, I sat on deck making and test flying paper planes until I had perfected the design. To think that all these years I had been making paper planes the wrong way! After such frivolous activity, I tidied up and put away my books, pens, and paper.

Sat, Jun 15, 1985: 25°33′N 129°20′W, Previous Day's Run: 60

Today the wind improved, and we started moving a bit better. I spent the day overhauling the typewriter as it was getting stiff and sluggish. I first washed it in methanol and then sprayed the machinery with a concoction of kerosene and gearbox oil. It worked like a dream now! I practised typing some more, but it was difficult with *Laiviņa* on the move all the time.

Sun, Jun 16, 1985: 25°40' N 127°23′W, Previous Day's Run: 106

I had a lazy day just practising typing, reading, and relaxing. At least the stronger wind gave us a good day's run for a change.

Mon, Jun 17, 1985: 25°47′N 126°42′W, Previous Day's Run: 38

Rats! The wind was light again today. This morning I found a small squid on deck, which I used to bait the fishing line, but with no luck. I made a pleasant day of it by baking a loaf of bread, sunbathing, and listening to the radio. I was only 650 miles from Los Angeles, and I could faintly hear the commercial stations throughout the day. At night when ionospheric bounce was in effect, the stations were so strong that I had to turn down the volume. This time, I listened to *The Adventures of Red Ryder* and *The Trial of Pickwick* from Charles Dickens' *Pickwick Papers.*

Tue, Jun 18, 1985: 25°49′N 126°13′W, Previous Day's Run: 26

It was another day of light winds. I took advantage of the calm conditions and overhauled the alternator, which wasn't charging the battery. I stripped it, greased the bearings, cleaned the brushes, and checked the diodes and windings. After assembling it, I ran the motor for a while, but the alternator only put out an amp, which was used up by the drain of charge to the field windings. So I stripped it again and tested the diodes singularly and the coils again, and everything tested out okay. After reassembling it and running the motor, it still didn't work. I could only assume that the battery was so flat that it didn't have enough power to excite the field windings. I decided to leave it and perhaps get it tested in Santa Barbara.

I found out later that although it was wired as a twelve volt system, it was a twenty-four volt system that needed two batteries in series for it to work. I had been getting by over the years by keeping the battery charged with a battery charger and being very conservative in my battery usage when at sea.

Wed, Jun 19, 1985: 26°00′N 124°54′W, Previous Day's Run: 72

The light winds were still with us, but I was able to get better mileage. I had a lazy day just reading under a heavy overcast sky through which the sun peeped only intermittently.

Thu, Jun 20, 1985: 26°32′N 124°25′W, Previous Day's Run: 41

When I left New Zealand, I calculated that I could be in Victoria on this day. Such were the ways of the sea. Again there was little wind, and our progress towards Santa Barbara was painfully slow. I relieved the blues by baking bread and working out puzzles.

Fri, Jun 21, 1985: 27°17′N 123°32′W, Previous Day's Run: 65

Today was midsummer. I broke out the noodles and had some mushroom noodle soup to celebrate. We were becalmed most of the morning but started to get a breeze during the afternoon. This was frustrating as there has been a week of light winds and we were crawling to Santa Barbara under an overcast sky and very little sunlight. There was a light sprinkling of rain, but it didn't amount to much.

Floating on the water were a lot of little sailboat-shaped creatures like Portuguese men-of-war except with a sail angled to their body, instead of an airbag, and with only short tentacles. I researched later and found that they were called velella. There were also clusters of pelagic barnacles, which were similar to gooseneck barnacles except they floated on the surface of the water. They grew their own ball of foam, which kept them afloat, and a whole colony was attached to it.

Figure 24.1: Pelagic barnacle eating a salp

I scooped one of the pelagic barnacles up with a bucket and watched it. At first, I thought that it filtered microscopic life out of the water until I saw an three-centimetre-long salp swim too close to one of the many mouths. In a flash, the tentacles closed on it, and the mass of jelly-like substance was quickly dragged into the shell mouth.

I spent the rest of the day catching salps with some screen wire I had and feeding my new pet. Boy! Could it eat! I might have had about a hundred salps swimming in a bucket, yet after an hour they were almost completely devoured.

The salps were like a tubular jellyfish that swam by sucking in water at the front end of the tube and expelling it out the rear. Sometimes, they escaped the jaws of the barnacle when they bumped into it, by reversing the process and going backwards. When salps are first born, there may be a hundred of them attached together, with their nervous system all connected. Each individual salp sucks in water and expels it in a synchronized fashion. As they grow, wave action slowly breaks up these linear colonies into smaller and smaller groups until eventually the fully grown individuals are on their own.

They can swim in two directions, forward and backward. The larger they are, the slower are their water-squirting pulses. If they bump into something going forward, they switch into reverse gear and go backward. Their backward speed is twice as fast as their forward motion. That helps them escape danger, and danger is anything they bump into.

Sat, Jun 22, 1985: 27°53′N 123°27′W, Previous Day's Run: 36

It was again another day of calms and light winds. It would take ages to get to Santa Barbara at this rate, and I was thoroughly fed up with these weather conditions. At this time of year, this entire area was supposed to have winds of average force 4. I was getting force 1. I spent the day reading and feeding my pet. I saw a ship heading north at noon.

Sun, Jun 23, 1985: 28°50′N 123°10′W, Previous Day's Run: 59

Now only 380 miles away from Santa Barbara, I was sleeping during the day and staying awake at night to keep a lookout for ships. All day and the previous night we ran with a spinnaker after having picked up a southerly wind when it was supposed to be north-northwest, but by late afternoon the wind had hauled around to the northwest and freshened.

Just after sunset I came on deck for a look around and was shocked to see a ship crossing my bow, with a huge "SANKO LINE" painted on the side. It was a bit too far away to read the name painted on its bow. By its course, I figured that it was coming from Japan and going to Panama.

Soon after, the sky cleared from the west, and I saw the stars for the first time in a week. With the stars, was a new moon just starting to wax.

Mon, Jun 24, 1985: 30°08′N 122°36′W, Previous Day's Run: 83

At last we had a decent wind and our daily runs were improving. My noon position showed us north of thirty degrees, so I opened Dug's second-last present, a tin of sour lemon candies. I had a lazy day reading and baking bread, and in the evening I listened to *The Adventures of Red Ryder* and *The Country of the Blind* by H. G. Wells. I was hoping we would arrive in Santa Barbara on Friday.

Tue, Jun 25, 1985: 31°21′N 121°22′W, Previous Day's Run: 97

I was excited to be getting closer to Santa Barbara. Every day the radio was getting stronger and stronger signals, and I could listen to it both day and night without putting it up against the backstay. I still had to take it outside, as the signal didn't get into the boat.

Today I tidied up *Laiviņa* and then repaired the broken carriage return on the typewriter. Next, I soldered up some loose connections in the flashlights and the radio batteries. After dinner I listened to *Sergeant Preston of the Yukon* and another radio serial. I hoped that the next day I might sight land.

I would cross my outward-bound track soon and would have succeeded in a non-stop solo circumnavigation. I was seeing more shipping now and saw another ship this evening. The surface of the water was covered with millions of velella.

Wed, Jun 26, 1985: 32°50′N 120°32′W, Previous Day's Run: 99

It was a nice day with a steady wind. Around 4 p.m. while reading down below in the cabin, I heard and felt a loud thump. I went on deck to discover that we had hit a small log. I checked and found no damage to the hull. At 8 p.m. I crossed my outward-bound track and had completed a non-stop circumnavigation.

CHAPTER 25

Nearing Santa Barbara

THU, JUN 27, 1985: 34°08′N 119°56′W, PREVIOUS DAY'S RUN: 84

I calculated that I would sight land sometime in the morning. At 2 a.m. I was on deck looking out for ships and land when out of the corner of my eye I saw a flash of light. At first, I thought that it was a ship just over the horizon, but it appeared again and again in a regular fashion. I counted the intervals between flashes. Six seconds. It was the lighthouse on Santa Rosa Island. I hadn't expected to sight it until 4 a.m. so we must have made good time, probably as a result of being inshore of the south-going California current.

I set a course straight for the lighthouse, and soon we were approximately two miles off. Unfortunately the wind started to die as we were getting into the lee of the island. I was close enough to hear the roar of the swells breaking on the rocky foreshore, so we turned and ran northeastward along the shore to meet the channel between Santa Rosa Island and Santa Crux Island, where I hoped to be at dawn. In the light, fitful airs, we ghosted back and forth, first one tack and then the other, as a fog closed in making navigation difficult. Although the lighthouse was obscured, occasionally I could see a dull glow through the fog. I could hear the engines of fishing vessels moving back and forth further inshore but only saw their lights for brief periods when they were nearer to me.

Dawn came slowly and subtly with a lightening of the grey sky and sea until I could see a little more around me. Occasionally the shore, now about a mile away, would appear, wraithlike, only to disappear quickly afterwards, swallowed up by a clinging, wet shroud. A couple of hours later, with the warming of the sun, the fog lifted up 100 metres, allowing me to see under its blanket the grey world around me. Inshore, a half-dozen fishing boats were working, and I could see the thick kelp beds marking the rock reefs that extended a half a mile from the water's edge. Working slowly along the shore, I saw the mast and hull of a motoring sailboat coming out of the grey fog astern of me. Here was an excellent opportunity to get a message to the Santa Barbara harbour master.

Although they were going to overtake me, they were giving me a wide berth. With one arm (as two arms means distress) I waved, and they waved back. I guess they thought that I was being friendly. I continued to wave my one arm, and they waved back again. They must have thought that I was a happy fellow. Still I waved, and still they waved back. They were now a hundred metres abeam of me, and it looked as though we would continue this pantomime. I had this vision of them disappearing into the mist ahead, still waving. Then I heard a voice.

"I think he wants something."

"Are you sure?" the skipper answered.

"Well, he's still waving," the voice replied.

They altered course and came alongside.

"Do you need help?" the skipper asked me.

"I don't need help, but could you do something for me?" I asked him.

"What would you like?"

"I've just sailed around the world without stopping, and I wonder if you could use your radio to get a message to the Santa Barbara harbour master for me. I'm three weeks overdue, and people may be worrying."

He smiled. "You're kidding me," he said.

I guess they were wondering about this raving lunatic swinging his arms around and making wild claims!

"No, I'm serious. I left Santa Barbara last November, rounded the Horn in January and went past New Zealand in April."

"I don't have the correct crystal in my radio, but I'll likely meet someone who can. What would you like me to tell them? Wait... wait. Let me get something to write this down," he said.

He went below and came up with a notepad and pencil.

"Tell the harbour master that *Laiviņa*, registration number Oscar November 380142, skippered by Peter Freeman, is currently at Santa Rosa Island and should be at Santa Barbara harbour tonight sometime."

"Okay, we'll do that for you," he assured me.

We talked for a bit, and then they motored ahead, leaving me behind wallowing in the oily swell. Later that morning, we made the entrance to the channel and the breeze improved, allowing me to work through between the two islands. At the other end of the channel the fog cleared away completely, and I could see Santa Crux Island. It was surprising to see a lot of large flying fish in spite of the cold water. Unfortunately we were becalmed again, so I sunbathed on deck amid the beautiful sparkling water and the arid landscape.

Eventually the wind came up, and we were able to get moving again. After a couple of tacks, we were clear of the channel; one tack would take us right across the Santa Barbara Channel, the main shipping channel. Unfortunately, this beautiful blue sky became obscured by smog, and I had to stop sunbathing as it had gotten colder. With a reasonable amount of sea room and heading away from land, I lay on deck in the smog listening to the radio. I was pretty tired, and in a very short time, without realizing, I fell asleep.

A couple of hours later I awoke having crossed the shipping lanes. I hadn't heard any foghorns (or smoghorns as they could more aptly have been called), which would have woken me up. Later, the smog lifted a bit, and I could see the mountains behind Santa Barbara. My eyes burned, and my head ached from the pollution.

As we got closer to land, the wind freed a little, and I set the spinnaker for a glorious reach towards Santa Barbara. I could now see the little city. A sailboat came towards me, going in the opposite direction. Before he flashed by, I hailed him, and we had a brief chat until our boats were too far apart for any further conversation.

As *Laiviņa* was getting pretty close to the entrance to the Santa Barbara harbour, I took down the spinnaker. Later, I lowered the genoa as the wind was getting quite fresh. The wind continued to rise, so I decided it would be prudent to motor into the harbour. By the time everything was shipshape, the anchor ready to let go and the chain faked out on the foredeck, we were abeam of the entrance.

I started the engine and opened the throttle. Promptly, the engine died. The throttle cable fitting had broken at the engine end. As a temporary measure, I jammed the throttle half open, and we chugged, just like the *African Queen*, into the boat harbour. I had to rehoist the mainsail to help us through the choppy seas. Once out of the chop, I lowered the mainsail and headed for the visitors dock with the throttle jammed half open.

I timed my final glide into the dock, and pulled the gear lever into neutral. The engine raced for a while until I could secure *Laiviņa* to the dock. Only then could I go below and shut down the engine.

I grabbed my papers and headed up the flight of stairs to the harbour master's office and told them my story. I was able to use their phone to call customs. The final thing I needed to do was to call Penny. For that call, I needed privacy. I went back down the stairs to the pay phone and put through a collect call. There was no answer.

The sun was going down, and I thought that Penny was out for the evening. I tried every quarter of an hour, until suddenly I was connected.

"Hello?" Penny answered.

"I have a collect call from Peter Freeman. He is on the line now. Will you accept the charges?"

"Peter? Yes. Yes! Of course!"

"Go ahead."

"Penny?"

"Peter! Where are you? In Santa Barbara?"

"Yes, I just got in an hour or so ago. How are you?" I asked her.

"I'm thrilled! But what about you?"

"I'm a bit tired, but very happy. I've just got to get up the coast now and then I'm home. I'll leave here tomorrow. I need some rest, and I want to clean the barnacles off the hull," I told her.

"Did you know you've broken the world record?"

"No. Really?"

"Yes!"

"Wow. I have to think about that. Listen, I don't want to talk for too long. I still have to go out of the harbour, and this phone call will get expensive. I wanted to let you know that I made it to Santa Barbara and to tell you that it will probably take me a couple of weeks to get to Victoria. When I get to the entrance of the Juan de Fuca Strait, I hope to meet a fisherman who can get a message to you to let you know when I expect to arrive at the entrance to Victoria Harbour."

"We'll be waiting for you. I'm so excited!"

"Me too. I'm looking forward to being home," I replied.

"I can't wait!"

"I love you and miss you."

"I love you too, and I miss you a lot."

"Bye, Penny."

"Goodbye, Peter. I'll see you soon!"

I stood there at the phone for a few minutes trying to understand my feelings. I knew the voyage was not yet over. I still had to get up the coast to Victoria, and only then could I relax my vigilance. But having spoken to Penny for the first time in over eight months, I was pining to get back to Victoria and be reunited.

Here I was, in Santa Barbara, standing on solid ground. I was able to walk around, I was able to run, I was able to visit people. I walked the docks until I found Al and Marley's boat, *Summer Solstice*, a Westerly 45, and knocked on the porthole. They were surprised to see me and even more surprised when I told them where I had been. We talked for an hour or so, and as I was leaving, they gave me a bag of fresh fruit, vegetables, candy bars, and tins of beef. When I was in Santa Barbara eight months before, Al drove me around town to show me the locations of the lumber yards.

It was getting late when I returned to *Laiviņa*. I started the motor with the throttle jammed open a bit and motored out to the anchorage beyond Stearns Wharf. I found a good spot, lowered the anchor, and bedded it into the bottom. I was weary, but I still had some chores to do. I tidied up the sails and secured them. Down below, I stowed the fresh food I had just received in my food locker and crashed on my bunk. I was asleep in seconds.

CHAPTER 26

Santa Barbara

Fri, Jun 28, 1985: 34°25′N 119°40′W, Previous Day's Run: 22

I awoke at 6 a.m. and, after a breakfast of porridge, decided to scrape the gooseneck barnacles from the hull. The water was very cold; I knew I wouldn't last long without some protection, so I put on a pair of woollen long johns, wool trousers, a wool undershirt, and a sweater, and then over the top of this, my cruiser suit. That would keep me warm, but now I would float like a cork.

I dug out some diving weights and other pieces of lead that I had in a locker, went on deck, and arranged the weights near the stern, where I could reach them once in the water. I didn't know how much lead I would need to neutralize the buoyancy of my cruiser suit. I didn't want to go over the side with the lead already in my pockets and find myself heading for the bottom at an accelerating pace.

I put on my mask, snorkel, and flippers and went over the side. What a shock! The water was cold as it rushed into my clothes, though after a while, the water next to my skin warmed up. As I expected, I floated high in the water from the buoyancy of the cruiser suit.

I first scraped off the barnacles close to the waterline. Next, I started putting the lead weights into my pockets until the buoyancy was neutralized. Diving down in the murky waters, I cleaned one side of the hull and started on the other.

I had most of it completed when I noticed that small fish were eating the barnacle pieces I had taken off the hull, and then larger fish were chasing the smaller ones. With the visibility no better than five metres, I was beginning to worry about the even larger ones. It could have been my imagination, but I started seeing large grey shapes moving around the boat. With my clothes full of water and the lead weights in my pockets, there was no way that I could get out of the water quickly. With discretion being the better part of valour, I left the remaining barnacles and, with much difficulty, hauled myself aboard. I didn't think I could have stayed much longer in the cold water anyway.

I rinsed the saltwater out of my clothes and gave them a good scrubbing to get the last few months of grime out of them. The wash water in the bucket turned a dirty brown-black, and I needed a lot of detergent to get them clean. Next, I repaired the throttle cable, and with the engine cover off, I noticed one of the engine water hoses was leaking. After fixing the water hose, we were ready to go back into the harbour to pick up my mail.

I decided to motor in and soon reached the visitors dock. I secured *Laiviņa* and went to fetch any letters that awaited me. The previous evening, the person on duty wasn't able to get my mail and suggested I come back the next day when the regular staff were on duty.

Penny had written me a letter and sent it to Santa Barbara knowing that I would receive it when I arrived. I read through the letter, savouring all the news and personal musings. After reading the rest of my mail, I phoned customs again. As soon as I was connected, the phone system prompted me to put in a lot of quarters. I just did not have enough as it was long distance to Los Angeles. I phoned the operator and told the man who answered that I was having trouble locating customs. He connected me to the customs office for free.

While getting *Laiviņa* ready for departure, I was visited by Al and Marley, who wanted a snapshot of me with them. I gladly obliged, enjoying the moment. Finally, after folding up my sails with the help of a female harbour official, I was ready for sea again. The last thing to do was to post my mail. I asked for directions to a shop where I could buy a large envelope for my diary notes, but no one could help me. I stood there with the sheets of paper in my hand, not knowing what to do, when who should walk up but Chris, the guy who lent me the many sturdy clamps I used to fix my rudder. I was amazed at the coincidence.

"Do you remember me, Chris? Last November, you loaned me all of your clamps so I could laminate up a new rudder after I broke mine off the coast."

"Oh, yeah. Peter. I didn't recognize you."

"Yeah, I know. I have a beard now."

"Where have you been?" Chris asked me.

"Around the world. After I left here last November, I headed south, past Easter Island, around Cape Horn, then around Antarctica, under Australia, under New Zealand and back up through the Pacific. I just arrived here last night."

"Wow! No kidding? Let me shake your hand. Congratulations!"

He thrust out his hand and I gripped it warmly.

"I really appreciated what you did for me. By the way, can you help me now. I need to post my diary notes and I'm looking for a place to buy a large envelope in which to put them so I can mail them to Canada."

"Give them to me I'll mail them for you," Chris offered.

"Can you? Let me give you some money for postage."

"No, no. Don't worry about it. That's my gift to you," he said.

We shook hands once more and he walked with me back to *Laiviņa.* I got on board, hoisted the mainsail, and cast off the lines. I pushed the boom out with my hands, backing the mainsail, and *Laiviņa* started to move slowly astern. By moving the tiller with my foot, and adjusting the force on the mainsail with my hands, I backed her away from the visitors berth slowly until we were clear and then swung the tiller over.

Laiviņa turned smoothly, and I followed the turn, continuing to push the boom further outboard with the main sheet falls loose. As soon as she had turned through a quarter circle, I pulled the boom in sharply by hauling on the mainsheet falls, and she started moving forward. As she gained steerage-way, I turned her downwind, and we sailed out of the harbour.

A small group of people waved to me as I left. After dodging ahead of a fishing boat, I headed out of the harbour. Up went the genoa, and we heeled over, gathering speed and heading towards the open water. A couple of tacks later, I changed the number two genoa for the number one genoa as the wind was lighter than anticipated. I put in a long tack across the Santa Barbara Channel to the rocky cliffs of Santa Crux Island. I wanted to be away from the mainland in the hope that I might have better winds through the night.

When I reached the island, the sun was setting and the dark cave in the island's cliff was made even darker by the deepening shadows. The wind now became quite fresh, and I was forced to change back to the number two genoa. A few hours later the wind eased, and I was back to the number one genoa.

CHAPTER 27

Last Leg

Sat, Jun 29, 1985: 34°21′N 120°13′W, Previous Day's Run: 28

Figure 27.1: Oil-pumping platform

During the night, the wind eased further until we were becalmed at the edge of the shipping lane. For the rest of the night and all of the next morning, we wallowed as the sails crashed back and forth. I watched the freighters steaming past me close by. In the afternoon, a light breeze came up, enabling us to get over to the mainland side of the channel, close to Point Conception.

As we moved further away from Los Angeles, the air was much cleaner, and visibility improved towards the west. To the east, a thick black cloud of smog obscured the land. Sailing along the beautiful coastline showed me what California must have been like before the coming of the Europeans. The air would have been pristine, marred only by the occasional lightning induced fire.

A hot land breeze began to blow, and I could hear and see freight trains rumbling along the shore. One train had 112 full-length wagons being pulled by five engines. Later, I sailed quite close to two oil platforms standing starkly against the smog-induced golden sunset. They must have been automated as I didn't see any life on them.

Just at sunset, a cool sea breeze replaced the hot land breeze, and we sailed close to Point Conception and its blinking lighthouse. The breeze freshened quickly, and by dark we were down to a number one jib and a reef in the mainsail. It was when I was winching in the headsail that the port jib fairlead sheared through exactly as the starboard one had done in the South Pacific. As a workaround until I could get it repaired, I swapped it for the repaired starboard one, just as I had done when the starboard fairlead had sheared through.

As it became dark, I saw a line of buoys up ahead. By the time I noticed that the buoys were supporting a net, it was too late to avoid it. Fortunately we were moving fast as we passed over it. The keel pushed the net down, I held the rudder amidships, and after the keel passed over it, it came up behind the rudder. It was possible that the net was set deeper than the floats, but had it become entangled in my rudder, it would have created quite a predicament for me.

For dinner that night, I cooked up a potato and an onion that had been given to me by Al and Marley.

Sun, Jun 30, 1985: 34°40′N 122°10′W, Previous Day's Run: 98

The wind continued to blow strongly all day, but it was nice and sunny, and I managed to bake a loaf of bread from the last of the flour. Still tired from the previous day's activity, I took things easy and read and slept.

Mon, Jul 1, 1985: 35°08′N 124°31′W, Previous Day's Run: 119

It was another beautiful day, a beautiful Canada Day. All through the morning, the sun shone out of a clear sky, and the wind slowly died until we were becalmed. For a short time, the wind came up and blew from the northwest, and then just as quickly it became calm again. I was very lucky to have any wind as I never expected to reach this point along the coast so quickly.

I started reading the C. S. Lewis *Space Trilogy* again. I had read it years before and had been given the books before my voyage. Later that evening, I listened to the radio and managed to pick up what was now becoming my favourite serial, *The Adventures of Red Ryder.*

Tue, Jul 2, 1985: 36°30′N 124°14′W, Previous Day's Run: 83

I spent the day relaxing, reading, and sleeping as the wind continued to freshen. A bit after 8 p.m. I heard a tearing sound. The North number one genoa had torn out all its hanks again. It was my fault as I should have reefed earlier, but I was hanging on to it and pushing *Laiviņa* as hard as I could. Damn! More work.

Wed, Jul 3, 1985: 38°12′N 123°22′W, Previous Day's Run: 110

The wind was still strong and steady, and I spent the morning repairing the broken jib fairlead. As the afternoon progressed, I sighted the Californian coast, and by sunset, I was close inshore, where I tacked and set the self-steering for an all-night tack back out to sea.

Thu, Jul 4, 1985: 39°00′N 123°50′W, Previous Day's Run: 53

Today was American Independence Day. At dawn, I changed tack and headed back inshore to meet the coast in the early afternoon. We were just a bit south of the town of Mendocino, and as the afternoon wore on I made short tacks up the coast close inshore. At sunset, the wind died, and I could see the current pushing us back down the coast. After it grew dark, the fireworks started, and I sat on deck watching them while I listened to the radio. Just off that part of the coast, I passed two buoys, one a bell buoy and the other a whistle buoy. After turning off the radio, I could hear their mournful sound against the background of surf breaking on the reefs. That evening, I took the hanks off the torn North genoa and put them back on the Hood genoa, which I was now using.

Fri, Jul 5, 1985: 39°10′N 125°20′W, Previous Day's Run: 71

At 2 a.m. I was awakened by the flapping of the sails. The wind had come up, and I had to get the old Hood genoa down before it tore. By the time I had it down, the wind had strengthened enough so that I skipped the number two genoa and set the number one jib. While at it, I put two reefs in the mainsail. By sunrise, we were down to a fully reefed mainsail and the number two jib. For the rest of the day, while we bashed to windward, I slept, read, and ate popcorn.

Sat, Jul 6, 1985: 39°20′N 127°38′W, Previous Day's Run: 107

At 8 a.m. I was down below when I glanced out of the porthole to see something on the horizon. I went on deck and saw a sailboat flying a blue and white tri-radial spinnaker about a mile away. From the boat's course, it looked as though it was returning to San Francisco or San Diego from Hawaii. I changed course a bit to get closer so we could greet each other, but they did not alter course, and we passed outside of hailing range. This was the closest high-seas encounter I had with a sailboat.

During the morning, I saw a lot of velella floating on the surface of the ocean. We were wallowing among them becalmed, and there were about six velella per square metre. By the afternoon, the concentration was so dense that it was like sailing through a carpet of them, they were all jammed up together.

It was mostly light wind all day, so I just listened to the radio, sunbathed, and folded up the sails from the previous days of strong wind.

Sun, Jul 7, 1985: 40°20′N 127°35′W, Previous Day's Run: 60

During the night, a rare southerly wind blew up, and by noon it was blowing quite fresh. We were zipping along under the spinnaker. I decided to head in a northwesterly direction as I wanted to be in a good position when this rare south wind ended. My noon position showed that we had crossed the forty-degree parallel, so I celebrated by opening up a can of beef, eating a carob bar, and drinking a glass of hot chocolate and a glass of apple juice.

Mon, Jul 8, 1985: 41°56′N 128°33′W, Previous Day's Run: 105

At 1 a.m. I woke up to find the spinnaker without the clew. The poor old sail was threadbare and tore so easily now. During the night hours, the spinnaker became damp and stuck to something. It subsequently tore after it caught on a genoa hank. I took it in and set twin genoas, the number one and number two. After sunrise, I awoke and noticed a metre-long tear in the Hood number one genoa. It was more work for me. I set a jib in its place and we were sailing fast again.

The weather was beautiful, the wind light, and we were sliding along well under the twin headsails while I sunbathed, read, and listened to the radio. During the evening, I managed to pick up CKDA, a Victoria AM radio station, but only faintly before it faded away. Unfortunately, a San Francisco station transmitted on the same frequency. There were still a lot of velella, and now we were passing some of the pelagic barnacles I had encountered before in the Pacific. These were big ones—about thirty centimetres in diameter.

Tue, Jul 9, 1985: 43°15′N 128°53′W, Previous Day's Run: 80

Another beautiful day as I sunbathed, listened to the radio, and read. I saw a propjet aircraft bound for Hawaii flying very close to the water. Later a seagoing tug passed ahead of me in the same direction, with two barges in tow. I spotted a loose orange buoy up ahead and managed to retrieve it in one neat manoeuvre. It was amazing what could be found at sea. During the evening, CKDA came on quite strong initially but later faded out.

Wed, Jul 10, 1985: 44°41′N 127°55′W, Previous Day's Run: 96

"And the good south wind still blew behind." I was amazed at my luck at getting such a wind. According to the weather reports on the radio, the Oregon coast was getting light and variable winds while I was getting this fantastic southerly wind. During the day, I again sunbathed, read, and listened to the radio. What a life!

Around sunset, we crossed the forty-fifth parallel. I opened the last of Dug's presents. It was a tin of candy. I also opened a can of beef, a carob bar, a hot chocolate drink, and a box of apple juice. I was stuffed.

Just on dark, the wind started veering quite quickly, and by midnight we were close-hauled in a northwest wind. I was pleased that I had steered a course to the northwest in anticipation of this wind, which I knew would eventually arrive. I was now in a perfect position to reach the entrance to the Juan de Fuca Strait on one long port tack. It also put me further out to sea and west of the opposing California current.

Thu, Jul 11, 1985: 46°00′N 127°00′W, Previous Day's Run: 88

I had finished reading all of my books, so I decided to trim the edges of the torn spinnaker in preparation for sewing. I was getting excited as my noon position showed us to have around 230 miles to go. At this stage, I hoped to arrive at noon on Sunday.

During the afternoon, I saw in the distance what must have been a ship firing off shells; I saw the smoke and the flash but couldn't see the ship. By nightfall, I had sewn up the tear in the Hood number one genoa to be ready for when the wind dropped light again.

Working my way up the coast, I was acutely aware of the hazards around me. I had encountered a lot more shipping, I was travelling close to the coast, and my gear was very worn. After achieving so much, I did not want to lose *Laiviņa* or my life so close to home.

CHAPTER 28

Familiar Waters

FRI, JUL 12, 1985: 47°36′N 125°30′W, PREVIOUS DAY'S RUN: 114

I had a beautiful night's rest, which I needed because I was approaching land and had to stay awake. Already there were signs of land: kelp, floating debris, and land-based birds. I was excited but also nervous at the prospect of the end of my voyage; I had butterflies in my stomach. There was a good chance of arriving Saturday afternoon if this wind held.

As I approached the entrance to the strait, I had a nearly overwhelming desire to turn *Laiviņa* around and run away. It was almost too much. I persevered, not because of any exercise of will, but rather the effort required to change the status quo. My status quo was to continue to sail to Victoria.

I had been so focused on my voyage that for the better part of a year I had lived only for sailing the oceans. As I sailed around the world, I never considered the end of my journey. It was such a huge undertaking that the only way I could be successful was to look just at the next piece of ocean.

I was about to transition abruptly from a seafaring existence to that of a landlubber. The shock of that realization hit me suddenly as I was approaching the entrance to the Juan de Fuca Strait. I started to experience a different kind of stress from what I had been living with the past nine months. I was very anxious about how I would be able to perform in social situations.

I knew I had lost my social skills; I even struggled at times with my verbal skills, in spite of reading to myself out loud. My brain could easily read written material because I was merely mimicking something that was already composed by others, but if I had to compose my own conversation, I found it difficult. During the many months of sailing, I had honed my seafaring skills considerably, and I knew that world intimately. I was confident in my ability to meet the challenges that the sea would send my way. Now I lost that confidence, that self-assurance.

My brain had wired itself during the voyage to make me a good sailor; I had to take apart that circuitry and reshape it to deal with the world of people.

After a while, this strong and disturbing feeling dissipated. I began to look forward to coming home and was excited at the prospect of having a life where I did not need to exercise constant vigilance in order to stay alive and healthy.

Just before noon, I crossed a ship bound for Portland, Oregon, and I saw the first land, the Olympic Mountains, which line the Juan de Fuca Strait. I could only see one mountain, but the remaining mountains gave away their position by the perpetual cloud hanging over them. I was also able to see the cloud hanging over the high land on Vancouver Island. Between the two cloud masses lay the Juan de Fuca Strait, dead ahead.

The noon position showed us to have only 120 miles to go. As I approached the entrance to the strait, the wind started to back, and I was able to free the sheets a bit and move a little faster. Luckily, I didn't need to tack up to the strait. Near sunset, we sailed into coastal water with its brown green colour, and I saw a few fishing boats. I quickly wrote a message on a piece of paper that asked the Coast Guard to contact Penny and to let her know of my location and latest estimated time of arrival. I sealed the message in a plastic bag that was weighted down by a small scrap piece of brass rod and placed it in the pocket of my wet-weather jacket.

I sailed towards the nearest fishing boat and manoeuvred as close as I could so that we were moving in the same direction, abeam of each other.

"Ahoy there!" I called. "Could you radio a message into the Coast Guard for me?"

"Sure. What do you want us to say?"

"I've got it written down on a piece of paper in this bag. I'll throw it over to you."

"Okay... just a sec," he replied.

My self-steering was holding my course fairly steady as I watched him walk into the wheelhouse and talk to the skipper. He came back out on deck, and the skipper brought our boats much closer together. I judged my throw carefully and flung the weighted bag across the intervening gap. It hit the deck cleanly, and there was a brief scrabble before he had the bag in his hand.

"Got it!" he said.

"Good. So if you get that message to the Coast Guard, I'd really appreciate it."

"No problem. Consider it done."

The fishing vessel broke away, and we continued on our own course. By midnight, the wind died completely, right at the entrance to the strait. We sat there wallowing and not going anywhere.

Sat, Jul 13, 1985: 48°31′N 124°47′W, Previous Day's Run: 62

We were becalmed all the night and well into the morning. This ruined my chance of arriving at Victoria in the afternoon. While I wallowed off Cape Flattery, a sports fisherman came nearby. I asked him to radio the Coast Guard in Port Angeles, who in turn would phone my position and a new estimated time of arrival through to Victoria.

At noon, a westerly wind started, gently at first and then gradually freshening through the day. *Laiviņa* started moving down the strait, slowly at first and then with gathering speed. I moved in close to the coast to see if anyone was watching for me, but the people I saw on the beaches and trails were not paying much attention and did not return my wave.

By sunset, I was approaching Race Rocks, so I took the twin headsails down and replaced them with the mainsail and number two genoa. We had a fantastic sail through Race Passage with a strong wind and current behind us. As *Laiviņa* shot out of the race and into the slack water, the last light in the sky was fading.

Up ahead, the brilliant lights of Victoria beckoned, and I wanted to continue and complete the final ten miles. However I thought there would be no wind during the night, and I didn't want to arrive at Victoria in the wee hours of the morning. Even if there were wind, it was already 11 p.m. I did not want to inconvenience my friends who wanted to see me arrive.

I took the sails down, started the motor, and chugged past William Head and the penitentiary on the point. I could see the high double fences topped by razor wire and the sodium vapour lights illuminating the land around, momentarily blinding me. I headed past William Head and into narrow Pedder Bay. A mile past the penitentiary, I found a spot off to the side, set the anchor, and tidied up the gear.

Docked at the marina was a large cabin cruiser with its cabin lights on. I saw a number of people moving around inside the cabin. My plan was to row over and ask them to phone Penny for me, to let her know that I had made Pedder Bay and that I would sleep the night here.

It was getting late, and I didn't want to lose the opportunity to contact Penny. I was afraid that the occupants of the cabin cruiser would either leave soon or head off to their bunks. I didn't have time to wash up and change into my clean shore-going clothes. I went into the cabin and grabbed a notebook and pen. On the top sheet of paper, I wrote Penny's phone number.

I unstrapped the dinghy and launched it over the side, climbed down into it, and fitted the oars. Checking my course, I started to row for the lights of the cabin cruiser. Inside, two couples were sitting in the main saloon, chatting and idly watching television. I rowed up to the stern of the vessel and knocked on the transom.

"What's that!" the slim woman said.

"I dunno, there's someone outside. I'll go and look," said her companion, a tall, thin man in his forties.

"No, wait!" she whispered.

"Why?"

"What if it's someone from the jail?" she whispered.

"What do you mean?"

"Who would be knocking on the back of our boat at this time of night?"

After I had knocked, I heard the conversation cease. I heard some words, but I couldn't understand them. Then it became quiet. I knocked on the transom again, this time a little harder.

"There it is again!" she whispered.

"Look, I gotta go and see," he whispered back.

"Be careful!"

"There are four of us here."

He first went over to the galley drawers, opened one of them, and withdrew a long, heavy knife. Holding the knife behind his back, he went to the louvred doors at the aft end of the saloon, and cautiously opened one of them. He peeked ineffectually through the opening into the dark narrow bay and saw nothing. I saw him look around and could tell that he didn't see me, sitting in the dark in my dinghy low down on the water. He was about to withdraw his head and close the door when I spoke.

"Hi! Can you help me?" I called up.

"Who are you?" he asked.

"I'm Peter Freeman. I'm from the sailboat anchored over there," I indicated with my hand. "She's called *Laiviņa*."

"Yes?" he said cautiously. "What do you want?"

I could only see part of his head as he had opened the door just enough to look outside.

"I'm wondering if you could call my girlfriend for me and let her know where I am," I asked him.

"Just a minute."

He withdrew his head and closed the door, and I heard the lock snap shut.

"Who is it?" his companion asked.

"Peter somebody. He wants me to call his girlfriend."

"What does he look like?"

"I dunno, I couldn't see him that well. He's pretty scruffy."

"He's scruffy? Are you sure he's not from the jail?"

"I dunno, he just wants me to call his girlfriend. He said he is off a sailboat anchored over there."

"Where is he?" she asked.

"In a tiny little boat... at the back of our boat."

"What if he's climbing up onto our boat?"

"I don't think so."

"Make sure!"

"Okay."

As I waited, I could hear the faint whisperings. After a while, I heard the lock snip and the door open. I saw his head in the opening again.

"Okay... ah... I can call your girlfriend. What's her phone number?" he asked me.

"I've got it written down here. I'll pass it to you."

"That's okay, just tell me what it is, and I'll write it down," he said.

I recited Penny's phone number.

"Just a sec," he said.

His head disappeared; the door closed and locked. I thought him very unfriendly and didn't understand his reluctance to engage in a decent conversation with me. After a while, I heard the lock snip and the door open a little way again, the outline of his head illuminated by the faint cabin lights.

"I wrote it down. Let me read it back to you to make sure I have it right," he told me.

He read the number back to me.

"Yeah. That's right," I confirmed

"What's her name?"

"Penny."

"And...um...what do you want me to tell her"

"Tell her I've arrived in Pedder Bay and I'll try to time it so I arrive at the Ogden Point breakwater at noon tomorrow."

"Okay. What's your name again?"

"Peter Freeman. I've just arrived back from sailing around the world by myself without stopping. I left Victoria last October, and all of my friends want to be at the wharf to greet me when I get there."

"Oh...okay," he answered dubiously.

"If you can call her, I'd really appreciate it."

"Yeah, sure...I will."

"Thank you."

I pulled on the handles of the oars and got the dinghy moving, glancing over my shoulder to adjust my heading so as to make *Laiviņa* in a straight line. As I rowed, I could see him standing in the doorway, framed by the cabin light. After a while he moved out onto the poop deck and was joined by another person.

I reached *Laiviņa* and climbed up over the stern. As I busied myself with lifting the dinghy aboard and strapping it down on the cabin top, I saw the couple go inside the cabin cruiser and close the door.

"Well, he does come from that sailboat. He's not from the jail," he said.

"Are you going to call his girlfriend?" she said.

"Yeah."

"But what if he is from the jail and he wants his girlfriend to pick him up?"

"You saw him, he went back to his boat."

"Well, he could have broken into that boat."

"I doubt it. He seems to be able to handle that dinghy all right. Anyway, I'm going to make the phone call."

Once I had *Laiviņa* shipshape, I crawled into my bunk, set the alarm for a five-hour sleep, and fell asleep straight away.

CHAPTER 29

Home

SUN, JUL 14, 1985: 48°25′N 123°22′W, PREVIOUS DAY'S RUN: 57

The sounds of early-morning fishermen powering out of the marina woke me. A glorious morning heralded the last day of my voyage, and I ate my breakfast with a lump in my throat. I gave myself a sponge bath at the sink, shaved off my beard and put on clean clothes. This was a special day, and I needed to look good for it.

After I came on deck, I noticed that the tide was almost low and the bottom of the keel was stuck in the mud where I anchored just off the side of the channel. I had calculated that I would probably just touch at low tide, but we were touching hard enough to be stuck. I started the motor and alternately went forward and astern while I rolled *Laiviņa* from port to starboard. Then I used the tiller to alternately turn to port and to starboard, repeating the process over and over again.

I managed to create a hole of about three metres in diameter in which I could manoeuvre. I then tried ramming a track back out to the main channel. Eventually I pushed my way free and chugged out of Pedder Bay. Once I reached the entrance to the bay, I hoisted the sails, and in the light breeze I motor-sailed towards Victoria. I wanted to arrive at the breakwater at noon, and being stuck in Pedder Bay had made me a little late. In the light winds, I would not make it by noon under sail alone. I would have preferred to sail with whatever the winds gave me, but I did not want to leave friends waiting.

We had to manoeuvre around a tug towing a log boom and then we were in the clear heading for Ogden Point. With my binoculars, I had a rough idea of the location of the Ogden Point breakwater ten miles away. This morning, there was a temperature inversion, which made all the buildings and docked ships look elongated vertically. A cruise ship at Ogden Point looked like a city skyscraper. It made it hard for me to identify the point, but as I got closer and closer, it became easy to see the breakwater and the white and red lighthouse on the end.

Figure 29.1: Friends on Ogden Point breakwater

Closer and closer I came. Knowing that my friends would be waiting there, I had some difficulty in stilling my beating heart. At first, I started to discern people through the binoculars, and eventually I could see them with my naked eyes. When I finally arrived, there was a large crowd of friends waving and cheering. They were holding up a large painted cloth sign that read, "WELCOME HOME PETER." When I saw the sign and all of the people, I felt the impact of seeing friends for the first time in many months, all in one place.

I looked at familiar faces and did not see them. Instead of seeing the rich detail in a friend's face, smile, bright eyes, hair, ears, and nose, I saw only a blur, a fog for a face. My mind was suffering from emotional overload, allowing me to recognize only a couple of my very closest friends. It was too much for me. I was in shock.

I immediately recognized my girlfriend, Penny, as I was longing to see her. Passing the end of the breakwater, I called out a few words, waved, and then continued my way into the outer harbour. As I was

Figure 29.2: Christy, Patrick, Robert, and Penny

going past Fisherman's Wharf, Bill Challand and his friends gave me a warm welcome by blowing foghorns as I passed by.

Ahead at the customs dock, I saw a large crowd waiting for me. Fortunately, I was focused on the task of docking safely. With my eyes, I judged the distance, *Laiviņa*'s speed, and the light wafting winds. There was a negligible current, so I was able to come neatly alongside the floating pontoon. As *Laiviņa* touched the rough boards, a small band played "Waltzing Matilda." My mooring lines were ready, and there were plenty of willing hands to secure *Laiviņa* to the dock.

"I got it, Pete. Just pass me your bow line!"

"We'll look after it!"

"Yer made it!"

"Good work!"

"Welcome home!"

I climbed over the lifelines and stepped onto the dock. Penny was right there in front of all the people. Without speaking, she placed a garland of flowers over my neck and gave me a big hug and a kiss. I did not want to let her go. This was the first time I had hugged anyone in nine months. Her face close to mine, she spoke quietly.

"We have a surprise for you," she said. "Are you ready?"

Figure 29.3: Approaching the customs dock

"Sure!" I was in everyone else's hands now.

She stepped back and then moved to the side. I looked at the faces of a row of tightly packed people standing in front of me. They parted and I saw another one that was very familiar, but I thought I must be mistaken. This person could not possibly be here. On the dock. In Victoria. In Canada. She should be in Noosa Heads, my hometown…

"Mom! What are you doing here? How did you…?"

My words were smothered in a big kiss and a hug that seemed to last forever.

"Welcome home, love! I'm so proud of you!" she said.

"But how did you get here? When did you get here?"

"A couple of weeks ago. I'm staying at Penny's. I'll tell you all about it later. Your friends want to talk to you now," she said.

I spent some time responding to the many questions fired at me. I felt nervous and uncomfortable, but persevered despite the emotional turmoil confusing my thoughts. After a while, I noticed a smartly dressed young woman in a blue uniform with a blue hat upon her luxuriant blond hair and a neat pair of black pumps. She was waiting patiently to talk to me.

"Excuse me. I'm from Canada Customs. I need to clear you into Victoria."

"Certainly, let me get my papers," I said.

I quickly climbed over the lifelines and went down the companionway into *Laiviņa*'s cabin. I came back on deck soon after and was about to climb back over the lifelines.

"Do you want me to go up to the customs building?" I asked her.

"No, there is no need. I can do it all here," she said.

"Welcome aboard!"

She gingerly climbed over the lifelines in her dress, taking care not to stumble in her dress shoes. I held her arm until she was aboard, then fetched a life cushion upon which she could sit. I felt embarrassed, as *Laiviņa* was looking worn out. The lines, although clean from the constant washing of the ocean, were tattered and worn and still in an untidy state. I had not had time to coil the halyards and cheese down my jib sheets. She was embarrassed too as she had to conduct her official business with a large crowd of onlookers noting everything she did and said. We completed the paperwork quickly.

"I have to go below and inspect your vessel," she told me.

"You'll have to forgive the state of the interior. It smells of the sea and nine months of unwashed habitation," I cautioned her.

I preceded her down the companionway, quickly stowing a few loose items I saw lying about.

"Don't go down into the cabin with him! He hasn't been with a woman for nine months!" someone yelled from the dock.

Her face reddened, and when she reached the bottom of the companionway, she spent a brief moment looking around, then turned and carefully climbed back onto the deck. I suspected she wanted to complete her formalities and get back to the safety of her office. I helped her over the lifelines onto the dock, then joined my friends as her receding blue uniform disappeared behind the throng of people.

"What food do you miss the most?" someone asked me.

"Strawberries and ice cream!" I replied, not really knowing what food I missed. It was just the first thing that came into my mind.

I spent the next hour chatting with my friends, when later, someone thrust a plastic bowl into my hands. Inside the bowl were scoops of ice cream topped with fresh strawberries.

"Thank you!" I told him as I gratefully ate the strawberries and then the ice cream. Everything tasted wonderful!

Figure 29.4: Clearing customs

After a while, people started to head home, and I prepared to take *Laiviņa* over to Fisherman's Wharf, where she would be moored for a while. Penny, my mom, and some close friends accompanied me. We motored over to Fisherman's Wharf, docked, and secured *Laiviņa* with my stout mooring lines. I put her properly to bed with lines coiled and tidied, frapping hooks on the halyards, a sail cover over the mainsail and boom, the sails folded and bagged, and the jib sheets cheesed down on the cockpit thwarts. *Laiviņa* was tired, but she was proud, and she could still dress herself properly. Her long voyage was over.

Figure 29.5: Back: Penny, Peter, Emma; Front: Patrick, Christy, Robert

CHAPTER 30

Epilogue

Figure 30.1: The author and Laiviņa in 1985

We all ended up back at Penny's house, where we continued our conversations. Fortunately, it was Sunday, so my friends were able to visit before having to go to work the next day. Penny had taken two weeks' vacation, and her children were on their school's summer vacation. In a day or so, they were going to spend a couple of weeks with their father. I suggested to Penny that we spend her vacation sailing around the Gulf Islands in Haro Strait near Victoria.

The next day we received a phone call from the couple who owned the large cabin cruiser that was moored in Pedder Bay. The local newspaper had a story of my voyage and the couple had read it. They realized that I was not the killer who had escaped from the William Head Penitentiary that was reported in the same newspaper as the story of my voyage. They called me to apologize for their cold treatment of me and told me how they reacted when I knocked on the transom of their boat.

I found eating new foods tasted incredibly potent to my hypersensitive taste buds. I was used to simple, bland rations. Fruit was ever so sweet, tangy, and textured. Spicy dishes seemed very rich in flavour and I savoured every morsel. I lingered over the flavour of vegetables that sat in my mouth before I swallowed them. Salads were ambrosia.

All that I planned came true. It had been a beautiful experience for me. My planning had been accurate and the food and equipment adequate. I was in excellent physical shape except for a low iron count. Although I took vitamin and mineral pills, the stress and exercise of the voyage had leached the iron out of my system. It would have been nice to have had the money to buy a new mainsail. If I were to repeat such a venture, I would change very little. Not that I would do the same trip again, as it was the challenge of the unknown that gave a voyage of this kind its meaning. Next, I would do something different.

I visited the dentist and had the two missing fillings repaired. The dentist found no decay in the holes left by the missing fillings. My diligence in keeping the holes cleaned out had paid off.

The next two weeks were a good interlude for me. I had not understood the extent of the psychological changes that had occurred in me from being at sea and alone for nine months, with only the occasional contact with other people. My one-on-one contact with Penny let me re-establish some of my communication skills in a safe environment. It helped me transition into an environment rich in complex social interactions. I needed time to engage with people and relearn the subtleties and nuances of personal connections.

After the two weeks were over, I went back to work. I owned an incorporated company that developed software and provided information technology solutions to business in Victoria. Before my trip, I had handed over active work to friends with similar skills to continue to support my clients. Now I needed to re-engage in the business world and start making a living.

I found it surprisingly difficult. I lacked confidence and had lost the ability to engage with different kinds of people in a fluid and understanding way. The loss of those skills crippled me for a while. Slowly, as

I worked on various projects, my confidence built and I was returning to my former self.

I gave talks and slide shows for yacht clubs, schools, and service organizations, and to raise money for local museums. I started writing this book and managed to complete about a quarter of it before life stepped in and scrambled my plans. About three years after my voyage, Penny and I had separated and *Laiviņa* was put up on the hard at Canoe Cove Marina, where I intended to overhaul her, but she languished there through my lack of finances and consuming work commitments.

In 1988, I met Mary while working as a contractor for the government of British Columbia. We married in 1990, and I moved *Laiviņa* from Canoe Cove Marina to the front yard of the house Mary and I had bought. Her tired appearance was rightfully not appreciated by my neighbours, so she was moved again and stayed on the hard at Jenkins Marine for a few more years.

In 1997, I became committed to overhauling *Laiviņa*. My career was doing well, we had paid off our mortgage, and our children had grown and were fairly independent. We had funds to spare. Mary and I spent the next year refitting *Laiviņa*, and we launched her on the first day of November in 1998, a grey, late-fall day.

We followed the large boat trailer that carried *Laiviņa* through the twisting roads and down to the launching ramp at Goldstream Marina. Yellow maple leaves lay rotting on the ground, and the salmon had finished spawning. *Laiviņa* slid back into the ocean; her fresh red antifouling paint touched the cold, clean saltwater for the first time in a decade. Her unblemished lily-white topsides glowed in the soft light coming from the heavy overcast sky as she floated free of her restraints.

We spent a few weeks erecting the mast and preparing her for sailing. She had a new mainsail and two new spinnakers, and her other sails had been thoroughly reworked by Leitch and McBride, a local custom sailmaker. She had a second spinnaker pole, and her twin forestays were properly fitted with their own turnbuckles. Her halyards, sheets, guys, and braces were new, and she had a new engine and new lockers below.

In inshore waters, Mary and I sailed to Desolation Sound, Chatterbox Falls in Princess Louisa Inlet, and the Sooke Basin, and we circumnavigated Whitby Island in Washington State. We sailed offshore to San Francisco, staying at the Sausalito Yacht Club, and then voyaged up the Sacramento River almost as far as Stockton. The return voyage from San Francisco to Victoria was hard. We beat into almost constant near-

Figure 30.2: Launching Laiviņa after a refit in 1998

gale conditions, fighting against current and wind. The stainless steel forestay turnbuckle failed from metal fatigue, but fortunately its bronze companion kept the top of the mast in place and we returned home without further incident.

In 2003, we built a waterfront house at Musgrave Landing on Salt Spring Island. *Laiviņa* was moored at the marina in tiny Smeeton Cove, named after Miles and Beryl Smeeton, famous circumnavigators who had made their home on Salt Spring Island close to Musgrave Landing. *Laiviņa* ventured very infrequently from her berth. I was consumed with other aspects of my life.

We sold our home at Musgrave Landing in 2014, and I bought land on Salt Spring Island closer to Ganges on which to build an energy-efficient home. Mary bought a house in Victoria to be closer to our grandchildren.

I moved *Laiviņa* onto my land and lived in her for a year and a half while I built my new home. My primitive life living in a boat so far from the ocean was made more comfortable by the care packages that Mary made up for me. I enjoyed grain salads, soups, bread, and other dishes too complex to cook on the fireplace or stove. Today, *Laiviņa* is waiting for another major overhaul to bring her back into her former glory. At thirty-eight years old, she is in her prime.

Appendix A

World Record

Nobby Clark's First Letter

October 19, 1986

Dear Peter,

Ian Smith of the Guinness Book of Records has just sent me your claim, together with back-up material. I see you have been kept waiting for a long time, which is a pity. I would have written to you a long time ago, but I was unable to trace your address. However, now we are in touch, I can promise you a reply by return of post (my standard practice, unlike 'by organizations'!)

Reading through your 'proofs' I see that you were in actual physical contact with some people. Strictly speaking this is not allowable for a NON STOP circumnavigation. However, this is not so important as acceptance of any sort of supplies during the voyage: food, water, spares, camera film, luxuries (e.g. cigarettes, drink etc.). If necessary, you should be prepared to swear this before a notary. Thirteen singlehanders have claimed nonstop circums to date, two of them have been disqualified for this reason: on taking aboard camera film and nothing else. Knox-Johnston was sufficiently careful that he refused to shake hands with well-wishers when he dried out SUHAILI off Bluff! However, I would not disqualify just for this.

So if you can assure me that you took nothing aboard throughout the voyage, please answer the following:

1. NAME OF YACHT (there seems to be 2 spellings!)
2. DIMENSIONS (LOA x BEAM x DRAUGHT)
3. RIG
4. Your full name; date and place of birth (under which flag did you sail?)
5. ROUTE: You sailed W–E, but please state how many of the 5 southernmost capes you rounded. Obviously GOOD HOPE & CAPE HORN, also LEEUWIN (S.W. Australia), but what about

SOUTH EAST CAPE, TASMANIA (or did you go through BASS STRAIT), and did you round SOUTH WEST CAPE, STEWART ISLAND, NZ?

6. DATE FOR ROUNDING CAPE HORN
7. PLACES AND DATES WHEREVER YOU STOPPED, or were you met at sea by any vessel to whom you passed mail.
8. DISTANCE OFF when you passed SANTA BARBARA on the homeward voyage.
9. POSITION where you crossed your outward track (i.e. tied the knot)
10. Best noon-to-noon run (or 24 hour run); dates, approximate position
11. Best 7-day run; dates, approximate position (i.e.which ocean?)

Once I have these facts I'll be able to isolate your precise record and let you know what you accomplished. Most important of all, please let me have your LOGGED DISTANCE sailed around the world and, if possible, the exact days, hours & minutes from/to SANTA BARBARA. I'm afraid that the happy-go-lucky days of yore have disappeared forever; in the good old days 50 years ago when I began listing Blue Water Game (BWG) records, 2½ years or whatever was good enough for everybody, now the round-the-world racers insist even on seconds!

Congratulations on your fine effort. Depending on your answers to my questions you'll be the 12th singlehander to attempt a nonstop circum.

One last point, if you can spare a photo (colour slide or black and white) of yourself & your yacht I'd be grateful.

Best regards,
Nobby

P.S. Everyone knows me as Nobby, so please feel free.

Nobby Clark's Second Letter

December 3rd, 1986

Dear Peter,

Many thanks for the picture, and for your long and very interesting letter. Let me put your mind at rest: sending and receiving mail is within the 'rules', and so is shaking hands. The official invasion of your yacht at Port Stanley (in view of the war) does not interfere with 'nonstop' because it was official business (you might, for example, have been ordered to heave-to at sea and boarded by the R.N. for inspection—or later by US coastguards suspecting drug smuggling; official invasion cannot alter the 'nonstop' category providing no food, water or other supplies are handed over to the singlehander). Passing mail to the Frenchmen on Kerguélen could have ended your 'nonstop' attempt if the barge had damaged LAIVINA and you were forced into Port-aux-Français, but fortunately you managed to avoid this disaster. I think I can ignore the 'help' given to you by the one Frenchman! The meeting with friends in Otago Harbour did not break any 'rules'.

You're wrong in suspecting you are the only singlehander to go round without radio contact. LES POWLES (GB) had even less money than you, very little food, no radio and no contact with land (he didn't even see any land for 325 days!!). He was on short rations within a week of starting from England in 1980, and he went on to half rations off NZ. He had no food on board for the last 10 days of his circum. A desperate voyage! SOLITAIRE was 34′ 0″ x 10′ 3″ x 5′ 6″, GRP Bermudan Sloop; she rounded all five capes, from/to England W–E (H4), 1980–1.

As I think I mentioned in my previous letter, I have you down as the 12th singlehanded nonstop circumnavigator, and at that time you held the record for the fastest nonstop singlehanded circumnavigation (all sizes of craft included). As you know DODGE MORGAN easily beat your time, but don't despair about this. Many years ago I divided up the sizes of all B.W.G. yachts as follows:

Now that singlehanders are consistently sailing major sized yachts seeking 'fastest' records, the time has come to break the fastest into size classifications.

THEREFORE you hold the record for the fastest singlehanded nonstop circumnavigation in a medium sized yacht: from/to SANTA BARBARA, W–E (H3), 1984–5, taking 236 days 10 hours 45 minutes. You can take this as official: offered by the Guinness Book of Records (but subject to counter-claims, I have to do this because it is impossible to be

Table A.1: World Record Classes

Category	Type	Size
	TINY SIZE	Under 4.00m (13′ 1½″) LOA
SMALL	MIDGET SIZE	From 4.01m to 6.50m (21′ 4″) LOA
	MEDIUM SIZE	From 6.51m to 15.50m (50′ 10″) LOA
LARGE	MAJOR SIZE	From 15.51m to 24.50m (80′ 5″) LOA
	GIANT SIZE	Over 24.50m

absolutely certain about any BWG record since so many nationalities are involved, and so many singlehanders—and other crewed yachts—do not report their voyages, and remain incognito for years). But you are at liberty to quote me as confirming all of the above, and I very much doubt if a counter claim is possible until someone goes out and actually beats your time. In the meantime, if you pass this to your publishers, it will do your book a lot of good.

Incidentally, you forgot to enclose a copy of the letter Penny received from the RYA dated 13.1.85 If you will send me this I'll write to them and put them into the picture. (I'm surprised they didn't know about me—most organizations and journalists do).

I'm so pleased we finally made contact. Sometimes it takes years before I manage to establish facts about a particular record. So if you hear of anybody who is thinking about BWG record, do give them my address. I always reply by return of post. Although this has been my hobby for over 50 years, I appreciate some payment in the initial stages to cover postal charges. So if you refer anyone to me, please take note of this sticker. (I'm not asking you for $5.00, but I will certainly appreciate a copy of your book)

I'll finish with congratulations on your record, and wish you a very happy Christmas and a very prosperous New Year.

All the best,
Nobby.

October 19th, 1986

Dear Peter,

Ian Smith of the Guinness Book of Records has just sent me your claim, together with back-up material. I see you have been left waiting for a long time, which is a pity. I would have written to you a long time ago, but I was unable to trace your address. However, now we are in touch I can promise you a reply by return of post (my standard practice, unlike the 'big organisations'!)

Reading through your 'proofs' I see that you were in actual physical contact with some people. Strictly speaking this is not allowable for a NON STOP circumnavigation. However, this is not so important as acceptance of any sort of supplies during the voyage (apart from receiving or handing over mail). I need your specific assurance that you received nothing to take aboard throughout the voyage: food, water, spares, camera film, luxuries (e.g. cigarettes, drink etc). If necessary, you should be prepared to swear this before a notary. Thirteen singlehanders have claimed nonstop circums to date, two of them have been disqualified for this reason: one taking aboard camera film and nothing else. Knox-Johnston was sufficiently careful that he refused to shake hands with well-wishers when he dried out SUHAILI off Bluff! However, I would not disqualify just for this.

So if you can assure me that you took nothing aboard throughout the voyage (from/to Santa Barbara), please answer the following:

1. NAME OF YACHT (there seem to be 2 spellings!)
2. DIMENSIONS (LOA × BEAM × DRAUGHT)
3. RIG
4. your full name; date and place of birth (under which flag did you sail?)
5. ROUTE: you sailed W-E, but please state how many of the 5 southernmost capes you rounded. Obviously GOOD HOPE & CAPE HORN, also LEEUWIN (S.W Australia), but what about SOUTH EAST CAPE, TASMANIA (or did you go through BASS STRAIT), and did you round SOUTH WEST CAPE, STEWART ISLAND, NZ?
6. DATE FOR ROUNDING CAPE HORN
7. PLACES AND DATES WHEREVER YOU STOPPED, or were met at sea by any vessel to whom you passed mail.
8. DISTANCE OFF when you passed SANTA BARBARA on the homeward voyage.
9. POSITION where you crossed your outward track (i.e. tied the knot)
10. Best noon-to-noon run (or 24 hour run); dates, approx. position.
11. Best 7-day run; dates, approx position (i.e. which ocean?)

Once I have these facts I'll be able to validate your precise record and let you know what you accomplished. Most important of all, please let me have your LOGGED DISTANCE sailed round the world and,

Figure A.1: Nobby's first letter (page 1)

if possible, the exact days, hours & minutes from/to SANTA BARBARA.
I'm afraid that the happy-go-lucky days of yore have disappeared forever;
in the good old days 50 years ago when I began listing Blue Water
Game (BWG) records, 2½ years or whatever was good enough for everybody,
now the round-the-world racers insist even on seconds!

Congratulations on your fine effort. Depending on your answers
to my questions you'll be the 12th singlehander to attempt a nonstop circum.

One last point, if you can spare a photo (colour slide or black &
white) of yourself & your yacht I'd be grateful

Best regards,

Nobby

P.S. Everyone knows me as NOBBY,
so please feel free

By air mail
Par avion
Aerogramme

26p

MR PETER FREEMAN
PO BOX 1622, STATION E
VICTORIA, BC
CANADA V8W 2X7

Royal Mail

Sender's name and address

D. H. CLARKE
"GABLES"
WOOLVERSTONE
IPSWICH
SUFFOLK IP9 1BA
ENGLAND

Postcode

An aerogramme should not contain any enclosure

Figure A.2: Nobby's first letter (page 2)

December 3rd, 1986

Dear Peter,

Many thanks for the picture, and for your long and very interesting letter. Let me put your mind at rest: sending and receiving mail is within the 'rules', and so is shaking hands. The official invasion of your yacht at Port Stanley (in view of the war) does not interfere with 'nonstop' because it was official business (you might, for example, have been ordered to heave-to at sea, and boarded by the R.N. for inspection — or later by the US Coastguards suspecting drug smuggling; official invasion cannot alter the 'nonstop' category providing no food, water or other supplies are handed over to the singlehander). Passing mail to the Frenchman on Kerguelen could have ended your 'nonstop' attempt if the barge had damaged LAIVINA and you were forced into Port aux Francais, but fortunately you managed to avoid this disaster. I think I can ignore the 'help' given to you by the one Frenchman! The meeting with friends in Otago Harbour did not break any 'rules'.

You're wrong in suspecting you are the only singlehander to go round without radio contact. LES POWLES (GB) had even less money than you, very little food, no radio and no contact with land (he didn't even see any land for 325 days!!). He was on short rations within a week of starting from England in 1980, and he went on to half-rations off NZ. He had no food on board for the last 10 days of his circum. A desperate voyage! SOLITAIRE was 34'0 x 10'3" x 5'6", GRP Bermudan sloop; she rounded all 5 capes, from/to England W-E (H4), 1980-1.

As I think I mentioned in my previous letter, I have you down as the 12th singlehanded nonstop circumnavigator, and at that time you held the record for the fastest nonstop singlehanded circumnavigation (all sizes of craft included). As you know, DODGE MORGAN easily beat your time, but don't despair about this. Many years ago I divided up the sizes of all B.W.G. yachts as follows:

SMALL	TINY SIZE	Under 4.00m (13'1½") LOA
	MIDGET SIZE	From 4.01m to 6.50m (21'4") LOA
	MEDIUM SIZE	From 6.51m to 15.50m (50'10") LOA
LARGE	MAJOR SIZE	From 15.51m to 24.50m (80'5") LOA
	GIANT SIZE	Over 24.50m

Now that singlehanders are consistently sailing major-sized yachts seeking 'fastest' records, the time has come to break the 'fastests' into size classifications.

THEREFORE You hold the record for the fastest singlehanded nonstop circumnavigation in a medium-sized yacht: from/to SANTA BARBARA, W-E (H3), 1984-5, taking 236 days 10 hours 45 minutes. You can take this as official: approved by the Guinness Book of Records (but subject to counter-claims; I have to do this because it is impossible to be absolutely certain about any BWG record since so many nationalities are involved, and so many singlehanders — and other crewed yachts — do not report their voyages, and remain incognito for years). But you are at liberty to quote me as confirming all the above, and I very much doubt if a counter-claim is possible until someone goes out and actually beats your time. In the meantime, if you pass this to your publishers, it will do your book a bit of good.

Incidentally, you forgot to enclose the photocopy of the letter Penny received from the RYA dated 13.1.85. If you will send me this I'll write to them and put

Figure A.3: Nobby's second letter (page 1)

Aerogramme, a Royal Mail product

them into the picture (I'm surprised they didn't know about me — most organisations and journalists do).

I'm so pleased we finally made contact. Sometimes it takes years before I manage to establish facts about a particular record. So if you hear of anybody who is thinking about a BWG record, do give them my address. I always reply by return of post. Although this has been my hobby for over 50 years, I appreciate some payment in the initial stages to cover postal charges. So if you refer anyone to me, please take note of this sticker. (I'm not asking you for $5.00, but I will certainly appreciate a copy of your book)

I'll finish with congratulations on your record, and wish you a very happy Christmas and a very prosperous New Year. All the best,

Nobby

A UNIQUE B.W.G. SERVICE

By air mail
Par avion

Royal Mail
1
GREAT BRITAIN
POSTAGE PAID

IPSWICH

MR PETER F. FREEMAN
P.O. BOX 1622, STATION E
VICTORIA
B.C. V8W 2X7
CANADA

Aerogramme

Name and address of sender

D. H. CLARKE
"GABLES"
WOOLVERSTONE
IPSWICH
SUFFOLK IP9 1BA
ENGLAND

Postcode

An aerogramme should not contain any enclosure

Figure A.4: Nobby's second letter (page 2)

Appendix B

Calculations

Maximum Hull Speed of Displacement Vessels

The formula that is used to show the maximum hull speed of a vessel with a displacement hull is:

$$SpeedInKnots = 1.34 \times \sqrt{WaterlineLengthInFeet} \tag{B.1}$$

When *Laiviņa* is sitting becalmed, the waterline length at around twenty-seven feet is considerably less than her length overall at thirty-two feet. Once she is travelling through the water at around seven knots, the waterline at the bow rises up the stem and forward while the waterline at the stern rises up and moves aft to the transom, so the waterline length is close to her length overall.

For practical purposes, when she is travelling close to her maximum theoretical hull speed, the waterline length is a bit under thirty-two feet because although the broad, flatter stern is well supported by the stern wave, the finer bow is not, so I reduce it by eight inches and make the waterline length at speed thirty-one feet and eight inches. If I plug in the figures for *Laiviņa*, it will come out as:

$$SpeedInKnots = 1.34 \times \sqrt{31.3333} \tag{B.2}$$
$$= 1.34 \times 5.597618541 \tag{B.3}$$
$$= 7.5 \tag{B.4}$$

Laiviņa's displacement hull needs to spread water apart and then fold it back together again behind her. As she picks up speed, she creates a pressure wave right in front of the bow. Behind this pressure wave, a trough is formed. Behind that trough, another wave is formed by *Laiviņa*'s speed through the water, a stern wave.

When *Laiviņa* is travelling at three knots, the distance between the bow wave and the stern wave is only five feet. When *Laiviņa* is travelling at a bit over seven and a half knots, the distance between the bow wave and the stern wave is thirty-two feet, her overall length. The depth of the trough is about one-seventh of the wave length, so the trough is about four feet deep. *Laiviņa* needs to be supported by water in order to float. At a speed of seven and a half knots, she is being supported at the bow by the bow wave and at the stern by the stern wave with very little support in the middle.

Speed in Light Winds

In very light winds when sailing slower than a knot, I would get a better figure for *Laiviņa*'s speed by dropping something that would float in the water just ahead of the bow and then time how long it would take to reach the stern. Sometimes, I would spit onto the calm surface of the water and watch the blob of spittle move aft. The formula is:

$$Knots = \frac{BoatLength \times SecondsInHour}{FeetInMile \times TransitTime} \tag{B.5}$$

If a chip of wood takes thirty-eight seconds to go from the bow to the stern over *Laiviņa*'s thirty-two foot length, then:

$$Knots = \frac{32 \times 3600}{6076.1155 \times 38} \tag{B.6}$$

$$= \frac{115200}{230892.389} \tag{B.7}$$

$$= 0.50 \tag{B.8}$$

The table on the next page shows speeds at different transit times.

Table B.1: Speed by Time over Boat Length

Seconds	Speed
10	1.90
11	1.72
12	1.58
13	1.46
14	1.35
15	1.26
16	1.18
17	1.12
18	1.05
19	1.00
20	0.95
21	0.90
22	0.86
23	0.82
24	0.79
25	0.76
26	0.73
27	0.70
28	0.68
29	0.65
30	0.63
31	0.61
32	0.59
33	0.57
34	0.56
35	0.54
36	0.53
37	0.51
38	0.50
39	0.49
40	0.47
41	0.46
42	0.45
43	0.44
44	0.43

Wind Chill

The formula used by Environment Canada for calculating wind chill is:

$$T_{wc} = 13.12 + 0.6215 \times T_a - 11.37 \times V^{0.16} \quad \text{(B.9)}$$
$$+ 0.3965 \times T_a \times V^{0.16} \quad \text{(B.10)}$$

Where:

T_{wc} is the wind chill index
T_a is the air temperature in degrees Celsius
V is the velocity in kilometres per hour

When I was experiencing the storm in the vicinity of Île Kerguélen, the wind was steady at sixty knots (111.12 kilometres per hour) and the air temperature was zero degrees Celsius. Using the formula, the wind chill is:

$$T_{wc} = 13.12 + 0.6215 \times T_a - 11.37 \times V^{0.16} \quad \text{(B.11)}$$
$$+ 0.3965 \times T_a \times V^{0.16} \quad \text{(B.12)}$$
$$= 13.12 + 0.6215 \times 0 - 11.37 \times 111.12^{0.16} \quad \text{(B.13)}$$
$$+ 0.3965 \times 0 \times 111.12^{0.16} \quad \text{(B.14)}$$
$$= 13.12 - 11.37 \times 111.12^{0.16} \quad \text{(B.15)}$$
$$= 13.12 - 11.37 \times 2.124842563 \quad \text{(B.16)}$$
$$= 13.12 - 24.15945994 \quad \text{(B.17)}$$
$$= -11 \quad \text{(B.18)}$$

Invisible Mountain Problem

After sailing from Australia to Canada in 1982, I amused myself by teasing out a solution to what I called the Invisible Mountain problem. I needed to find out how far I was from an island that had a mountain of significant enough height to be seen from far out to sea. I wanted to obtain a position line using the mountain instead of using celestial navigation in case I was unable to see the sun, moon, or stars during overcast conditions.

Assume that you are sighting the mountain from the deck. Your height of eye is three metres above the water, and the height of the mountain is 1,000 metres.

You are sailing on the ocean and heading for an island of volcanic origin that has a high mountain. The island and peak of the mountain are shown in your charts with the height of the mountain noted.

You sail towards this island, which you eventually sight many miles from the island's shore. You see only the uppermost part of the mountain because of the curvature of the earth. The rest of the mountain is below the horizon. As you sail closer and closer, more of the mountain appears to come out of the ocean. Eventually you are close enough to see it all. I call this the Fully Visible Point.

With the curvature of the earth and based on the height of your eye being three metres above the surface of the ocean, the sea horizon is about three and a third nautical miles away, a bit over six kilometres. You don't get to see the whole island until you are this distance from its shore. At this spot, you can calculate how far you are from the mountain, knowing its height above the ocean and by using a sextant to measure the angle between the top of the mountain and the water licking at the base of the mountain. It's basic trigonometry.

$$\tan(A_{tb}) = \frac{H_m}{D_{em}} \tag{B.19}$$

$$\begin{aligned} A_{tb} &= \arctan\left(\frac{H_m}{D_{em}}\right) && \text{(B.20)} \\ &= \arctan\left(\frac{1}{6.183}\right) && \text{(B.21)} \\ &= \arctan\left(0.1617337862\right) && \text{(B.22)} \\ &= 9^\circ\ 11.227' && \text{(B.23)} \end{aligned}$$

You would read a bit over nine degrees on the sextant when able to first see the whole mountain at the Fully Visible Point. If closer to the mountain than the Fully Visible Point, you could calculate the distance from the mountain by using the formula in a transposed manner:

$$D_{em} = \frac{H_m}{\tan(A_{tb})} \tag{B.24}$$

Where:

A_{tb} is the angle between the mountain's top and bottom read by the observer in degrees
H_m is the height of the mountain in kilometres
D_{em} is the distance from the mountain to the observer's eye in kilometres

Assume there is a bright rotating light on the top of the mountain. At night, when approaching the mountain from far out to sea when the whole mountain is still below the horizon, the first visible thing is the beam of light or "loom of the light" sweeping the night sky, not the light itself as it is below the horizon. Eventually the light will be visible as it comes up from below the horizon. Knowing the height of the light above the water and the height of your eye above the water, you can gauge how far you are away from the light and the top of the mountain using *Norie's Nautical Tables*, a set of mathematical tables first published in 1803. The tables calculate this distance based on the diameter of the earth.

You can get a position line (or in reality a position circle) when you first see the top of the mountain when it is level with the horizon. You can also get a position line (or circle) from the point where you can first see the base of the mountain, that is, the sea horizon distance from the base of the mountain, or at the Fully Visible Point. You can get an infinite number of position circles from the Fully Visible Point right up to the shoreline of the base of the mountain.

The challenge is to obtain a position line between the point where you can just detect the top of the mountain level with the horizon and where you can see the whole mountain at the Fully Visible Point. Given that mountains usually do not have bright lights atop them and that you will most likely be approaching the mountain during daylight hours, you will not detect the mountain until a substantial amount of it appears above the horizon.

My Invisible Mountain problem was to find a position line after measuring the angle of the top of the mountain to the water horizon when only a portion of the mountain was above the water horizon.

Two years before, I figured out an iterative solution to the problem. The idea was to take a guess and then feed that guess into a formula that returned a better guess. The process was repeated until the differences between successive guesses became so small that there was no point in refining the answer any more.

I felt that there must be a simpler, more direct solution. I started on the problem as I was crossing the doldrums on the outbound part of my voyage and solved it a few weeks later. The cabin was littered with the fruits of my labour spilled over the chart table. A pile of sheets, some taped together, showed long sprawling trigonometrical formulas that extended over multiple sheets of letter-sized paper. Eventually, I arrived at a solution that was not iterative. I revised it even more and found an even simpler solution.

As I sailed towards a mountain that was completely below the horizon, I would reach a point where the top of the mountain was precisely level with the horizon. Using my sextant, if I read the angle between the top of the mountain and the sea horizon, it would be zero degrees. If I continued to sail towards the mountain, it would slowly appear to rise up above the horizon, exposing more and more of its flanks. I would eventually reach the precise spot where the complete mountain would be exposed, that is, at the Fully Visible Point. This would occur at the point where:

$$D_{es} = D_{em} \tag{B.25}$$

Where:

$\mathbf{D_{es}}$ is the distance from the observer to the sea horizon
$\mathbf{D_{em}}$ is the distance from the observer to the mountain

Assuming my eye is three metres above the surface of the ocean, it can easily be calculated. A simple formula is:

$$D_{es} = 3.57\sqrt{H_e} \tag{B.26}$$
$$= 3.57\sqrt{3} \tag{B.27}$$
$$= 3.57 \times 1.732050808 \tag{B.28}$$
$$= 6.183\ kilometres \tag{B.29}$$
$$= 6.183 \times 0.5399568 \tag{B.30}$$
$$= 3.338\ nautical\ miles \tag{B.31}$$

An even more simple and approximate formula can be used when the height of eye was in feet and the distance to the sea horizon can be calculated in nautical miles:

$$D_{es} = \sqrt{H_e} \tag{B.32}$$
$$= \sqrt{9.8425197} \tag{B.33}$$
$$= 3.137\ nautical\ miles \tag{B.34}$$

A more universal formula that will work with any unit, kilometres, nautical miles, statute miles, metres, feet, etc., is:

$$D_{es} = \sqrt{2 \times R \times H_e} \tag{B.35}$$
$$= \sqrt{2 \times 6,371 \times 3 \times 0.001} \tag{B.36}$$
$$= \sqrt{38.226} \tag{B.37}$$
$$= 6.183\ kilometres \tag{B.38}$$
$$= 6.183 \times 0.5399568 \tag{B.39}$$
$$= 3.338\ nautical\ miles \tag{B.40}$$

Where:

D_{es} is the distance from the observer to the sea horizon in kilometres

H_e is the height of the observer's eye above the sea surface in kilometres (3 metres or 0.003 kilometres in this example)

R is the radius of the earth in kilometres

The radius of the earth and the height of eye must be expressed in the same units, i.e., metres or feet or nautical miles.

Similarly, I can work out the distance from an observer on top of the mountain looking to the sea horizon.

$$D_{ms} = \sqrt{2 \times R \times H_m} \tag{B.41}$$
$$= \sqrt{2 \times 6,371 \times 1} \tag{B.42}$$
$$= \sqrt{12,742} \tag{B.43}$$
$$= 112.880 \ kilometres \tag{B.44}$$
$$= 112.880 \times 0.5399568 \tag{B.45}$$
$$= 60.951 \ nautical \ miles \tag{B.46}$$

Where:

D_{ms} is the distance from the mountain to the sea horizon in kilometres
H_m is the height of the mountain above the sea surface converted to kilometres. (1,000 metres or 1 kilometre in this example)
R is the radius of the earth in kilometres

The radius of the earth and the height of the mountain must be expressed in the same units, i.e., metres or feet or nautical miles.

These calculations ignore the effect of atmospheric refraction caused by the ocean being hotter or colder than the air above it. They also ignore the fact that the base of the mountain is closer to the observer than the top of the mountain, but the calculations are sufficiently accurate to obtain a position line when still at a safe distance from the mountain. Other navigational methods should be used when reefs or other navigational hazards are present in the zone measured by this Invisible Mountain formula.

The Extreme Range is the furthest distance that an observer can see the top of an object such as a lighthouse or mountain when at sea, assuming there is no intervening object such as an island. I call this the Extreme Range Point.

To find the distance at which I will first see the top of the mountain as I sail towards it, I add the distance from my position to the sea horizon to the distance from the top of a mountain to the sea horizon from the perspective of an observer on top of the mountain.

$$D_{em} = D_{ms} + D_{es} \tag{B.47}$$
$$= 60.951 + 3.338 \tag{B.48}$$
$$= 64.289 \; nautical \; miles \tag{B.49}$$

Where:

$\mathbf{D_{em}}$ is the distance from the observer to the mountain
$\mathbf{D_{ms}}$ is the distance from the mountain to the sea horizon
$\mathbf{D_{es}}$ is the distance from the observer to the sea horizon

The theory behind my solution to the Invisible Mountain problem is based on the knowledge that I can:

- Calculate the distance to the sea horizon from my eye
- Calculate the distance to the sea horizon from the mountain top
- Calculate the extreme range distance by adding the two previously calculated distances together
- Assume that I would read an angle of zero degrees between the top of the mountain and the horizon when I was at the extreme range
- Calculate the angle I would read between the top of the mountain and the sea horizon when I am at the sea horizon distance from the mountain

Two factors independently cause the measured angle between the top of the mountain and the sea horizon to increase proportionally to the decrease in distance from the Extreme Range Point to the Fully Visible Point.

First, even if the ocean were flat instead of spherical, the measured angle would increase as the mountain is approached solely based on the distance. Halfway between the Extreme Range Point and Fully Visible Point, the measured angle would be halfway between those measured at the Extreme Range Point and Fully Visible Point respectively. It is using the principle of proportionality.

Second, because the ocean is on the surface of a sphere, each nautical mile sailed from the Extreme Range Point to the Fully Visible Point increases the measured angle by one minute of arc because a nautical mile is an angular measurement of one minute of arc subtended at the earth's centre.

Together, the two factors cause an increase in the measured angle proportional to the decrease in distance when sailing from the Extreme Range Point to the Fully Visible Point. Using the principle of proportionality enables the formula to be less complicated.

When I first worked out an iterative solution, the formula was fairly straightforward but complex in operation. Later I found a non-iterative solution, but it involved a lot of trigonometrical terms and made the solution unwieldy.

For example, if the distance between the Extreme Range Point and the Fully Visible Point were forty nautical miles (NM) and the measured angle between the top of the mountain and the sea horizon at the Fully Visible Point were eight degrees, then:

- 40 NM from the Fully Visible Point, the angle would be 0°
- 30 NM from the Fully Visible Point, the angle would be 2°
- 20 NM from the Fully Visible Point, the angle would be 4°
- 10 NM from the Fully Visible Point, the angle would be 6°
- 0 NM from the Fully Visible Point, the angle would be 8°

The general formula is:

$$D_{em} = D_{er} \times \frac{A_{ts}}{\arctan\left(\frac{H_m}{D_{es}}\right)} + D_{es} \tag{B.50}$$

As an example, assume a mountain height of 1,000 metres, a height of eye above the water surface of 3 metres, and a measured sextant angle of 4° 35.613′, which is half of the angle of 9° 11.227′ that would be measured at the Fully Visible Point.

$$D_{em} = D_{er} \times \frac{A_{ts}}{\arctan\left(\frac{H_m}{D_{es}}\right)} + D_{es} \tag{B.51}$$

$$= (D_{ms} + D_{es}) \times \frac{A_{ts}}{\arctan\left(\frac{H_m}{D_{es}}\right)} + D_{es} \tag{B.52}$$

$$= \left(3.57\sqrt{H_m} + 3.57\sqrt{H_m}\right) \times \frac{A_{ts}}{\arctan\left(\frac{H_m}{3.57\sqrt{H_m}}\right)} + 3.57\sqrt{H_m} \tag{B.53}$$

$$= \left(3.57\sqrt{1000} + 3.57\sqrt{3}\right) \times \frac{4.5932^\circ}{\arctan\left(\frac{1}{3.57\sqrt{3}}\right)} + 3.57\sqrt{3} \tag{B.54}$$

$$= 112.880 \times \frac{4.5932^\circ}{9.1865^\circ} + 6.183 \tag{B.55}$$

$$= 112.880 \times 0.5 + 6.183 \tag{B.56}$$

$$= 62.623 \textit{ kilometres} \tag{B.57}$$

$$= 62.623 \times 0.5399568 \tag{B.58}$$

$$= 33.813 \textit{ nautical miles} \tag{B.59}$$

Where:

- $\mathbf{D_{em}}$ is the required distance to the mountain
- $\mathbf{D_{er}}$ is the Extreme Range Distance, i.e., the distance from the mountain when the top of the mountain is level with the horizon
- $\mathbf{A_{ts}}$ is the angle measured between the top of the mountain and the sea horizon expressed in degrees and decimals of a degree (D.dddd)
- $\mathbf{H_m}$ is the height of the mountain expressed in metres
- $\mathbf{H_e}$ is the height of eye on the boat above the sea surface in metres
- $\mathbf{D_{ms}}$ is the distance from the top of the mountain to the sea horizon in metres
- $\mathbf{D_{es}}$ is the distance from the observer on the boat to the sea horizon in metres

Halfway between those two points I would read an angle of half of 9°11.227′ or 4°35.613′.

Appendix C

Repairs

Bolts

1. Cut a length of threaded rod with a hacksaw.
2. Thread a nut on the end exposing a millimetre of rod.
3. Centre-punch the thread.
4. Peen over a millimetre of protruding rod to lock the nut in place.

Grommets

1. First repair the sail.
2. Use a length of stainless steel tube the size of the grommet.
3. Heat the end of the rod until it is red hot over the stove.
4. Burn a neat hole through the many layers of sailcloth.
5. Cut pieces of this tubing between one and two centimetres in length depending on the number of layers of sailcloth and the size of the tube.
6. Clamp a ball-peen hammer in the vice with the ball uppermost.
7. Hold the tube on top of the ball.
8. Slip a washer over the tube.
9. Slip the sail over the tube.
10. Slip another washer over the tube.
11. Place a second ball-peen hammer on top of the tube.
12. Hit the ball-peen hammer with a blacksmith's hammer.
13. Keep striking until the tube is folded outwards over both washers to produce a grommet.

Sealing a breach

First steps:

1. Immediately shove any available material into the hole to slow the influx of water (squabs, cushions, life jackets, clothing, or whatever is handy).
2. Brace the material in place against the water pressure.
3. Heave to on a tack that places the hole higher in the water or even above the water to reduce the pressure (if on deck and the hole can be seen, do this step first).
4. Bucket water out of the inside of the boat.
5. Pump the bilge.
6. Monitor the inflow rate.

Once the situation is stable, a better seal may be created by using the smaller, thick rubber collision mat, assuming the hole is large enough:

1. Hold the end of the line in the right hand.
2. Hold the line close to where it went through the hole in the collision mat in the left hand.
3. Force the mat through the hole from the inside.
4. Make sure that the rubber wraps around the left hand to protect it from jagged edges.
5. Once the mat is on the outside of the hull, pull the mat back a bit with the line until it is sucked against the hull.
6. Secure the line to something strong inside the boat.
7. Seal the inside of the breach with cushions, plastic, tape, or other material.

Should the hole be too small or in a place where the previous method will not work, use the larger, thinner collision mat and fother the hole from the outside if the position of the hole allows. Most likely the hole will be in the bow or forward on the port or starboard side:

1. Attach a line to each corner of the mat.
2. Go on deck with the mat.

3. After passing two of the lines under the boat, work the mat into position over the hole (in good weather, go over the side).
4. Secure the mat tightly in position.

Major Mast Repair

Before leaving Victoria, I conducted an experiment to see if I could lower and raise my mast using only the equipment I carried on board. I adopted a "falling derrick" system, using the spinnaker pole as a strut. The test was successful, and I erected the mast the same way after I had replaced the old rigging with its new stainless steel set. If I had been dis-masted, I knew that I could re-erect the mast at sea.

Extreme care needs to be exercised. All lines and securing must be checked many times throughout the lowering process. All lines used must be Dacron, not nylon, as nylon stretches.

1. Slide the spinnaker pole ring on the mast track and set it to the lowest position.
2. Clip the spinnaker pole to the ring.
3. Secure the end of spinnaker pole to the mast with lashings as a precaution.
4. Loosen the forestay turnbuckle.
5. Detach the forestay eye from the turnbuckle.
6. Clip the other end of the spinnaker pole to the forestay eye and secure with lashings as a precaution.
7. Shackle a strong turning block to the bow fitting.
8. Attach at least a twelve-millimetre-diameter Dacron line to the forestay eye. (This line, called the initial lowering line, will be used to bring the mast down from a vertical until the mast is level with the top of the jury mizzen-mast.)
9. Lead the initial lowering line through the turning block and then aft down either the port or starboard side to a headsail sheet winch.
10. Wind the initial lowering line onto the headsail sheet winch and take up the tension until it is tight.

11. Attach two stabilizer lines of at least ten millimetres diameter to the forestay end of the spinnaker pole and lead each line to the port and starboard side, respectively.
12. Temporarily secure the stabilizer lines to the cap shroud chain plates.
13. Using a heavy mooring line, secure the base of the mast by tying a clove hitch in the centre of the mooring line.
14. Lead one end of the mooring line forward and secure it to the base of the port stanchion that is forward of the mast, so the line makes approximately a forty-five-degree angle to the fore and aft line.
15. Lead the other end of the mooring line forward and secure it to the base of the starboard stanchion that is forward of the mast, so the line makes approximately a forty-five-degree angle to the fore and aft line.
16. Using a second heavy mooring line, secure the base of the mast by tying a clove hitch in the centre of the mooring line.
17. Lead one end of the mooring line aft and secure it to the base of the port stanchion that is aft of the mast, so the line makes approximately a forty-five-degree angle to the fore and aft line.
18. Lead the other end of the mooring line aft and secure it to the base of the starboard stanchion that is aft of the mast, so the line makes approximately a forty-five-degree angle to the fore and aft line. (This will hold the base of the mast in position.)
19. Remove the boom from the mast.
20. Attach a turning block to the clew end of the boom.
21. Rove a ten-millimetre-diameter line through the turning block and secure the ends. (This line, called the final lowering line, will be used to lower the mast the final distance to the deck.)
22. Measure the distance from the stern at the pushpit rails to the base of the mast.
23. Measure the same distance up the mast from the base of the mast and note the location.
24. Climb the mast with one end of the final lowering line.

25. Attach one end of the final lowering line to the mast using a fisherman's bend with the standing part coming away from the forward part of the mast.
26. Lash the bitter end to the standing part of the line.
27. Attach a turning block at the tack end of the boom.
28. Lead the final lowering line through this turning block to the spare sheet winch.
29. Secure the other end of the final lowering line to a deck cleat or pushpit rail.
30. Attach two ten-millimetre-diameter lines to the clew end of the boom to be used as stays.
31. Erect the boom vertically as a jury mizzen-mast by securing it amidships to the pushpit rails.
32. Secure one of the rope stays of the jury mizzen-mast to the base of a port stanchion using a trucker's hitch.
33. Tension the rope stay.
34. Lash the hitches so the knot cannot fail.
35. Secure one of the rope stays of the jury mizzen-mast to the base of a starboard stanchion using a trucker's hitch.
36. Tension the rope stay.
37. Lash the hitches so the knot cannot fail.
38. Carefully loosen off the cap shroud turnbuckles a small amount so they have no tension but very little slack.
39. Carefully loosen off the forward lower shroud turnbuckles.

The lowering process starts by easing off the initial lowering line a small amount until the forward lower shrouds draw tight. The masthead should move aft a bit. The slack can be taken up in the final lowering line until it is firm. This will stop the mast from swaying from side to side too much. The forward lower shrouds will be loosened some more and this process repeated until the forward lower shrouds are completely disconnected.

As this process is repeated so that the initial lowering line is loosened about thirty centimetres each time, the tension on the spinnaker pole stabilizer lines needs to be constantly adjusted so they are snug. The cap shrouds may need to be loosened from time to time, and the slack must be taken up in the final lowering line. The heavy mooring lines holding the base of the mast will need to be constantly adjusted as the mast slowly comes down.

At first, the spinnaker pole, the forestay eye, and the mast will naturally want to lie in a vertical plane. About the time that the mast has almost reached the level of the jury mizzen-mast, the spinnaker pole will want to flop over to the port or starboard side. The spinnaker pole stabilizer lines are important at this stage, so they must be adjusted with care as the spinnaker pole must be kept in a vertical plane to prevent the mast from crashing to the deck.

As soon as the mast is starting to slide down the side of the jury mizzen-mast, all the slack in the final lowering line can be taken in and the final lowering line can take the weight of the mast. The mast can be lowered the remaining distance to the deck by carefully loosening off the rope stay holding the top of the mizzen-mast secure to get it out of the way.

The process is reversed when re-erecting the mast.

Appendix D

Self-Steering

To have a sailboat steer itself efficiently, a perfect system would need to mimic a skilled helmsperson who functions reactively and proactively to changes in course and who keeps the vessel within an acceptable tolerance.

Reactive When hand steering, a skilled helmsperson will allow a vessel to go off course a certain amount before moving the tiller or turning the wheel to bring the vessel back on course.

Proactive Bringing the vessel back onto the correct course, a skilled helmsperson will move the tiller towards the balanced position a bit before the correct course is reached to avoid going past the correct course.

Reactive/Proactive When sailing with a wind coming over the quarter and the seas striking the stern at an angle, a skilled helmsperson will proactively anticipate the effect of the seas attempting to turn the vessel into the wind by steering more downwind while at the same time reacting to the sensation of the approaching sea lifting the stern.

Unattended self-steering should maintain an even course within an efficient tolerance. For example, if the vessel needs to stay on a close-hauled course on the port tack, a self-steering system should maintain that course within a few degrees. If the vessel needs to sail a broad-reaching course on the starboard tack, it should maintain that course within ten degrees. A course could be either a compass course or a course relative to the direction of the wind.

Course relative to compass A self-steering system that keeps a boat on a compass course won't be able to take advantage of the efficiencies gained from small changes in wind direction and strength.

If the wind were to shift ten degrees on a close-hauled course, the sails would either be constantly luffing and producing very little power or creating drag from a large turbulent area formed on the back of the sails. With larger wind shifts, the sails might be damaged by flogging, or the vessel might heave to by itself or gybe, possibly causing damage.

Course relative to the wind A self-steering system that keeps a boat on a course that is relative to the wind will be able to follow the wind when it makes minor shifts, keeping the sails working at maximum efficiency. It may or may not be able to compensate for more than minor changes in wind strength, and unless the skipper conducts regular course checks, it may even end up sailing in the opposite direction.

A self-steering system will only work properly when all the forces are accounted for. The relevant factors include:

Sail balance Sails must be adjusted so that the rudder is close to amidships and has no weather helm or lee helm. For example, the position of the spinnaker pole and the position of the spinnaker clew must be adjusted so the centre of effort of the spinnaker is to weather of the central fore and aft line of the vessel to compensate for the centre of effort of the mainsail being on the leeward side of the fore and aft line.

Wind speed variation If the wind increases on a close-hauled course, the vessel will heel more, and the centre of effort of the sails will move to the port or starboard side of the central fore and aft line of the vessel. This will increase the weather helm and may require either the self-steering, the sails, or the helm to be adjusted.

Swell Swells can force a vessel to broach, so a self-steering system needs to anticipate the turning force applied by the swell upon the vessel. Swells can also cause the vessel to surge forward and increase speed, in turn causing the apparent wind to move forward.

Angle of heel As the vessel heels over, the centre of effort of the sails moves more to leeward, inducing a turning force on the vessel and attempts to turn the vessel into the wind.

Apparent wind directional changes There are three factors that can change the apparent wind direction:

1. Increase in wind speed
2. Increase in boat speed
3. Change in boat heading relative to the wind direction

As a vessel deviates from its course, the angle that the apparent wind makes to the fore and aft line of the vessel may change. I say "may" because there are situations in light winds where the vessel can deviate from the true wind, yet the apparent wind angle stays the same, particularly when sailing on a broad reach in light airs.

Wind Vane

The basic concept is for the vessel to have a wind vane, similar in principle to the weather cock atop barns that farmers use to see the direction from which the wind blows. The cock always faces into the wind. On a sailboat, the wind vane always points into the wind. This is a sensor that measures the wind direction and provides an output in the form of its rotational position.

Should the vessel deviate from its course, for the briefest of time, the wind vane no longer points into the wind before the wind pressure on one side of the wind vane increases and pushes the vane around until it is again pointing into the wind.

If one holds the wind vane and stops it from "weather cocking" and pointing into the wind, as the boat goes more and more off course, eventually the wind will be striking one side of the vane at right angles. The wind will be applying the greatest force on the vane and subsequently the greatest turning momentum. This force as a percentage of the maximum force at other angles can be calculated. The formula is:

Table D.1: Wind Pressure

Angle	% Maximum
0	0.0%
5	8.7%
10	17.4%
15	25.9%
20	34.2%
25	42.3%
30	50.0%
35	57.4%
40	64.3%
45	70.7%
50	76.6%
55	81.9%
60	86.6%
65	90.6%
70	94.0%
75	96.6%
80	98.5%
85	99.6%
90	100.0%

$$PercentMaxForce = \sin(WindAngle) \tag{D.1}$$

Vane-to-Tiller System

To correct the vessel and put it back on course, the input provided by the wind turning the wind vane would need to produce an output that would turn the boat by using a rudder. To understand the forces and processes involved, consider a tiller attached to the rudder instead of a wheel. If we mechanically connected the wind vane directly to the tiller and expected it to move the main rudder, the vane would need to be very large, potentially a square metre in size or greater. The wind would need to be strong enough to turn the tiller sufficiently to bring the vessel back on course.

Practically speaking, such a system would work only a small percentage of the time and would need to be under constant attendance by a crew member. The huge wind vane needed would become a liability in gale-force or storm-force winds.

Vane-to-Servo-Blade System

The solution to problems inherent in a vane-to-tiller system is having a more compact wind vane turning a long, narrow, and balanced blade rudder in the water. If a vessel were sailing at four knots, turning this servo blade at an angle of thirty degrees would require little effort from the wind vane but would generate tremendous force on the blade. This force would be much greater than the force used to turn the tiller in a vane-to-tiller system.

The long, narrow, and balanced blade would attempt to force the stern to port or to starboard and thus turn the vessel; however, it still would not have sufficient force to actually turn the vessel, except perhaps in more gentle conditions. The force it generated could still be harnessed by connecting it to the main tiller.

The commercial Aries system uses this principle. The blade in the water is hinged so it can swing from port to starboard, and attached lines on either side of the blade are led through turning blocks and connected to the end of the tiller.

This system still has its weaknesses. The main problem is that it turns the main rudder with no ability to judge how much to turn the rudder. It can easily turn it too much, with the result that it overcorrects, sending the vessel swinging wildly back on course and then continuing to go to the other side of the course before wildly swinging back again. The result is that the vessel travels a route that can swing through up to ninety degrees, going off course forty-five degrees on one side of the course line and forty-five degrees on the other side of the course line.

Vane-to-Trim-Tab and Auxiliary Rudder System

The oversteering problems that occur when connecting the servo blade to the main tiller are solved by hanging a smaller balanced auxiliary rudder off the transom. The main rudder is used first to balance the boat, and the auxiliary rudder is used to make course corrections. The tiller of the main rudder is held in place by two lines, one from the port side and the other from the starboard side. Thc lines are secured with clove hitches to the tiller and are easily slipped off the end of the tiller when manual intervention is required. The main rudder is set with the correct amount of weather or lee helm to achieve balance.

To turn the auxiliary rudder, a narrow blade or trim tab is attached to the trailing edge of the auxiliary rudder. The trim tab now needs to turn only a smaller high-aspect-ratio balanced auxiliary rudder, so components can be smaller as the forces are lesser.

Feedback System

There is still one oversteering problem that remains. When driving a car down a winding road, drivers get feedback from the road in a visual form, telling them that the curve they are steering around will be coming to an end soon. The driver starts straightening the wheels before the car is out of the curve so that just as the vehicle leaves the curve and enters the straight, the wheels are straight.

Similarly, we need a self-steering system to anticipate the fact that the vessel is almost back on course and to start reducing the angle the auxiliary rudder makes to the fore and aft centreline and thus reduce the turning effect. Unfortunately the wind vane does not provide input to the auxiliary rudder to tell it to stop turning until it is back on course. It tells the auxiliary rudder that it is back on course only after the vessel has passed its course line while the auxiliary rudder is still turning the vessel. A good self-steering design needs to incorporate a feedback mechanism.

This is achieved by sending output from the auxiliary rudder as input to the wind vane, which in turn sends output back to the auxiliary rudder. The auxiliary rudder continually outputs its turning angle, or its angle to the fore and aft line of the vessel, as input into the wind vane.

The steps in this process are as follows:

1. The wind vane system axis turns in response to the vessel going off course.
2. Because the wind vane system axis is directly attached to the trim tab axis, it turns the trim tab in a synchronized fashion.
3. There is a slight delay, less than a second, before the trim tab causes the auxiliary rudder to turn.
4. Because the auxiliary rudder axis is directly attached to the wind vane blade axis, it turns the wind vane blade in a synchronized fashion and lessens its angle of attack to the wind.
5. There is a slight delay, a fraction of a second, before the wind vane blade causes the wind vane system to turn.
6. The wind vane system now brings the trim tab closer to the fore and aft line.
7. There is a slight delay, less than a second, before the trim tab causes the auxiliary rudder to move back closer to the fore and aft line.
8. The auxiliary rudder turns the vessel less.
9. The amount of rotation of the auxiliary rudder, directly and in a synchronized fashion, turns the wind vane blade and increases its angle of attack to the wind.
10. This process is repeated over and over and has the effect of reducing the turning effect of the auxiliary rudder as the vessel gets closer and closer to the correct course.

The key reason for this design success is based on the natural delay that occurs between the moment in time that the trim tab turns and the later moment in time when it forces the auxiliary rudder to turn. It is this delay that allows the wind vane, the trim tab, and the auxiliary rudder to reach a point of stability between the angular momentum or turning moment and how far off course the vessel has gone. The further off course the vessel, the greater the turning moment.

The feedback effect allows the vessel to come back to its correct course as the auxiliary rudder and the trim tab slowly move closer to the fore and aft line synchronized with the vessel approaching its proper course. It is just like the driver of a car coming around a corner bringing the vehicle wheels back into a straight line as the car reaches the straight road ahead.

Power Multiplication System

Unlike the traditional weather cock, the wind vane has a built-in power multiplication system. The movement of the wind vane is like that of the windscreen wipers of a bus or truck, where the wiper blade stays vertical as it sweeps from side to side, as opposed to the wipers of a car, which sweep across the windscreen like a door opening.

An almost parallel control arm allows the wind vane to maintain almost the same angle of attack to the wind after the vessel has gone off course. The amount by which the control arm is away from the parallel allows the wind vane to ultimately feather into the wind, but only after it has turned considerably. This ensures that the trim tab will be turned significantly.

Design and Construction

I was working in Australia in 1982 for an engineering and surveying company doing property surveys. I spent a number of months designing and drafting a self-steering system for *Laiviņa.* An engineering company in Noosaville built the components using a combination of stainless steel, aluminum, and hot-dip galvanized steel.

As this was a prototype, I designed in numerous adjustments to balance the auxiliary rudder, the trim tab, the force multiplier in the wind vane, and the feedback quantity. Sailing *Laiviņa* to Canada, I was able to determine the best adjustments to balance the auxiliary rudder and trim tab.

In the spring of 1984, I built casting patterns, and Smith Brothers Foundry in Victoria cast and machined bronze rudder gudgeons that had built-in gudgeons for the trim tab shaft. They also made a single stainless steel pintle to replace the two existing hot-dip galvanized ones.

The following are plans I drafted in 1982 while working in Noosa Heads prior to my voyage to Canada with Arvita. The drawings are of the prototype system. I later simplified some of the fittings because I did not need the adjustments in balancing the auxiliary rudder and trim tab. I also used nylon ball bearings for the linkage arms instead of the corrodible steel ones that I had originally fitted.

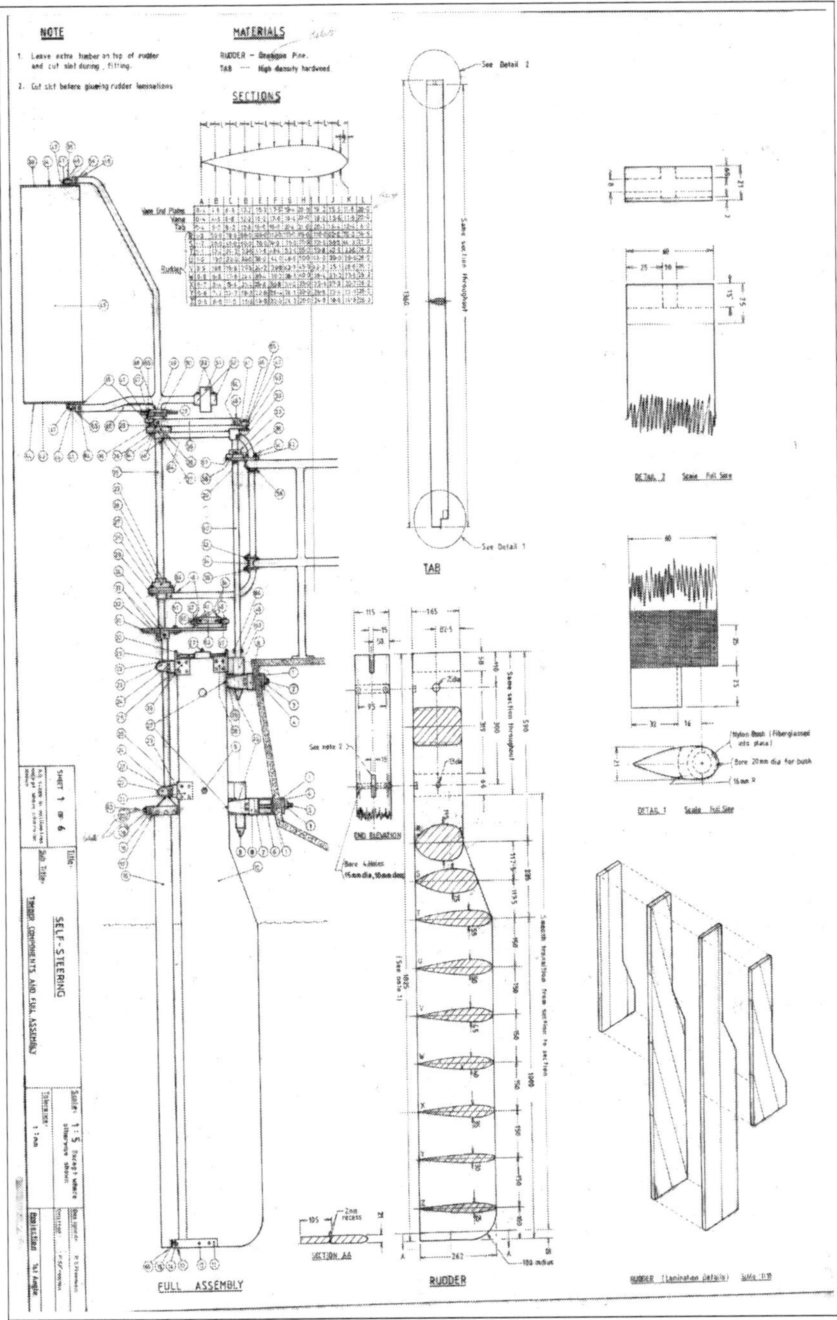

Figure D.1: Self-steering system (sheet 1)

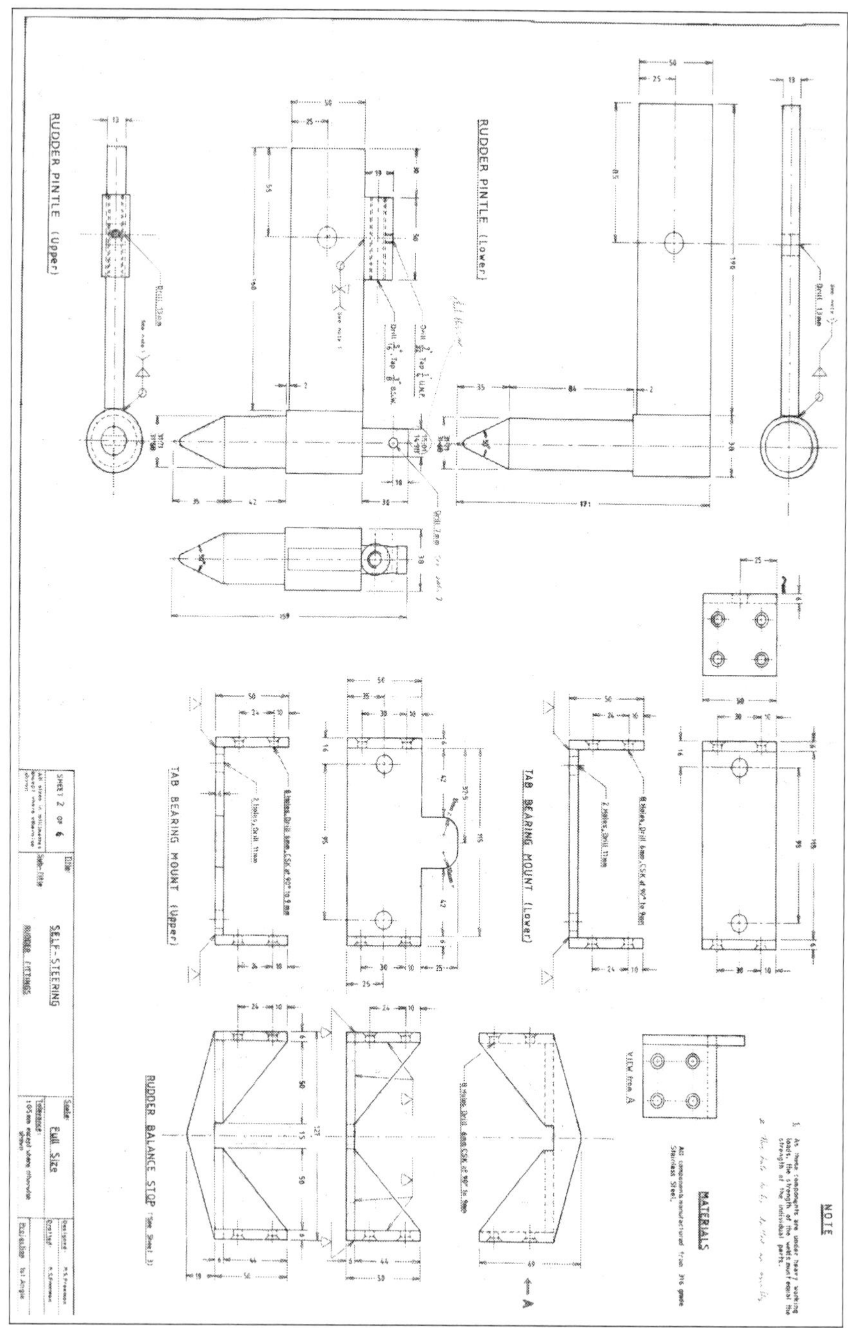

Figure D.2: Self-steering system (sheet 2)

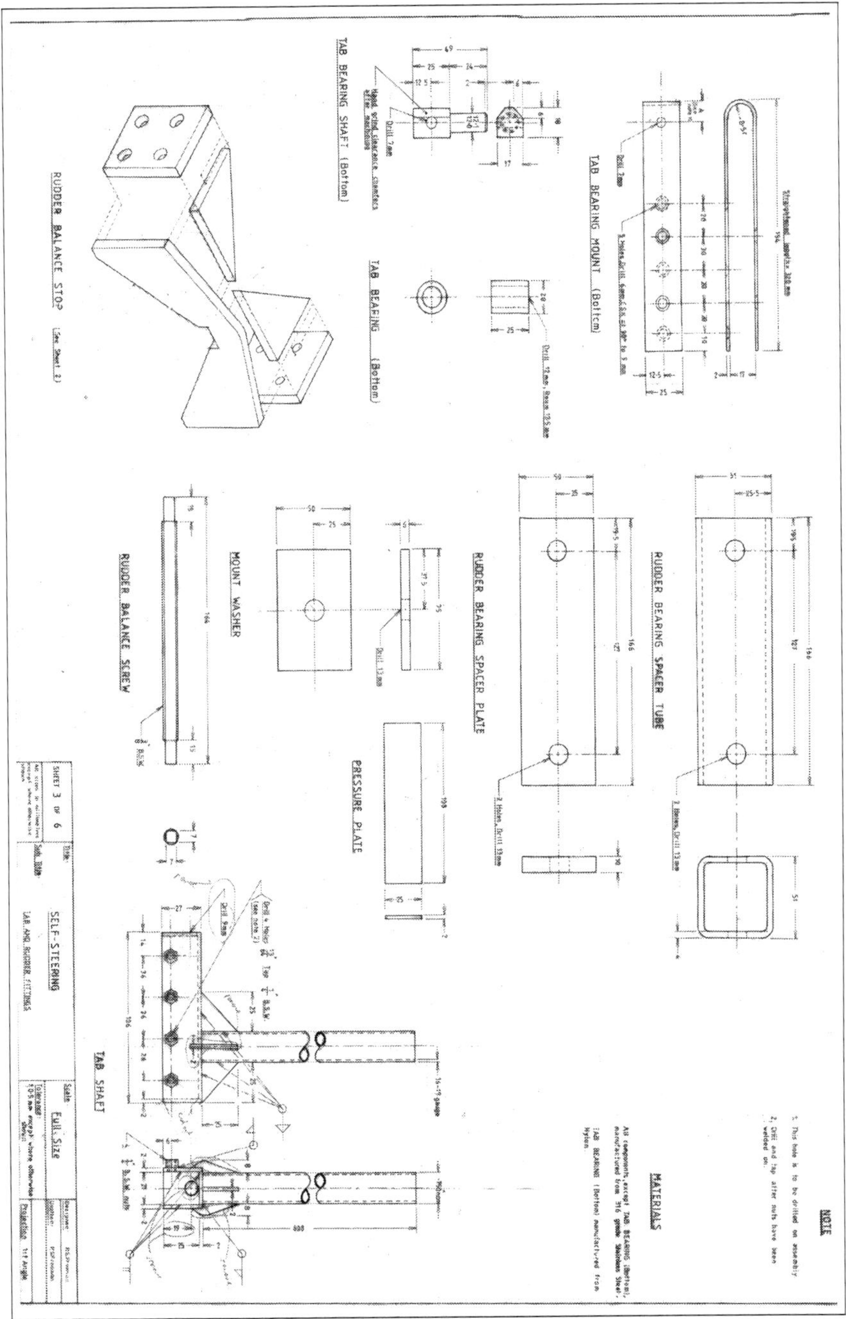

Figure D.3: Self-steering system (sheet 3)

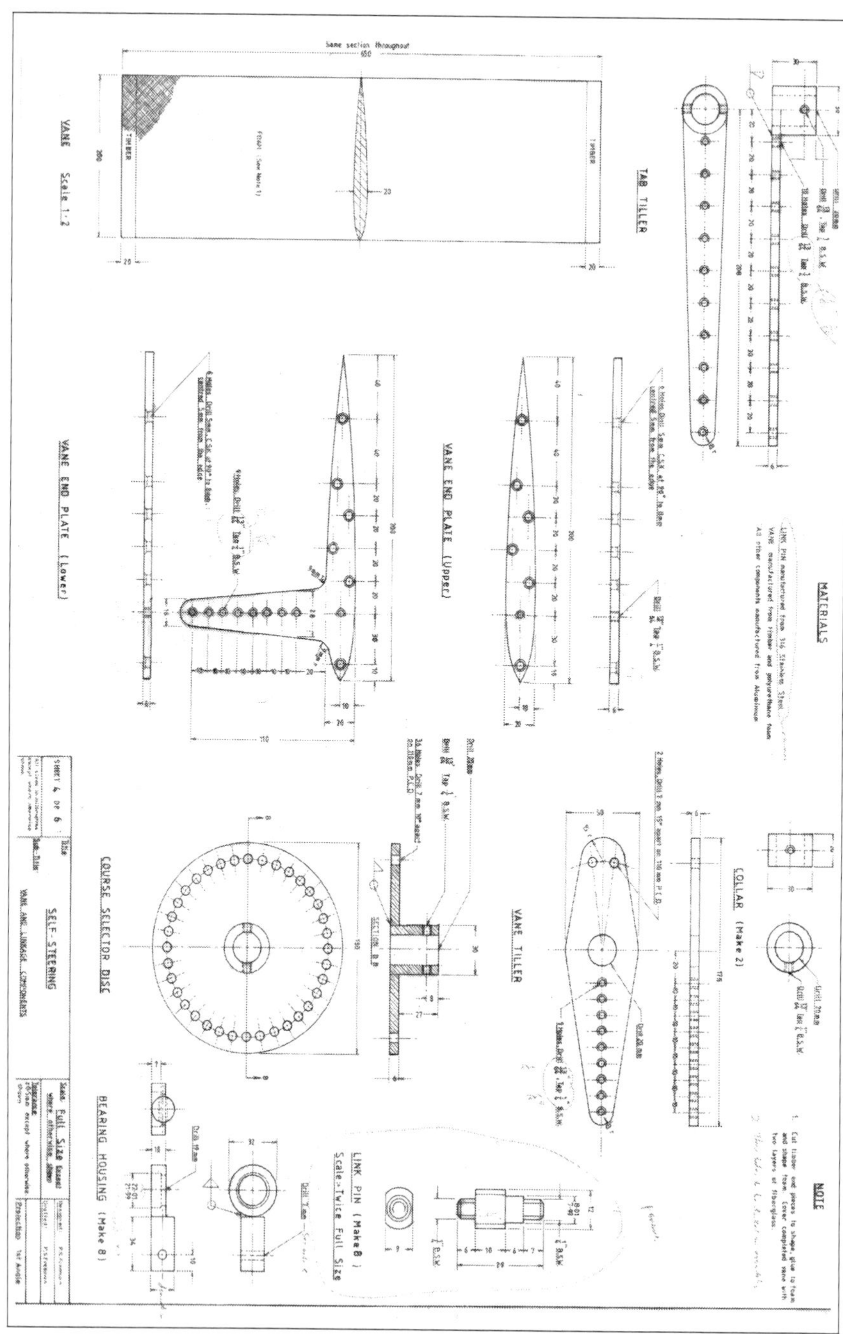

Figure D.4: Self-steering system (sheet 4)

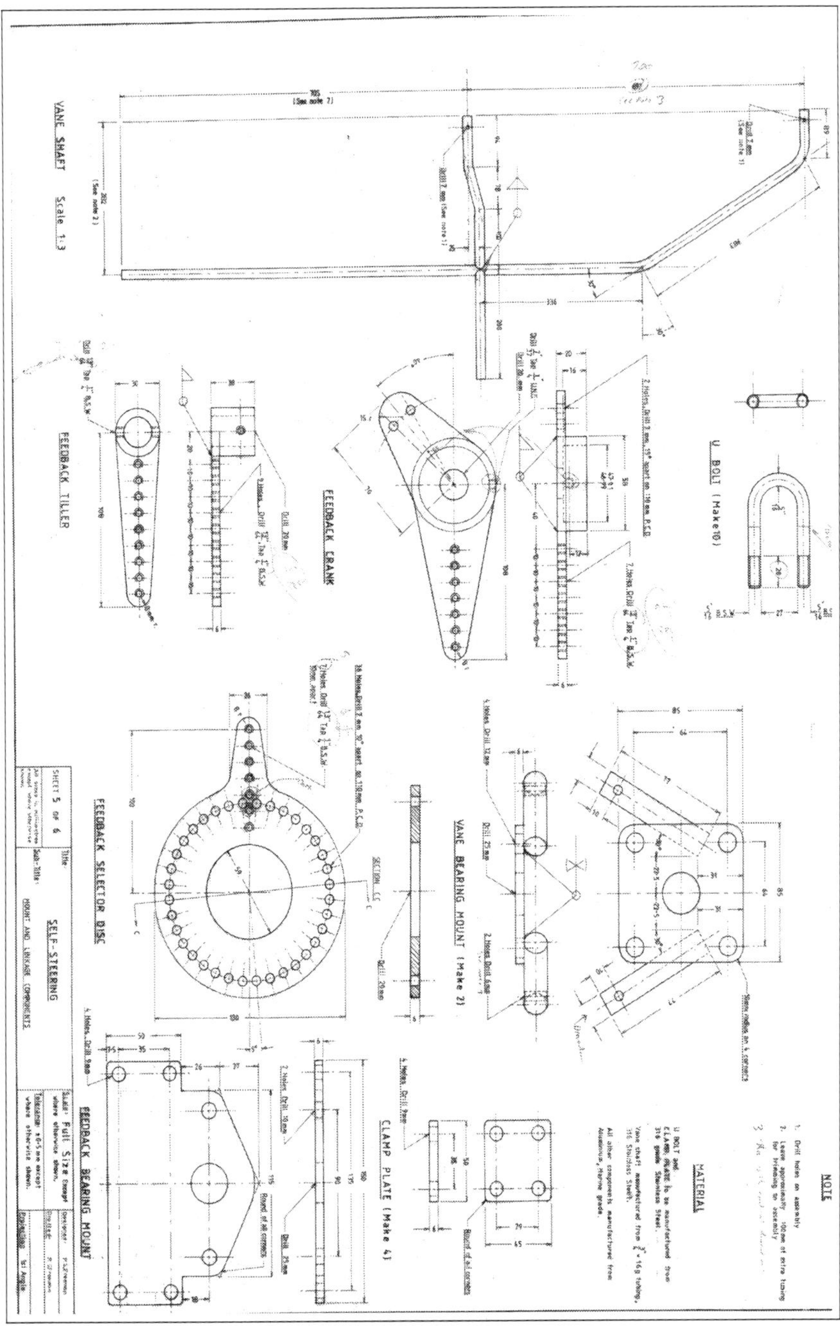

Figure D.5: Self-steering system (sheet 5)

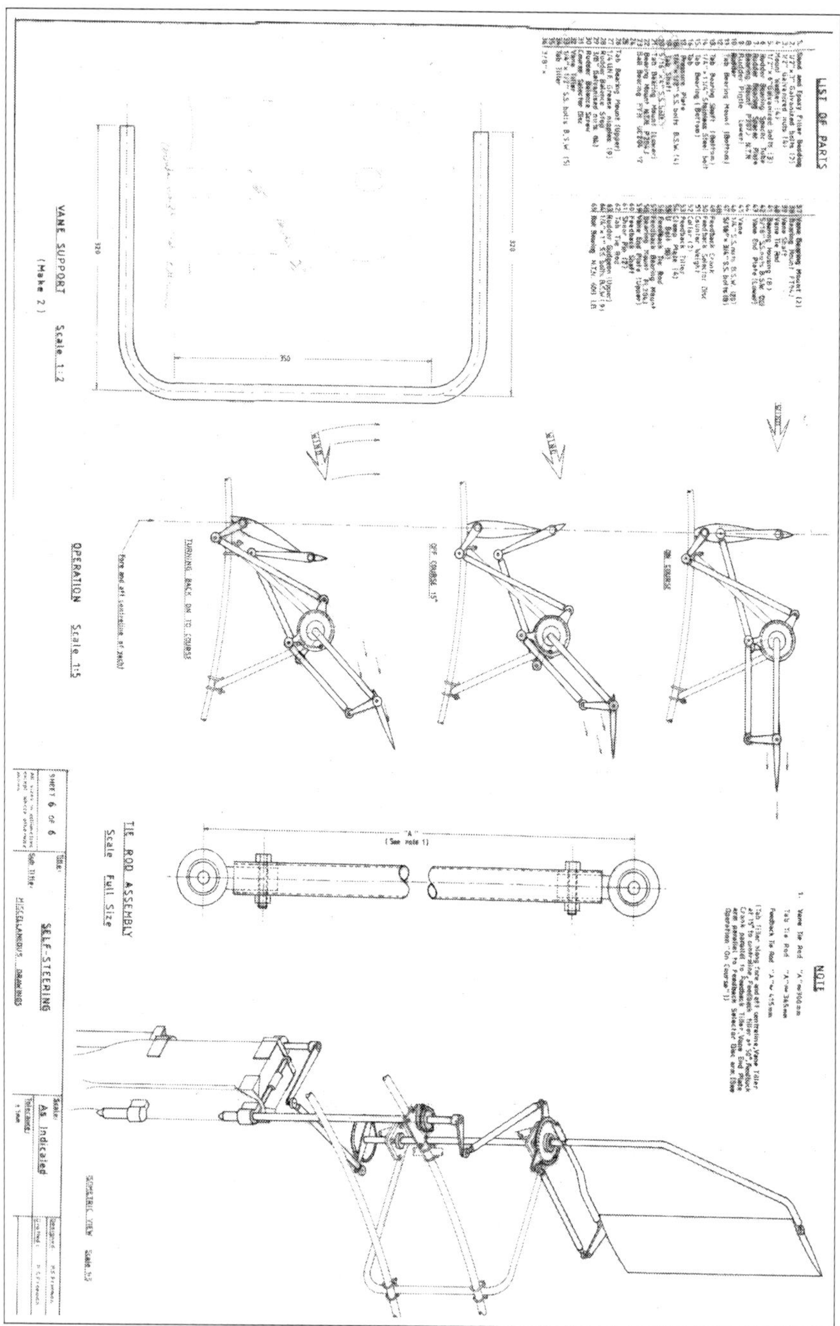

Figure D.6: Self-steering system (sheet 6)

Notes on Self-Steering Plans

Sheet 1 I replaced the sealed ball bearings at the end of the tie rods with nylon balled sheaves. It was part of my move to use more off-the-shelf products.

Sheet 2 This shows the original cross lamination which was not the best layup. The new rudder I built keeps the laminations parallel, rather than using cross-laminations, as much more force is applied to the rudder over its length than over its width.

Sheet 3 This shows the pintles that were later replaced by a solid stainless steel shaft that went through bronze cast gudgeons.

All of the parts on this sheet were no longer needed when I replaced this part of the design with solid bronze cast gudgeons.

Sheet 4 This shows the rudder balance screw and the rudder balance stop that were not needed in the later design. I found that the auxiliary rudder did not need any adjustment and could be set in the central or straight up and down position. The casting of new bronze gudgeons locked the auxiliary rudder in place.

Sheet 5 This shows the link pins which I later replaced with regular stainless steel bolts. The bearing housing was later replaced with a stainless steel rod bent to make a U-bolt that followed the groove of small nylon ball bearing sheaves I had purchased.

The vane tiller and the course selector disc were made of aluminum. When *Laiviņa* was moored at a dock, the vane was allowed to feather into the wind. Unfortunately, the constant movement wore a groove in the vane tiller. I would now make the vane tiller in stainless steel.

I was moving towards a design where more and more components could be purchased off the shelf instead of having to be fabricated as a special order.

Sheet 6 This shows the set of adjustment holes in the feedback crank. I found that there was no need for this adjustment as I regulated the amount of feedback by changing the hole to which the tie rod was connected on the feedback tiller.

Appendix E

Planning

Planning any voyage is an iterative process.

First, I drew straight lines on a Mercator projection chart so that the lines did not cross over land and were an appropriate distance from the land for safety. Next, I adjusted the route to pass on the downwind side of high-pressure systems. For example, heading south, that meant going to the east of the North Pacific high-pressure system and to the west of the South Pacific high-pressure system.

I then adjusted the course to sail close-hauled in the trade wind zone so as to make sufficient easting in one hemisphere to compensate for the loss of easting in the next hemisphere. For example, I stayed hard on the wind when heading south while I was in the northeast trades to compensate for being pushed west when passing through the doldrums and the first part of the southeast trades near the equator.

Then I broke the overall route into legs of similar weather or sailing conditions as shown in the table on the following page.

The original decision was to travel the Southern Ocean along the 45°S latitude after passing Cape Horn and the Falkland Islands. Later I decided to risk going further south to 50°S latitude knowing that most iceberg encounters were higher than 55°S latitude and in particular at the 57°S latitude. I did try going further south to 53°S latitude, but I was running into easterly winds at the time so headed back to 50°S latitude.

Choosing the time to depart was critical. Hurricanes occur in late summer and early autumn to the west of Mexico, so I needed to pass that area both outward and homeward-bound outside of that period. Statistically speaking, Cape Horn has two relatively quiescent periods: in the winter around June, and between Christmas Day and New Year's Day. I wanted to avoid making passage through the Southern Ocean in winter, so I planned to round Cape Horn on New Year's Day.

The average speed and distance I had to travel each leg was easy to calculate, so I could estimate the time it would take to transit each

Table E.1: Route Legs

#	NM	Leg
1	62.3	Victoria to the Juan de Fuca entrance
2	1254	Juan de Fuca entrance to start of the NE trades
3	1239	Start of the NE trades to start of the doldrums
4	382	Start of the doldrums to end of the doldrums
5	2081	End of the doldrums to Easter Island
6	2731	Easter Island to Cape Horn
7	446	Cape Horn to Port Stanley
8	8558	Port Stanley to Hobart
9	1100	Hobart to Dunedin
10	2293	Dunedin to start of the SE trades
11	2786	Start of SE trades to start of the doldrums
12	336	Start of the doldrums to end of the doldrums
13	1966	End of the doldrums to Santa Barbara
14	1274	Santa Barbara to Juan de Fuca entrance
15	62.3	Juan de Fuca entrance to Victoria

leg. From New Year's Day at Cape Horn, working backwards set the date of departure from Victoria, B.C., at October 14. The same backward calculation provided the expected dates and times to transit from one leg to the next. Working the other way from Cape Horn, I set the date and time of arrival at the start of each successive leg and the date I expected to arrive back in Victoria.

By choosing New Year's Day to round Cape Horn, I was also in oceans at times when I would not expect to encounter a hurricane.

I was able to accurately estimate the depletion of consumables such as kerosene for the two-burner pressure stove and methanol for warming the kerosene prior to lighting the stove.

I estimated the use of a bit under a litre and a half of water per day for drinking and cooking, using some seawater for cooking. For a voyage of 300 days, I would need 450 litres of water.

With two water tanks, each holding 100 litres and four twenty-five litre jerrycans, I had only enough space for 300 litres of water. There was no room to safely carry extra water, and the extra weight would affect *Laiviņa*'s speed. To supply the extra water I needed, I would collect rainwater off the mainsail when it rained.

Appendix F

Sails and Rigging

I left on this trip with all new stainless steel standing rigging to replace the original galvanized wire rope rigging, the old stainless steel forestay, and some new running rigging. My friend Barry Carter and I shared the cost of a spool of stainless steel wire rope to save money and to rig both our boats.

I fitted the old stainless steel forestay soon after passing Easter Island to give me a twin forestay rig for easier sail changes when running wing-and-wing with genoas and jibs. I kept the old rigging aboard for emergency repairs.

I took the sails shown in the Sail Inventory table with me. All of the sails were the original sails except for the new number one genoa built by North in Victoria.

Table F.1: Sail Inventory

Sail	Maker	Area	Weight
Reaching spinnaker	Hood	820 ft^2	1.5oz
Mainsail	Hood	215 ft^2	8oz
Number one genoa	North	370 ft^2	8oz
Number one genoa	Hood	370 ft^2	8oz
Number two genoa	Hood	310 ft^2	8oz
Number one jib	Hood	238 ft^2	8oz
Number two jib	Hood	130 ft^2	8oz
Storm jib	Hood	70 ft^2	10oz
Trysail	Hood	70 ft^2	10oz

The jibs and the number two genoa all had reefing eyes that would reduce their sail area to that of the next-smaller headsail, which was useful when reducing sail just a little without having to actually change the headsail, particularly if I didn't anticipate the wind to continue to stiffen and blow harder.

Because Hood built my original sails, I initially approached them to build a new number one genoa. Before I could get together a fifty percent deposit on the sail, the local company went bankrupt. Had I already paid the deposit, it would have had a significant impact on my extremely tight budget. I was lucky.

In spite of my emphasizing and reiterating that I wanted a strong and tough number one genoa, and asking for extra reinforcement placed on the foot and leech, the sail that North built was poorly designed. The North sail was flawed because it had fewer hanks than my Hood number one genoa. Also the luff tape was sewed at least a centimetre away from the edge of the sail so that when the grommets were fitted, they were half on the edge of the sail and half on the two layers of luff tape.

After I passed Moruroa Atoll on my return crossing of the South Pacific Ocean, a strong gust of wind tore out all the grommets and bolt rope on the luff of the North number one genoa. I recut the luff to remove some of the stretch in the sail and sewed on the luff tape so that it was butted up to the luff of the sail. This gave me the proper number of cloth layers to fully support the grommets I made and fitted.

During 1997-1998, Leitch and McBride Custom Sailmakers had overhauled the suit of sails that *Laiviņa* carried. They built a new mainsail, a standard spinnaker, and a storm spinnaker. Having sails built by local sailmakers is important to sailors whose lives may depend on them. The last thing sailors want to hear is a sail tearing as they are trying to claw away from a lee shore in a gale because it was made with minimal reinforcing.

Table F.2: Sail Use in Hours

Sail Set	Hours
Mainsail (full)	3712
Mainsail (first reef point)	233
Mainsail (second reef point)	81
Mainsail (third reef point)	383
Number one genoa (North)	3356
Number one genoa (Hood)	837
Number two genoa	1266
Number one jib	1050
Number two jib	332
Storm jib	169
Trysail	197
Spinnaker	603

The amount of time I used the trysail and storm jib shows the need to have these sails on board. Having a spinnaker that increased speed by a knot put me ahead 603 nautical miles or almost a week. A spinnaker is an important sail, even for singlehanders.

Appendix G

Barometer Record

The following readings are specific to the days of my voyage.

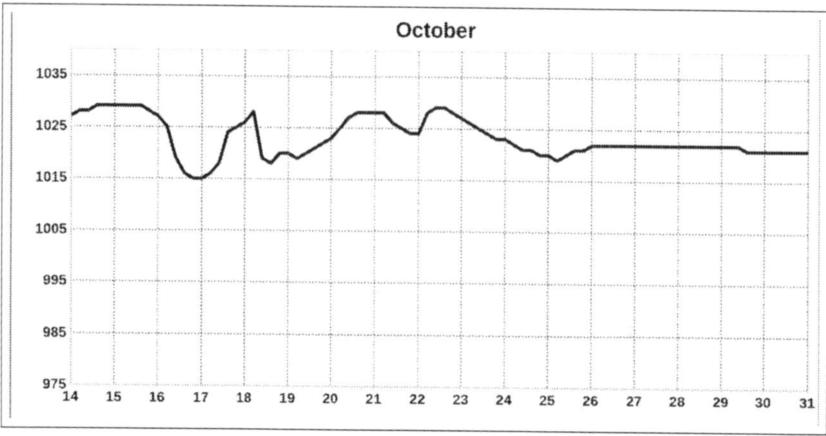

Figure G.1: October 1984

The steep descent on the fifth day, the 18th, shows the closeness of the isobars that usually indicates strong wind.

- As the barometer started to drop on the end of the day of the 15th, the wind picked up.
- The sharp drop on the 18th caused the wind to blow up to gale force.
- The strong following seas built by the wind that came out of the steadily dropping barometer on the 23th was the partial cause of the rudder breaking.
- The barometric dip on the 25th caused the wind to drop away and becalm us.
- Outside Santa Barbara on the 27th, we had light airs as indicated by the flat barometric pressure.

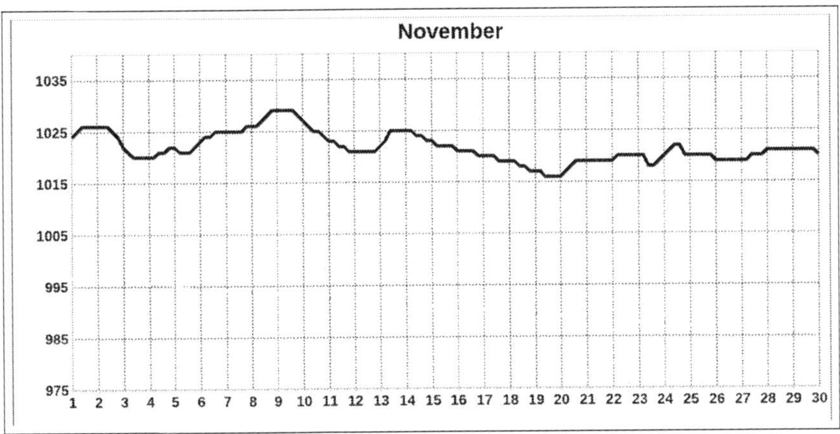

Figure G.2: November 1984

Once I reached the northeast trades, the barometric pressure began to drop steadily and evenly until the doldrums. There, the pressure stayed fairly steady until the southeast trades.

- Until the 7th, the winds were light.
- From the 7th until the 12th, the winds were strong and blowing from behind.
- On the 13th, the trade winds started.
- The doldrums started on the 19th when the barometer reached the lowest point in this area.
- The trade winds started at the end of the day on the 27th.

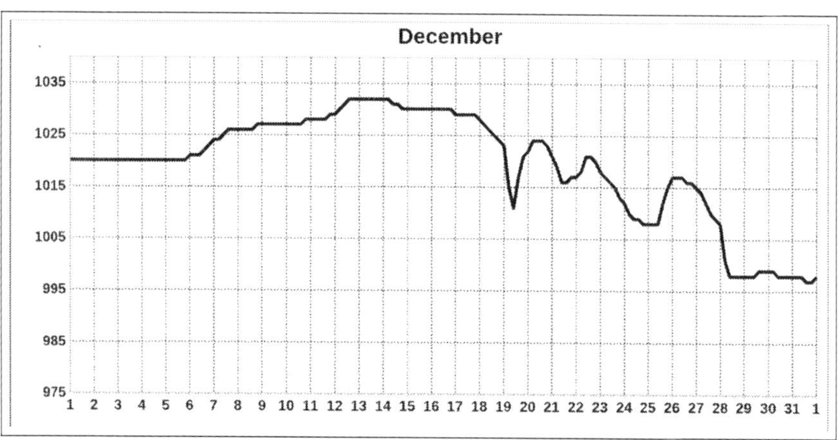

Figure G.3: December 1984

The barometric pressure rose steadily until the horse latitudes, close to the South Pacific high-pressure system. It then decreased evenly until the Roaring Forties. The steep descent and ascent indicate a strong wind leading to gale number two. In the Southern Ocean, the barometric pressure fluctuates considerably as low-pressure systems are formed from the mixing of the warm, moist subtropical air and the cooler, dry Antarctic air. The average barometric pressure is much lower around fifty degrees south than it is at thirty degrees south.

- The trade winds were steady until the 6th, when they freshened with the rise.
- The wind started to back on the 8th near the South Pacific high-pressure system.
- From the 14th to the 19th, the winds were light as we skirted past the high.
- With the dropping barometer on the 19th, and having crossed the parallel at forty degrees south, it blew a gale.
- At the top of the rise on the 20th, the winds became very light.
- Although the barometer fluctuated, the winds were strong and consistent in strength.
- The barometer was flat when the vortex formed in the clouds on the 30th.

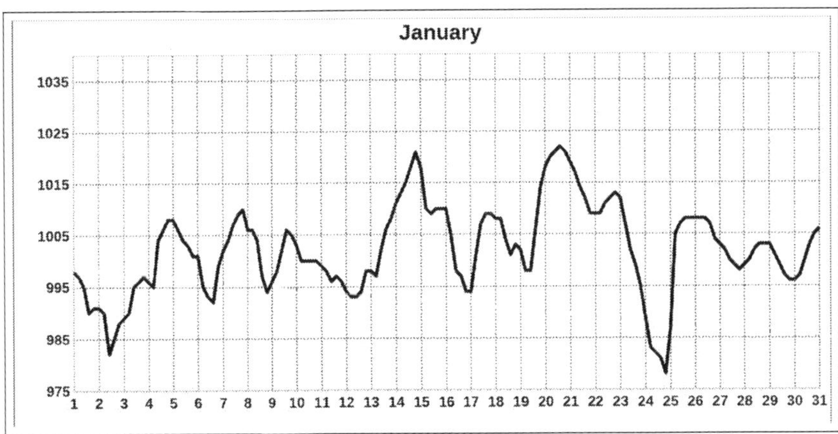

Figure G.4: January 1985

The steady progression of depressions in the Southern Ocean creates a relatively predictable weather pattern of wind direction and strength.

- On the 1st, it rained as the barometer dropped and blew a gale when it rose on the 2nd.
- On the 4th, I was fortunate to be rounding Cape Horn at the top of a barometric pressure rise, when the wind was at its calmest.
- The wind increased as the barometer dropped on the 8th leaving Port Stanley.
- The steady barometric pressure rise on the 14th provided us with the fastest day's run of 181 miles.
- We had a cold southwest gale as the barometer rose on the 19th.
- It was a nice calm day on the 20th at the top of the rise.
- Heavy rain fell as the barometer dropped on the 23rd and blew a storm as it rose on the 24th after a very deep drop.

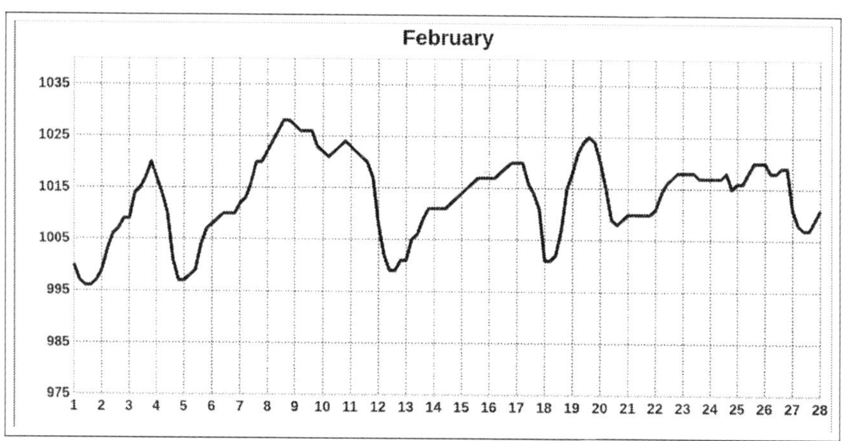

Figure G.5: February 1985

The regular up and down of barometric pressure shows the weather pattern in the Southern Ocean.

- Calm conditions prevailed at the top of the barometer on the 3rd.
- The wind suddenly increased at sunset on the 6th when there was a corresponding sudden rise in the barometer.
- The calm conditions on the 9th provided an opportunity to fix the self-steering system.
- Heavy rain fell as the barometer dropped on the 12th.
- The steep drop on the evening of the 17th signalled the storm that almost rolled *Laiviņa* over. Winds gusted to hurricane force.
- Fitful winds blew in the middle of the day on the 19th in Port-aux-Français at Île Kerguélen. The barometer was at the top of the rise.
- Blowing a gale by the morning of the 20th.

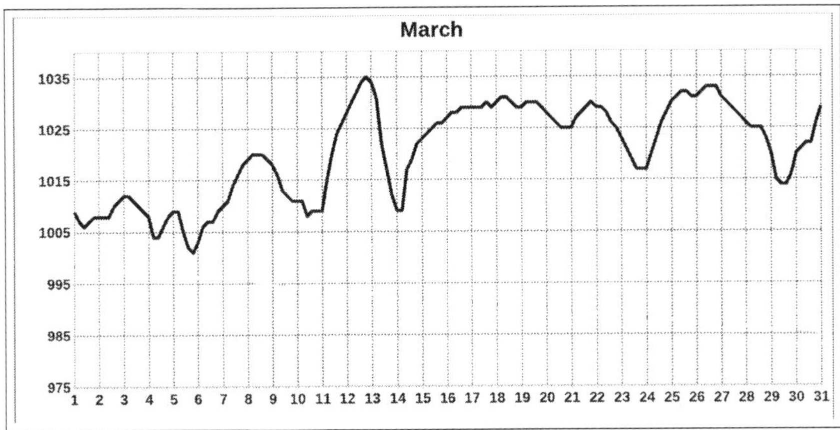

Figure G.6: March 1985

On March 14th, a lightning storm occurred as the cold front passed and the barometric pressure reached its lowest point. The hailstorm on the 30th occurred during the point when the barometer stopped rising and then jumped up again. Sometimes, the barometer does not foretell events, but records them.

- Gale-force squalls occurred when the barometer rose on the 2nd
- Even though the barometer was dropping on the 9th, it was calm.
- The wind suddenly increased at midnight on the 11th, as shown by the sharp rise.
- On the 13th, the barometer suddenly dropped with a gale from the east.
- A lightning storm hit when the cold front passed through on the 14th, and the barometer started to rise again.
- Light winds blew from the 18th through to the 20th off the south-west corner of Tasmania.
- On the 21st, the breeze came up and enabled me to get to Peach Bay.
- The plateau on the 26th gave light winds.
- A gale on the 30th kicked up as the barometer was rising.
- The wind died at the top of the rise on the 31st.

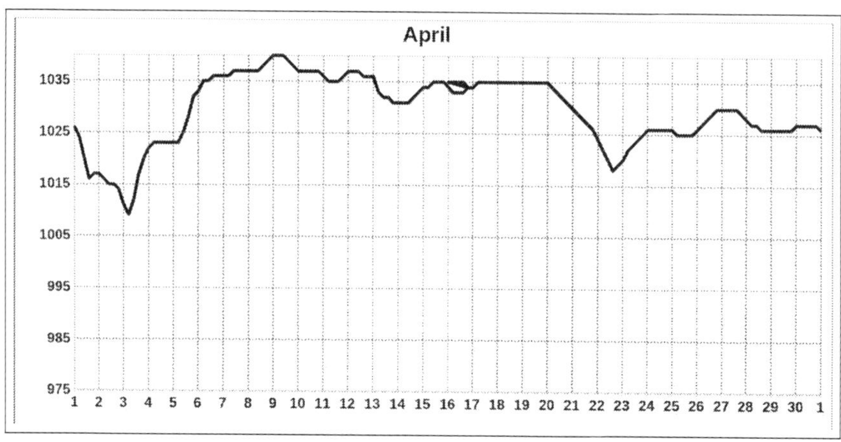

Figure G.7: April 1985

The pressure slope on the 1st, April Fool's Day, did not indicate a storm; rather, it may have indicated a gale. The storm-force winds may have been from a gale that was being accelerated by forcing air around the bottom of New Zealand and through Foveaux Strait. The high pressure at the horse latitudes is consistent with the light winds in that zone.

- The first storm struck on the 1st, as shown by the sharp drop.
- The second storm occurred on the 3rd, as shown by the sharp rise.
- The 4th had light winds, as indicated by the flat barometer.
- The wind picked up soon after the start of the race, as shown by the rising barometer on the 5th.
- By the 7th, we had light winds.
- The calmest condition occurred on the 8th, resulting in a low day's run of 48 nautical miles.
- We had good winds when the barometer dropped on the 10th and 11th, but calm at the plateau on the 12th.
- The drop near the 14th gave good winds.
- The plateau from the 15th through to the 20th produced frustratingly light and variable winds.
- The double line on the 16th represents crossing the International Date Line and having two April 16th days.
- Good winds prevailed from the 20th to the 23rd.
- We had strong winds on the 29th.

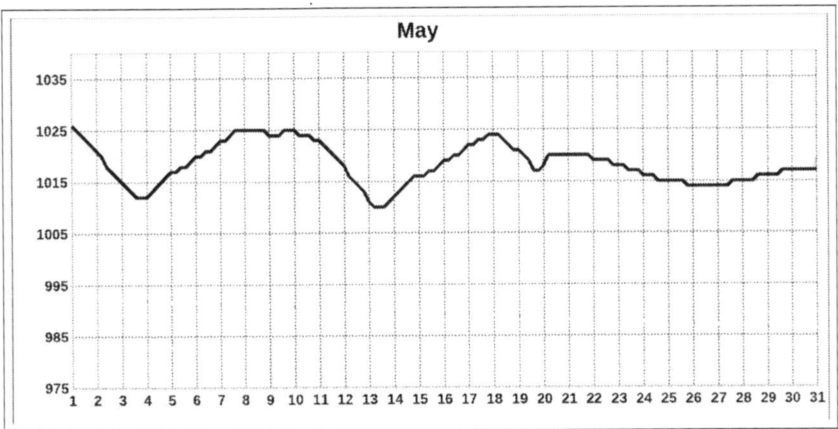

Figure G.8: May 1985

On the 17th, I reached the trade winds, just near the top of the barometric pressure rise. This time, sailing towards the doldrums, the drop in barometric pressure was not consistent, and the sharp drop reflected near-gale-force winds. The barometric pressure actually started to rise again before crossing the equator and before reaching the doldrums.

- The plateau from the 8th to the 10th produced light winds.
- We had strong winds on the 14th, but weak winds from the 15th to the 17th just before the trade winds were reached.
- The sharp drop in the barometer from the 18th to the 20th gave near-gale trade winds.
- The wind blew up again on the 23rd. By the 26th, it had eased.

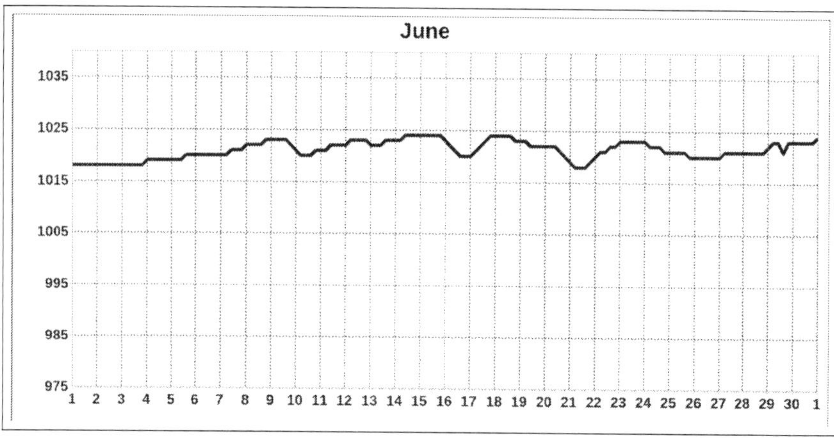

Figure G.9: June 1985

After we reached the start of the northeast trades, the barometer rose consistently until north of the northern limit of the trades. We then had frustratingly light winds at times until California.

- The flat barometer changed on the afternoon of the 3rd. It started to rise, signifying the end of the doldrums.
- The winds were lighter on the 9th, as indicated by the plateau.
- The winds were again light from the 13th through to the 16th as shown by other plateaus.
- We had fresh winds on the 15th and 16th, as shown by the drop in barometric pressure.
- Light winds blew at the bottom of the barometer on the 17th and 18th.
- We had light winds on the 20th and on the 22nd when the barometer was flat.
- With the dropping barometer, there were good winds after the 24th, which pushed us to the Channel Islands.
- We were becalmed on the 26th, but finally got some winds to get to Santa Barbara on the 27th.
- We had calm winds on the 28th, as shown by the flat barometer, but the wind freshened on the 29th when the barometer started to rise.
- The sharp down and up on the 29th continued to give us strong winds.

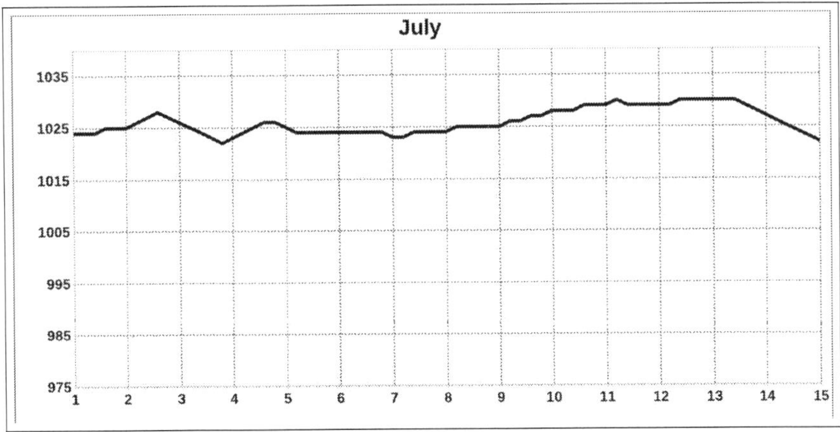

Figure G.10: July 1985

The light winds we experienced in July on the final leg home are reflected in the minimally variable barometric pressure recorded. The North Pacific high-pressure system persists to the west of California, Oregon, and Washington. We were sailing between this high-pressure system and the coast. As the winds are descending and are rotated in a clockwise direction, they are usually coming from the north and require tacking back and forth to make the entrance to the Juan de Fuca Strait.

- The dropping barometer from the 2nd to the 4th gave strong fresh winds.
- Calm winds prevailed when the barometer stopped dropping on the 4th.
- Winds came up on the 5th after the barometer finished its rise.
- On the 7th, the southerly wind started to blow.
- On the 10th, the southerly wind veered around to the northwest. The barometer had reached the top of its slow rise.
- We were becalmed while the barometer was steady on the 13th.
- When the barometer started to drop on the afternoon of the 13th, the west wind filled in.

Appendix H

Winds

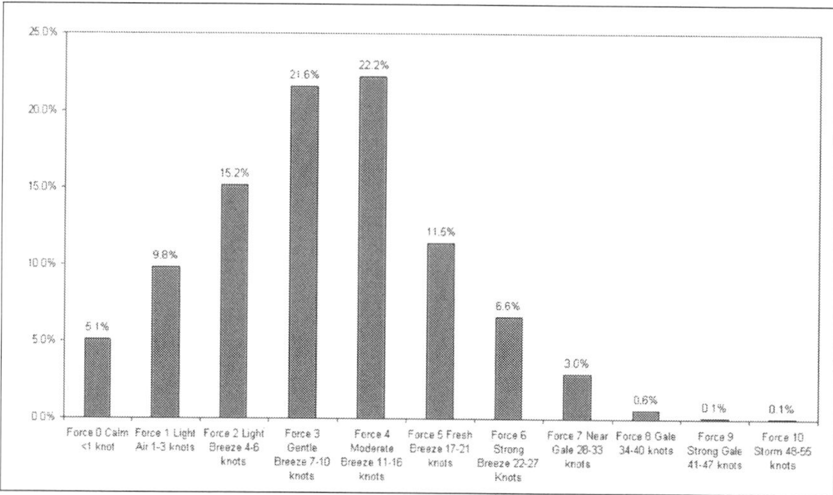

Figure H.1: Percentage of different-force winds

Above is a graph of the percentage of winds at different Beaufort scale force recorded during my voyage. Contrary to the popular idea that sailors are always battling strong winds on the open ocean, most of the time we in fact need more wind. Going to windward, force 3–4 is best; reaching, force 4–5 works well for displacement craft; downwind, force 5–6 is the best for displacement craft.

The table shows the amount of time spent on different points of sail. It shows the importance of having a sailing craft that is efficient at beating to windward.

Table H.1: Point of Sail

Point of Sail	Hours
Close-hauled	2,795
Beam reaching	1,031
Broad reaching	1,609
Running	793

Planing hulls can take a lot more wind going downwind as the apparent wind force decreases considerably when they are zipping along over twenty knots.

Acknowledgements

I would like to thank the following people:

Ed and Jen Buscall – Ed provided me with photos and the Buscalls supported me in many other ways.

Laura Cappello Bromling – Laura proofread the manuscript and she provided valuable advice. Her keen eyes and skill caught numerous grammatical errors and gave this book a more professional look.

Barry Carter – Barry is a watchmaker who supplied me with about eight watches to ensure that I would always have accurate time for my sextant sights.

Bill Challand – The late Bill Challand was the builder and skipper of the *English Rose.* A gregarious individual, Bill helped out with my preparations, giving me advice, and telling me many seafaring tales. Sadly, Bill died before he could do any serious sailing voyages.

Mary Freeman – Mary helped me edit the manuscript, and get it ready for publication.

Arvita Cotter (née Grundmanis) – It would not have been possible to have undertaken this voyage without Arvita's help. She was the co-builder of *Laiviņa*, sailed *Laiviņa* with me in the races, skippering in one race, and sailed *Laiviņa* with me to Australia, and later to Canada.

Dug Gammage – Dug sailed with me frequently, and helped me deliver a three-masted schooner from Victoria to San Diego. Dug was always there to help. He painted *Laiviņa*'s bottom prior to the trip, and helped with numerous other chores.

Al and Marley Elliott – Owners of the sailing vessel *Summer Solstice* docked in the marina at Santa Barbara. Al drove me around Santa

Barbara to show me where I could buy mahogany, and later gave me food for the final leg back to Victoria.

Anna Ford and Guy Jodoin – Anna and Guy helped translate from French into English, the letter from the scientists at Port-aux-Français on Île Kerguélen.

Rose Harvey and Tony Thurstans – Rose and Tony mailed my letters and slide film for me and were a contact point for mail from Canada. They looked after my brother, Carl, during his stay in Hobart.

Christina Heinemann – Christina created the cover design for this book, and advised me on the content style.

Mhora Hepburn – Mhora packaged up numerous puzzles for my trip, helping to keep my brain active during the voyage.

Joe Janson – Joe is the publisher that I needed and wanted. He advised me on critical decisions that ultimately shaped this book to bring it into its final form. Cape Horn Birthday needed his commercial judgment to produce a book that gave value to the reader, the publisher and author.

Penny Love – Penny helped me package up the food for the trip, organized the surprise party, and was an important shore contact, collecting mail and writing letters, which kept my spirits up.

Fred Pishalski – Fred was always there to help with various chores, picking me up and helping me to buy groceries.

Don Reed – Don showed me the trick of using an unhanked genoa as a spinnaker, and I have used this technique ever since. It was a great way of balancing a boat in strong winds on a broad reach.

Leslie Sheldon-Giles – Penny's friend Leslie helped me with various things, particularly in organizing the surprise party.

Chris – Chris was a woodworking instructor in the Santa Barbara area. He loaned me the many clamps to rebuild my rudder.

Peter – Peter was a sailor who was docked at the marina in Santa Barbara and helped me charge my battery.

Many others helped me make this voyage a reality. If I have forgotten anyone, it's because of the long passage of time between sailing the voyage and writing about it. It would be a pleasure to have you contact me so I can include your name in subsequent printings.

Afterword

Diary: In putting together the story of my voyage, I used the information recorded in my ship's log, such as wind strength and direction, sea state, barometric pressure, sails set, and random events that occurred from time to time. When I had the opportunity, I wrote in my diary, where I expanded the terse notes I had made in my ship's log into a coherent story. On those rare occasions when I encountered people, I put the diary pages that I had written into an envelope along with any rolls of exposed slide film and asked that they be mailed to Penny, back in Victoria. I was able to do this at Stanley in the Falkland Islands, Île Kerguélen, Hobart in Tasmania, Dunedin in New Zealand, and Santa Barbara in California.

As there was always a possibility that I might encounter a situation in which I would lose my life, I wanted my friends to have a record of my journey up to the last port of call.

After the completion of the voyage, I collected my diary from Penny, who had kept it safe for me, and started writing this story. I had completed the first month, when life took over my free time and I spent the next thirty years focused on raising children, advancing my career, and pursuing other adventures.

Photography: Most of the photographs were taken using an old Russian Zenit E SLR camera with a roller blind shutter. I had purchased this camera with a set of lenses and extension tubes from a second-hand store in Brisbane, Australia, in 1979. Having a limited amount of money, I could only afford three rolls of slide film.

Unfortunately, part of the second roll of film was either defective or the development process was flawed in that the one roll was developed with aged chemicals or the passage of time has deteriorated the dyes on the transparencies. I found that a set of images from Île Kerguélen to the Tasman Sea had a greenish-blue hue. Short of colourizing selected pixels, no amount of post-processing of the scanned images would bring up reds and browns that should be inherently in the scene. I originally scanned the images circa 1996 and they were re-scanned in 2017. There is no red left in the 2017 scans, yet there was a lot more red remaining in the 1996 scans, so I suspect that the dyes are deteriorating in this batch of film.

One afternoon, when I was living in Dunedin, New Zealand, I was showing a neighbour's young daughter my camera. I had no film in it and I had opened the back to show her how the roller blind shutter worked. As I pressed the shutter trigger a number of times, she watched in fascination. Before I could react, she suddenly poked at the roller blind shutter with her finger. It was too late. The blind was not badly damaged and I managed to get it working again. However its operation was never as smooth as it had been and occasionally my slides showed a band of slightly over-exposed film.

Some photographs were taken by friends. I am not always sure of the original photographers so I would like to acknowledge their contribution. If anyone recognizes images, please let me know so I can attribute them to you. The black and white photo at the start of the epilogue was taken by John Yanyshyn of *The Vancouver Sun.*

Standards: Except where a US citizen was giving me directions on land, references to miles in this book mean nautical miles, abbreviated to NM. I have tried to use metric measurements where possible, however I have used imperial measurements when mentioning lumber and hardware sizes as they are commonly used in Canada and the United States of America. I used square feet for sail area and feet for the sail dimensions and panel widths as those were the measurements used when I had the sails made. A rough conversion is to divide square feet by ten to get square metres. Because *Laiviņa* is a Hartley 32 class sailboat, the 32 referring to its length in feet, I have used feet and inches in describing its dimensions. My depth sounder measured depth in feet and fathoms, so I have used those measurements. Sometimes I have used feet to describe horizontal distance across the water because of its direct relationship to the fathom and approximate relationship to a cable.

Poetry: The two poems in this book, "Southern Ocean" and "Passage" are of my own creation and were written recently.

Name: The name *Laiviņa* is an unusual one, as it comes from the family heritage of my first wife, Arvita. Arvita's family fled Latvia during the Second World War with her parents eventually settling in Canada. The letters that we received from Arvita's grandmother were written in Latvian.

One evening, Arvita was translating a letter from her grandmother for me. Her grandmother was asking how progress was going on our boat building project. She referred to the boat as "*Laiviņa*"; Arvita explained that in Latvian, "laiva" means sailboat, and her grandmother was personalizing the word by adding the "-iņa" suffix. She had turned it into a term of endearment. Loosely translated, *Laiviņa* means "Our dear little sailboat." We had a name!

Laiviņa is pronounced "LIE-vin-yah," not "lie-VEEN-a" as most people pronounce the name. To help people remember the pronunciation, I tell them that they should come sailing with me and *Laiviņa* will "liven ya" up!

Purpose: I have been asked many times why I undertook such a voyage. The reasons are complex and are interwoven with childhood experiences, attitudes, beliefs, needs, and wants. I don't know if I can properly answer the question when I ask it of myself. In part, it was a need to prove to my father, Kevin, that I was like him, a man who loved the sea since he was young, working and voyaging in boats along the East Australian Coast. When I was a child, he would regale me with tales of his adventures in boats. One of my favourites was his story about sailing on Errol Flynn's yacht, *Sirocco.* My mother wrote about it in her book, *Hastings Street: Stories from Noosa's Past.*

> By strange coincidence, in the sixties my husband Kevin became a deck hand on a yacht that once belonged to Errol Flynn. It was then owned by John Archer, who sailed into Laguna Bay just as an anchored fishing trawler was about to run aground in a strong nor'- east wind. Our children were on the beach playing at the time and they noticed the trawler getting dangerously close to the surf. They came in breathlessly telling us the news. Kevin got me to ring the pub where he guessed the crew might be and then hurried to the beach, wading out into the surf in an attempt to get to the trawler. John Archer saw the predicament from

> his yacht and manned his dinghy, picking Kevin up. When the two boarded the trawler the motor wouldn't start. Next thing, my phone call to the pub had brought results as the crew arrived on the beach then ran through the breakers and swam to the floundering vessel. Quickly boarding, they got the motor started just in the nick of time, turning the trawler away from the choppy surf.
>
> Over dinner at our place that night, John Archer invited Kevin to join him on his famous yacht to sail to Brisbane the following day.

My father owned many boats, his first being the *Miss Laguna II*, built by my uncle and used by my father to make a living taking tourists on river and coastal cruises. My father sailed single-handed up the Queensland coast and back in a Hobie Cat he owned, sailing through the surf each evening to camp on the beach each night. While that was not a particularly challenging feat, he did all of his solo sailing encumbered by Eisenmenger's syndrome, which seriously affected his cardiovascular health. He managed his condition well and lived to a ripe old age, finally succumbing to his illness in his seventies.

But the main reason I undertook this voyage was simply that I love a challenge. I wanted to explore that age-old question about the meaning of life. I believe in the importance of finding that real meaning. We are not just hunter-gatherers, spiritual beings, or mere transients on the face of this planet. We are storytellers and sharers of knowledge, often gained at great risk and cost to ourselves.

We truly know ourselves and our world when we know our limits. As we gain experience by going close to our limits and thus get to know ourselves better, that experience moves our limits further away. This leaves us with the conundrum of never really knowing ourselves yet knowing ourselves intimately...because we kissed the lips of eternity and breathed the air of existence.

Peter Freeman

Index

Printed in Great Britain
by Amazon